FOOD LOVERS'
GUIDE TO
NEW JERSEY

Help Us Keep This Guide Up to Date

We would love to hear from you concerning your experiences with this guide and how you feel it could be improved and kept up to date. Please send your comments and suggestions to:

editorial@GlobePequot.com

Thanks for your input, and happy travels!

FOOD LOVERS' SERIES

FOOD LOVERS'
GUIDE TO
NEW JERSEY

The Best Restaurants, Markets & Local Culinary Offerings

3rd Edition

Peter Genovese

gpp

Guilford, Connecticut

Copyright © 2012 Morris Book Publishing, LLC

Editor: Amy Lyons
Project Editor: Lynn Zelem
Layout Artist: Mary Ballachino
Text Design: Sheryl Kober
Illustrations by Jill Butler with additional art by Carleen Moira Powell and MaryAnn Dubé
Maps: Rusty Nelson © Morris Book Publishing, LLC

ISSN 1550-8951
ISBN 978-0-7627-7944-4

Printed in the United States of America
10 9 8 7 6 5 4 3 2 1

All the information in this guidebook is subject to change. We recommend that you call ahead
to obtain current information before traveling.

Contents

Strawberries with Crème Anglaise (Diane K. Muentz, Alexander's Inn), 309

About the Author

Peter Genovese is a feature writer for the (Newark, NJ) *Star-Ledger*. He is the author of nine books, including *New Jersey Curiosities* (Globe Pequot Press); *Roadside Florida* (Stackpole Books); and *Roadside New Jersey; Jersey Diners; The Great American Road Trip: US 1, Maine to Florida; The Jersey Shore Uncovered: A Revealing Season on the Beach* (Rutgers University Press); and *Jersey Eats* and *A Slice of Jersey* (Pediment Publishing). His 10th book, Pizza City: *The Ultimate Guide to New York's Favorite Food,* will be published in Fall 2012.

To my mom, the best cook in Trenton,
who always made me eat my vegetables

Acknowledgments

How do you even begin to tell the food story of the nation's most densely populated state? With the help of a lot of people. Food—even more than politics or sports—is the number-one topic of conversation and debate among New Jerseyans, who are only too happy to tell you about their favorite restaurants, shops, markets, and other food sources.

At the top of the thank-you list, though, are a couple of out-of-staters, who hopefully will allow me to let them stand for all the good people at Globe Pequot Press. The first is Amy Lyons, Editorial Director for Travel, who got the ball rolling on this book. The second is Lynn Zelem, project editor for this book. To both of you: my heartfelt thanks.

A great big bushel of thanks, of course, must go out to all the shop and restaurant owners, farmers, suppliers, cooks, and others who were kind enough to talk to me during the research and writing of this book. The Garden State gets a bad rap around the country—no state is more maligned—but I have found New Jerseyans to be unfailingly kind, generous, and helpful in the 25-plus years I have spent here as a reporter and author. Special thanks goes to Brooke Tarabour, who pens the paper's excellent "Taste of New Jersey" feature, for her suggestions. And to Jim Willse, former editor of the *Star-Ledger*, who started me on the road to food writing back in 1998 when he put me behind the wheel of the Munchmobile, the paper's roving food patrol.

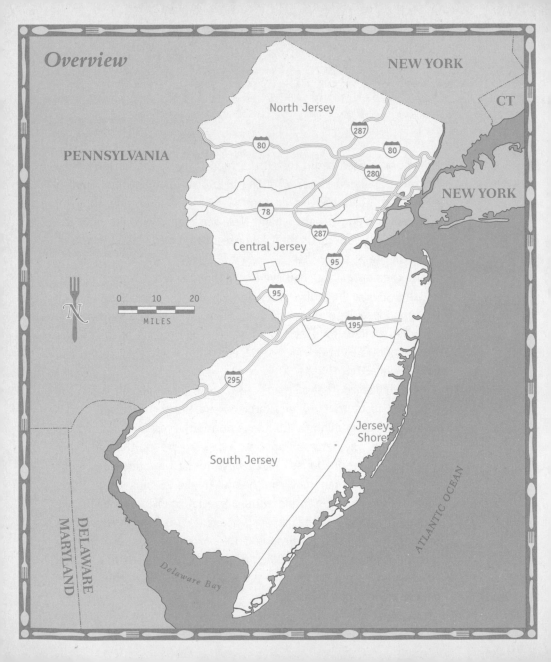

Overview

NEW YORK

CT

NEW YORK

PENNSYLVANIA

North Jersey

287

80

80

280

78

287

Central Jersey

95

95

195

0   10   20
MILES

N

295

Jersey
Shore

South Jersey

ATLANTIC OCEAN

DELAWARE
MARYLAND

Delaware Bay

Introduction

Is any state more dizzingly diverse, dining-wise, than New Jersey? Scores of ethnic cuisines—a United Nations of food—can be found in North Jersey alone. New Jersey is the nation's most densely populated state, yet South Jersey is overwhelmingly rural and home to scores of farms and roadside farm markets.

You really can get anything you want to eat in the Garden State; no longer does one need to head into New York City to find Turkish or Malaysian or Sri Lankan restaurants, to name just a few.

In this tiny, teeming state, everything is done on the run. The Garden State's 8.8 million residents are forever on the go, navigating the perpetually clogged major highways and twisty back roads that make up the state highway system. New Jersey can be a maddeningly frustrating state to negotiate and, for that matter, to like. We have been the butt of jokes since time immemorial.

But if there is one thing we're good at, it's eating, which includes knowing where to eat. Backyard barbecues and cookouts are a summer staple. We'll think nothing of driving 50 miles or more to our favorite restaurant. We know where to find good food and, in true Jersey fashion, the quickest way to get there.

We're equally at home in the poshest restaurant and the most ramshackle seafood shack. We can describe the virtues of filet mignon or a chili cheese dog. We love to share inside

food information—hot new chefs, just-opened restaurants, random finds and discoveries—with friends, family, even strangers.

New Jerseyans are more passionate about food than any other subject—more than politics, traffic, development, even sports. Debate about the state's best restaurant, ultimate thin-crust pizza, or freshest seafood can get lively, if not heated; enter a food argument with a New Jerseyan at your own risk. The Garden State? Call it the Food Fanatic State.

This book is the first comprehensive guide to good food in New Jersey. It is not meant to be the final word; consider it more Baedeker than Bible, a culinary roadmap to a state that leads the nation in highways—and, very likely, restaurants—per square mile.

It is the culmination of years of wandering New Jersey as a reporter for the state's largest newspaper, for both stories and, well, places to eat. But it is not simply a rundown of my favorite restaurants, shops, markets, and the like; many are the result of suggestions and tips from people who know the state and its food.

This book will tell you about hundreds of worthy food shops and stops; you'll undoubtedly add your own favorites to the list. Hopefully, it will take you down roads—culinary and otherwise—you've never taken and will allow you to sample, enjoy, and appreciate the richness and diversity that is the New Jersey food scene.

How to Use This Book

This book is divided into four chapters, using boundaries every New Jerseyan is familiar with: North Jersey, Central Jersey, South Jersey, and the Jersey Shore.

North Jersey includes Bergen, Essex, Hudson, Morris, Passaic, Sussex, Union, and Warren Counties. Central Jersey includes Hunterdon, Middlesex, Monmouth, and Somerset Counties. South Jersey takes in Atlantic, Burlington, Camden, Cape May, Cumberland, Gloucester, Mercer, Ocean, and Salem Counties. The Jersey Shore includes all the shore towns from Highlands to Cape May.

Restaurant Price Key

$	inexpensive; most entrees under $10
$$	moderate; most entrees in the $10 to $20 price range
$$$	reasonable; most entrees in the $20 to $30 price range
$$$$	expensive; most entrees over $30

Each chapter includes a map of the region to help you plan your food excursions. Within each chapter you'll find the following categories:

Made Here

This section spotlights local makers of everything from fresh cider and cheesecakes to peanut brittle, pork roll, and popcorn. Most of the companies listed sell directly to consumers at the plant or farm store, or through the mail and Internet. You can also buy many of these products at gourmet and specialty shops around the state. In this section you'll find the nation's largest distributor of pâtés and *foie gras* and the nation's only maker of madeleines.

Specialty Stores & Markets

This section is devoted to shops where you can find the best, freshest, most unique ingredients to assemble a great lunch or dinner. It includes pasta purveyors, patisseries, seafood suppliers, coffee and tea vendors, and natural-foods merchants. Don't worry—there will also be listings for quite a few things not so good for you but irresistible nevertheless.

Farmers' Markets

South Jersey is the state's agricultural belt, but farmers' markets can be found all over the state, even in the downtowns of the state's biggest cities. What is better than wandering amid the tables, baskets, and crates of an open-air farmers' market, sniffing the air for the freshest Jersey tomatoes, blueberries, strawberries, and other fruit and produce? New farmers' markets pop up all the time, and established ones often change times and locations, so it's always wise to check beforehand; contact websites are provided.

Farms & Farm Stands

The farm stand, laden with just-picked produce, is a New Jersey roadside fixture. Many farms allow you to pick your own fruits and vegetables; we'll tell you about some of the more notable ones. An increasingly popular feature, especially among kids, is the farm maze; we'll steer you to some of the better ones.

Food Events

The calendar is jammed year-round with food-related fairs, festivals, concerts, and other events, from the Dandelion Festival in Vineland and the Lima Bean Festival in West Cape May to the State Barbecue Championship in North Wildwood and ChowderFest on Long Beach Island. Lists are divided by region, but see Appendix C: Index of Food Events (p. 322) for a complete list of events in this book.

Learn to Cook

Want to finally learn how to cook or to refine those rusty kitchen skills? You can, at any number of cooking schools around the state. Some are held at their own facilities, others in restaurants, still more in kitchen supply stores such as Chef Central in Paramus and Sur La Table in Marlton.

Learn about Wine

Under this heading in several chapters, you will find information about wine schools helpful to both novice and serious oenophiles.

Landmark Eateries

There are thousands of places to eat in the Garden State; the ones listed here are landmarks because they are long-established local institutions of note or restaurants that absolutely must be visited for a particular specialty or for a one-of-a-kind atmosphere or unparalleled view.

Brewpubs & Microbreweries

In 1995 the Ship Inn in Milford opened, becoming the first establishment in New Jersey licensed to make beer since Prohibition. Today 20-plus breweries dot the state, turning out top-quality ales, lagers, porters, and seasonal brews. Many, particularly the Trap Rock Restaurant Brewery in Berkeley Heights, also offer first-rate menus.

Wine Trail

Wine has been made in New Jersey since 1870, when Renault started production in Egg Harbor City. Today several dozen winemakers, from the top of the state to the bottom, call the Garden State home. Many have won awards at prestigious wine competitions.

Recipes

The recipes included in this section (starting on p. 273) reflect the state's ethnic and culinary diversity. You'll find contributions from some of the state's most creative chefs, everything from duck bacon carbonara and seafood risotto to French silk chocolate pie.

Keeping Up with Food News

New Jerseyans are passionate about their favorite food and restaurants—and there is no better place to discover this than on the Internet. Here are some websites devoted to New Jersey food:

Artful Diner, www.artfuldiner.com: The Artful Diner is the Jersey-born-and-raised son of a chef, Arthur Namendorf, who has "a decided aversion to shelling out good money for strictly mediocre fare." His site includes reviews for scores of restaurants statewide. Sample from a review of Barnacle Ben's in Maple Shade: "Bus boys and girls ferry huge tubs of dishes, clean tables, hurriedly replace silverware, and dispense water; no nonsense waitresses scurry to and from the kitchen and chatter with patrons like long-lost relatives; the patrons themselves flit from table to table—laughing, joking, exchanging gossipy tidbits—moths in search of a conversational flame. Have you, perhaps, inadvertently stumbled into a family reunion?" The Artful Diner, also the food critic for New Jersey Online, compiles annual top-10 lists for romantic, holiday, and Jersey Shore dining.

Chowhound, www.chowhound.com: Chief Chowhound Jim Leff lives in New York and writes about "hidden culinary treasures" in neighborhoods around the city. He is the author of *The Eclectic Gourmet Guide to Greater New York City,* and his work has appeared in *Best Food Writing 2000* and *Food: True Stories of Life on the Road* (Travelers' Tales Guide). Want to find good, cheap food in the big city? Look no further than the Chowhound. The message boards on the Chowhound website are full of postings about restaurants not only in New York but also in New Jersey, Connecticut, and around the country.

Eating in South Jersey, www.eatinginsjersey.com: Lisa and John Howard-Fusco are a Forked River couple who admittedly don't make much money from their blog but love doing it anyway. Lisa, for one, says she finds it safer to use her 10 years of New York publishing and film experience to "yammer on" about her culinary obsessions, "instead of accosting people on street corners."

Ed Hitzel, www.edhitzel.com: Probably no one knows the South Jersey restaurant scene better than Hitzel, who publishes *Ed Hitzel's Restaurant Newsletter* and *Ed Hitzel's Restaurant Magazine.* The former, which includes reviews, ratings, recipes, statistics, and columns, is available by subscription only. The quarterly magazine can be picked up for free at restaurants and select locations in South Jersey and Philly. Hitzel also does a 3-hour Saturday morning food and restaurant radio show on WOND 1400 AM.

Grumpy Gourmet, www.grumpygourmet.net: Iona Konwaler and Dan Bellware are two North Jersey foodies whose mission is "to simply tell others of our restaurant experiences, what we did or didn't like." They have posted reviews of 60-plus New Jersey restaurants to date.

Hollyeats.com, www.hollyeats .com: Holly Moore—"First of all, I'm a guy," he says—writes about his "favorite roadside cafes, barbecue pits, diners, holes-in-the-wall, greasy spoons, down-home cooking restaurants" around the country. There is a good, detailed section on New Jersey hot dog haunts and other eateries. Nice, crisp photos accompany all reports. "Three or four times a year, I hop in my car, pick a state or two, and eat my way through them," Holly says.

Jersey Bites, www.jerseybites.com: Deborah Smith's blog is packed with restaurant reviews and recipes. She employs correspondents from around the state. Sample from review: "The Mixing Bowl Restaurant is a cozy little place serving breakfast and lunch in Sussex County, NJ. Go there on a Saturday or Sunday morning and there is sure to be a wait, heck, go there on a Tuesday morning and there is sure to be a wait. But let me tell you, the wait is worth it!"

Munchmobile, www.nj.com/munchmobile: No one covers New Jersey's food scene like the *Star-Ledger's* summertime food patrol. North Jersey, Central Jersey, South Jersey, the Shore: The van with the 8-foot-long hot dog on the roof covers the entire state, unlike other region-centric blogs. The Big Dog, as it is known, takes particular pleasure in uncovering little-known, out-of-the-way restaurants.

New Jersey Tables, http://newjerseydiningoutonline.com: A glossy, full-color magazine devoted to the best restaurants of North and Central Jersey. You can view menus on the website; the magazine, available in bookstores, also includes recipes and stories.

NJ.com, www.nj.com: For lively if not heated opinions about restaurants and food joints statewide, the best places are the Dining and Munchmobile forums on NJ.com.

Rosie's Food Bytes, http://home.att.net/~saferstein: For the latest on the New Jersey restaurant scene, the best source is Rosie Saferstein, who compiles the "Table Hopping with Rosie" feature on *New Jersey Monthly*'s website (www.njmonthly.com). Get restaurant news, information on openings and closings, and a complete list of food events around the state. Rosie also coordinates the New Jersey forum on http://egullet.com, an international forum on cooking, wine, restaurants, and other food topics.

North Jersey

It's impossible to describe New Jersey in 25 words or less, and North Jersey resists easy characterization more than any other part of the state. The densely packed towns along the waterfront—Jersey City, Hoboken, Union City, Weehawken, North Bergen—are as different as night and day or, for purposes of this book, a burger and prime rib.

Jersey City, fueled by urban gentrification and headquarters-switching by once-Manhattan-based companies, has undergone a recent renaissance, and so has the local food scene. Vietnamese, Korean, Cuban, French, Moroccan—you can find cuisines from dozens of countries in downtown alone. In staid, pricey Bergen County, you'll find some of the more celebrated—and expensive—restaurants in the state. For South and Latin American food, you need to look no farther than Paterson and Passaic. Newark's famous Ironbound is renowned for its amazing wealth of Spanish/Portuguese restaurants, markets, and bakeries. Upscale Morristown boasts an eclectic range of restaurants—Chinese to Afghan, bagels to chili dogs.

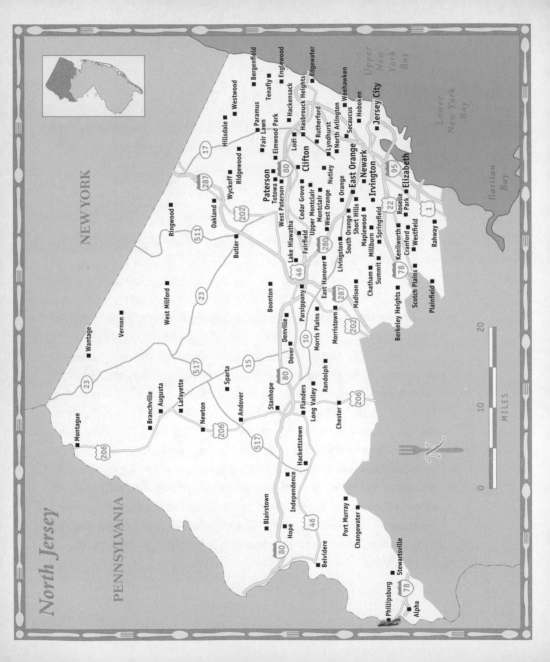

North and west of Morristown—Warren and Sussex Counties—is farm and dairy country, dotted with small towns that seem scarcely to have changed in the past 50 years. Here, in the most rural part of North Jersey, you'll find an abundance of roadside markets, fresh produce, church dinners and festivals, juicy homemade pies and other baked goods, and winding country roads that will make your food explorations fun.

In this chapter we'll visit everything from a 100-year-old Italian-ice maker and the maker of the state's best cheesecakes to an all-Japanese food store and the nation's leading supplier of *foie gras,* pâtés, and organic game and poultry.

Made Here

Antonio Mozzarella Factory, 71 Springfield Ave., Springfield; (973) 379-3738; www.antoniomozzarella.com. Antonio's is a factory all right, a 10,000-square-foot neoclassical building that makes 16,000 pounds of "mutz" every week. It's good stuff. Owner Tom Pugliese, who worked for two years in his cousin's cheese company in Italy, numbers among the next generation of mozzarella makers. He's in his early 30s. Here you can watch cheese coming off the assembly line on its way to being braided, salted, and smoked. Or, if you can't wait, you can buy balls of mozzarella in the well-stocked on-site retail store. There are nearly 40 kinds of sandwiches and 10 salads for sale, too. "Mozzarella is an easy thing to make, but so many people make it so many different ways," Pugliese says. "We try to keep it handmade."

Applegate Farm Ice Cream, Multiple locations (see below); www .applegatefarm.com. Since before the Civil War, families in North Jersey have enjoyed fresh dairy products from Applegate Farm. Now one of the largest retail outlets for ice cream on the East Coast, Applegate offers a taste of the country a half hour from the big city. They make more than 30 flavors of ice cream, from Moose Tracks, Rocky Road, butter pecan, and mint chocolate chip to rum raisin, strawberry cheesecake, Dutch apple, and orange pineapple. Sherbets, Italian ice, sorbets, low-fat yogurt, and low-net-carb/no-sugar-added ice cream also are available. There are several locations: 397 Centre St., Nutley, (973) 661-1166; 134 Ridgedale Ave., East Hanover, (973) 884-0222; 616 Grove St., Upper Montclair, (973) 744-5900; 400 Minnisink Rd., Totowa, (973) 256-4711; 356 W. Main St., Freehold, (732) 577-5545; 1401 Hudson St., Hoboken, (201) 942-9005; 14 Beechwood Rd., Summit, (908) 522-9731; 1092 Main Ave., Clifton, (973) 246-9909; 619 Ridge Rd., North Arlington, (201) 997-3276.

Argentina Bakery, 1611 Bergenline Ave, Union City; (201) 661-5801; www.bakeryunioncity.com. This place is tiny—when it gets busy you might have to wait out on the sidewalk—but there's a big assortment of delicate, delicious pastries. They make their own whipped cream, central to many of the baked goodies. Two of my favorite things here: *pasta flora,* a shredded coconut-topped pastry made with quince, and the white chocolate–topped caramel cookies called *alsajor.*

Bobolink Dairy, 42 Meadowburn Rd., Vernon; (973) 764-4888; www.cowsoutside.com. Jonathan White and Nina Stein White are dairy farmers and dreamers; they envision Bobolink, named after the ground-nesting bird that frequents their meadows and pastures, becoming an important center for promoting grass-based, sustainable, profitable, family-size dairy farming "as an alternative to the industrial, confinement-based farms that typified the dairy industry in the late 20th century." Their operation, also known as the Grasslands Cheese Consortium, makes artisanal cheeses from raw milk from grass-fed herds, plus wood-fired rustic breads. Their best-selling cheese is a cave-ripened cheddar. The Whites even offer agritourism as well as academic and seasonal internships lasting from one day to 10 or 12 months. Jonathan White spent time in Tibet in an effort to introduce Tibetan cheese to American markets. The farm is open year-round.

Cait and Abby's Daily Bread, 15 Sloan St., South Orange; (973) 763-2229. What a wonderful world this would be if there were a bakery like Cait and Abby's at every train station. The bakery, at the South Orange train station, is named after a previous owner's daughters. Warning, chocolate lovers: This place will

Ding Dongs and Animal Crackers

Many well-known food companies are headquartered in New Jersey. **Goya** is in Secaucus, and **Manischewitz** is in Jersey City. **Best Foods** (Hellmann's mayonnaise, Thomas' English muffins, Mazola oil) is located in Englewood Cliffs. Half the world's M&Ms, the world's best-selling candy, are made at **M&M/Mars** in Hackettstown. Ring Dings and Ding Dongs, the most famous tintinnabulary food duo of all time, are made at **Drake Bakeries** in Wayne. And every single one of Barnum's Animal Crackers is made at the **Nabisco** bakery on Route 208 in Fair Lawn.

test your limits. It offers chocolate shortcake, German chocolate cake, chocolate fudge cake, and Truly Chocolate Cheesecake, among other items. Throw in fruit pies, crumb pies, cream pies, elephant ears, muffins, strudel, bread, and other goodies, and you may never leave this station. There is another Cait and Abby's at 518 Millburn Ave., Millburn; (973) 564-9661.

Calandra's, 201 1st Ave., Newark; (973) 484-5598; www.calandras bakery.com. The most comforting neon sign in New Jersey? My vote would be the Hot Bread Every Hour until 9 p.m. sign in the window at Calandra's, the state's best-known bread maker. Luciano Calandra opened the bakery in 1960; today, Calandra's delivers breads to 700-plus supermarkets, restaurants, delis, and even the Atlantic City casinos. The Newark Calandra's is a cozy little bakery just off

Bloomfield Avenue. A bigger, brightly lit outlet opened on Route 46 in Fairfield in 1992.

Casa di Trevi, 534 Westfield Ave. (Route 28), Roselle Park; (908) 259-9000; wwwcasaditrevi.com. Let's get right to the point: You won't find better homemade ravioli than the ravioli at Casa di Trevi. From the outside, it doesn't look like much—a white-walled building that resembles a warehouse more than a stuffed-pasta outlet. Owner Michael Aiello and crew make 25 kinds of ravioli, five kinds of manicotti, and three kinds of stuffed shells, along with cavatelli, tortellini, gnocchi, lasagna, sauces, and other items. There's no sit-down; buy your ravioli fresh or frozen, and cook it at home. Grazioso's favorite is the Gorgonzola and walnut ravioli, but the plain cheese ravioli is a knockout; she uses top-of-the-line Impastata cheese. Casa di Trevi does a lot of private-label work for gourmet shops and delis. One stop here, and you'll never eat supermarket ravioli again. See Casa di Trevi's recipe for **Summer Pasta Salad with Fresh Rigatoni** on p 297.

D'Artagnan, 280 Wilson St., Newark; (800) 327-8246; www.dar tagnan.com. Named after the "Fourth Musketeer" in Alexandre Dumas's novel *The Three Musketeers,* D'Artagnan bills itself as the nation's leading purveyor of *foie gras,* pâtés, sausages, smoked delicacies, and organic game and poultry. Founded in 1985 by Ariane

Daguin and George Faison, the company provides 600-plus items to the world's top restaurants, hotels, cruise lines, and airlines. Mousse of duck *foie gras,* pâté de campagne, pheasant terrine *herbette,* plus rabbit, quail, venison, and even wild boar sausage and strip loin are available. You can shop online, through the mail-order catalog, or by phone. The company's motto: "Everything but the quack." See D'Artagnan's recipe for **Duck Bacon Carbonara** on p. 284.

Di Cosmo's Homemade Italian Ice, 714 4th Ave., Elizabeth. Italian-ice making has largely gone the way of chain operations, but Di Cosmo's still makes it the old-fashioned way, with real fruit frozen in a 100-plus-year-old wooden barrel. You never have far to go to find the owners here; John and Nancy Di Cosmo live right next door. John's grandparents, Katherine and Giovanni, started the business in 1915, and to this day old-timers talk about "going to Katarina's for lemon ice." John is in the little green shack cranking away, while Nancy spoons the ice to customers outside. They make 20 flavors, but no more than 3 or 4 are available at any one time. Lemon is the benchmark, but I like the pineapple best. Open from May to the end of September.

Donna & Company, (908) 272-4380; www .shopdonna.com. Diane Pinder left a nursing job behind to open her artisanal chocolate shop, named after her late sister. The shop is no longer open, but you find her chocolates at Whole Foods markets in Madison, Marlton, and

West Windsor; 18 Kings markets throughout New Jersey, and elsewhere. She offers conventional chocolates, plus many unusual and equally delicious varieties—a German chocolate cheesecake made with Swiss chocolate cream cheese ganache and praline pecans, and a Drunken Plum made with dried plums soaked in Courvoisier cognac and added to Belgian dark chocolate ganache. And don't forget the Cranford Clunky, a block of Belgian milk chocolate with dried cranberries and peanuts.

Feed Your Soul, 520 Jersey Ave., Jersey City; (201) 204-0720; www.feedyoursoulcookies.com. Mya Jacobson walked away from a well-paying job on Wall Street to open a cookie factory in Jersey City. Her cookies can be found in 15 supermarkets and stores, including Dean & DeLuca. The varieties include chunky peanut butter, chocolate chip graham, and white chocolate snickerdoodle, but I keep going back for the chocolate brownie chunk cookie, the best chocolate cookie I've had in years. Feed your soul, and your cookie cravings, in downtown Jersey City.

Fiore's, 414 Adams St., Hoboken; (201) 659-1655. This humble shop, opened by Alphonse Fiore in 1913, is probably the longest-established mozzarella maker in New Jersey. In 1965 current owner John Amato, who started working at Fiore's in 1950 as a delivery boy, took over the business. Not much seems to have changed over the years. The shelves are filled with olives, artichokes, pastas, and other items; giant wheels of cheese seem poised to roll out the door and down the street. Amato ships his mutz nationwide.

Fossil Farms, 81 Fulton St., Boonton; (973) 917-3155; www.fossil farmsostrich.com. Brothers Todd and Lance Appelbaum are two of the more unusual food suppliers in the state. They started in 1993 raising and selling ostriches as a low-fat, low-calorie alternative to beef and chicken. In their first year of business, the company rang up $250,000 in sales; the following year sales nearly doubled. By 2003 sales had reached $2.5 million. The brothers call the company Fossil Farms because "Fossil" was the nickname they gave their dad, Stephen, when they were kids. But Fossil Farms is about more than just ostrich; the Appelbaums supply buffalo, bear, rabbit, wild boar, antelope, alligator, caribou, elk, as well as snapping turtles, rattlesnake, and cobra. The latter is one of the most sought-after snake meats because of its unique taste (somewhat like conch) and texture (akin to tender chicken). "Our Ossi burger has fewer calories and cholesterol than chicken, turkey, beef, pork, anything you want to compare it to," says Lance. Ostrich, bear, and cobra meat may not be for everyone, but it's worth a look, if not taste.

Gimmee Jimmy's Cookies, 27 Utter Ave., Hawthorne; (800) 4-Jimmys; www.gjcookies.com. Gimmee Jimmy's is located in a low-slung brick building alongside a strip mall. Don't let appearances fool you; there's a whole lot of good baking going on inside. Owner Jimmy Libman started baking from his house in the early 1980s, using his mother's cookie recipe. Today Gimmee Jimmy's ships as many as 600 tins of cookies a week to customers around the country, even the world. What makes Jimmy's unique is that Jimmy is deaf, as are 6 of his 12 employees. When the orange light inside

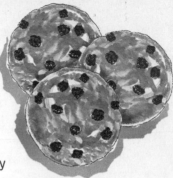

the kitchen goes on, it means a customer has walked through the front door. White means that Jimmy is on the phone; red, the fire alarm is on. "We're totally high-tech deaf," Jimmy says with a smile. There are 20 varieties of cookies; start with the double chocolate chip walnut, and see if you can stay away from the other 19.

Happy Herbert's, 444 Washington Blvd., Jersey City; (800) SO-HAPPY; www.happyherberts.com. Happy Herbert's, named after a cafeteria worker in the Brooklyn grade school attended by owner Gary Plutchok, makes nearly 40 kinds of crunchy, wholesome snacks. The lineup includes multigrain and organic pretzels, honey wheat pretzel sticks, organic spelt and kamut pretzels (made of "ancient" grains, for those allergic to modern wheat), white cheddar corn puffs, popcorn, and other items. Stop right there, you're thinking. Organic pretzels? Tasteless, surely. Happy Herbert's organic pretzel sticks, made from organic unbleached wheat flour, organic barley malt, and organic canola oil, are mighty good. Gary, a Brooklyn native, studied at Rutgers University's Food Science Department before finding work in the food industry. He started Happy Herbert's in 2000; since then, Happy Herbert's has contributed 10 percent of its pretax profits to children's charities such as Save the Children and UNICEF. I first discovered Happy Herbert's pretzels in a hotel gift shop and was instantly hooked. The snacks can be found in specialty shops statewide, or you can order direct from Happy Herbert's.

J. Emanuel Chocolatier, 457 Main St., Chester; (908) 879-0500; www.jemanuel.com. This high-end chocolate shop is located in a little mall less than a mile from downtown Chester. The truffles are the star here; J. Emanuel makes 35 kinds, from mocha cinnamon and almandine to Bailey's Irish Cream, dark French Bordeaux, and black and tan, with Guinness blended in with the ganache. The shop's trademark treat is Chester Crunch, a rich buttery toffee with almonds and pecans that is available in milk or dark chocolate. It's just great, and you can buy a 1.5 pounds in an attractive silver decorative tin. The bark here is terrific, too. And good luck resisting the cinnamon espresso beans.

MAKE MINE MANISCHEWITZ

B. Manischewitz Co., headquartered in Jersey City, is the nation's largest manufacturer of processed kosher food products and the world's number one baker of matzo, or unleavened bread. The company traces its roots to 1888, when Rabbi Dov Behr Manischewitz opened a small matzo bakery in Cincinnati. The bakery soon evolved into a thriving business. By the end of the century, demand for matzo was so high that Manischewitz switched from the old coal-fired ovens to gas-fired ovens, which allowed for more control over the baking process. In 1932 the company built a second factory, in Jersey City; it became the model for machine-made matzo bakeries worldwide. In the 1940s Manischewitz started making wine; in 1954 it purchased a processing plant in Vineland. The Vineland facility now makes all the company's canned and jarred products, including gefilte fish, borscht, and chicken soup. Workers pack two million pounds of fish and one million pounds of beets every year. In all, Manischewitz produces hundreds of kosher foods, including pasta, baked goods, soups, snacks, and juice. They can be found in supermarkets and groceries throughout the tristate area.

Jersey Pork Roll, 177 Stelton Rd., Piscataway; (866) 4NJ-PORK. Mention the words *pork roll* or *Taylor ham* outside New Jersey, and you're apt to encounter glazed-over expressions. But Taylor ham, made in only one place—Taylor Provisions in Trenton—could lay claim to the title of the state's official food. A pork roll egg and cheese is a diner/luncheonette standard, but good luck finding one west of the Delaware. You can buy Original Taylor Ham Pork Roll from Jersey Pork Roll, and save the trip to Trenton. Then pork roll comes in various sizes—1.5-pound boxes, 1-pound rolls, even massive 6-pound rolls. How big is pork roll in New Jersey? Trenton-based Loeffler Gourmet Inc., another pork roll maker, supplies it to more than 300 school districts in the state.

Lee Sims Chocolates, 743 Bergen Ave., Jersey City; (201) 433-1308; www.leesimschocolates.com. Never judge a chocolate shop by its appearances. Lee Sims, squished between a 99 Cents Up and Less store and Chilltown, a clothing store, is a narrow, fluorescent-lit, tile-floored shop. But its customers are loyal and legion. Lee Sims makes 75,000 pounds of chocolates a year. "We've been here 50 years, more or less," says owner Valerie Vlahakis. "Maybe more on the more side." Her parents, Nicholas and Catherine, started the business. You'll love the honeycomb-like sponge pillows, sweet and crackly. The dark chocolate coffee beans are addictive, and the dark chocolate breakaway is marvelous. The chocolate here overall is rich, creamy, and first-rate. Forget the surroundings, and walk in.

Mara's Cafe & Bakery, 281 Speedwell Ave., Morristown, (973) 682-9200; 25 Jefferson Ave., Westwood, (201) 666-0886; 25 E. Main St., Denville, (973) 625-0901; www.marasdesserts.com. The best cheesecakes in New Jersey, in my opinion, come from an airy shop in Morristown, where the only decorations to be found are the 1903 Oldsmobile carriage against the window and framed vintage lyrics ("Why Did You Make Me Care?"). Mara Magley and her crew make 300 to 400 cheesecakes a month; most of them are destined for restaurants, but you can stop in and pick one up. They range from the merely marvelous to the outright sensational. A few favorites: the almond brownie chocolate cheesecake, baked atop a chocolate cookie crust, studded with brownie chunks, and topped with chocolate ganache and sliced toasted almonds; or the caramel apple streusel, with its great crumbly crust.

Mazur's, 323 Ridge Rd., Lyndhurst; (201) 438-8500; www.mazurs bakery.com. This hometown bakery is consistently voted the top bakery by the readers of *New Jersey Monthly*, and one look at the glittering display cases tells you why. Cherry turn-overs, Vienna crumb cake, peach floats, fruit boats, chocolate truffle cheesecake, cream puffs—Mazur's is a sugar lover's fantasy and a dentist's nightmare. They make a rich Danish here, using 3 pounds of butter for every 10 pounds of dough. The bakery is especially proud of its wedding cakes. One was in the shape of Giants Stadium, with the bride and groom standing at the 50-yard line. Others have resembled cathe-drals, trucks, teapots, and Madison Square Garden.

Pierogi Palace, 713 Grand Ave., Rahway; (732) 499-4660. Pierogi Palace is anything but: No prince or princess would be wowed by the plain storefront. The inside is utilitarian: white walls, display case, front counter. But the pierogies made here are just about the best anywhere, which is saying something, considering the large Polish population in nearby Linden. Jessica Avent, who started working in the store for then-owner Larry Schall, now owns the operation. She and her staff do everything by hand; no commercial mixes are used. During the holidays, they make 250 dozen pierogies daily. The most popular varieties are the sauerkraut, the potato and cheese, and the potato and onion. Two must-tries: the sweet cabbage pierogi and the jalapeño cheese–potato pierogi.

Specialty Stores & Markets

A S Pork Store, 281 Browertown Rd., West Paterson; (973) 256-0115. Liveliest deli crew in New Jersey? It might be the gang at A S Pork Store, which sells much more than just pork. It's a full-scale Italian deli, with meats (including mortadella from Italy), pasta, olive oil, and other items. There's homemade focaccia and meatballs, sautéed broccoli rabe, and stuffed artichokes. We haven't even gotten to the best part. The subs and sandwiches here are great. Forget the corny names—the Guido, the Paisano, and the Marco Pollo—and just bite into them. The freshness of the meat and the spectacularly crunchy, crusty rolls used here add up to sandwich heaven.

Clove Brook Market, 800 Rte. 23, Wantage; (973) 875-5600; www .clovebrookmarket.com. Sussex County, at the state's tippety-top, is a long drive from just about anywhere. About 5 miles down the road from High Point State Park (at 1,803 feet, the state's highest elevation) is this market. The owners are Kim Sytsema and her husband, Rich, a dairy farmer. For 15 years Kim made the baked goods at Abma's Farms in Wyckoff. Tired of the commute and dreaming of her own business, she opened this deli/market in 2003. You'll find plenty of good sandwiches here, but the baked goods make the drive worth it. The mouthwatering selection includes blueberry, apple, strawberry rhubarb, and other pies; cinnamon raisin, raspberry almond, and cranberry scones; muffins, turnovers, cannoli, cheesecake, chocolate cake, strudel, and other treats. A personal favorite: the  summer smash pie, made with blueberries, peaches, cherries, and strawberries. Kim puts out samples on a table, making the decision-making process easier—or harder—for you.

Denville Seafood, 61 Broadway, Denville; (973) 627-2987; www .denvilleseafood.com. In 1951 Tony Aguanno, a former butcher, opened Denville Seafood with $200 to his name. His wife, Ann, passed away in 2001; the restaurant is named Codmother's Cafe in her honor. In the front is a clean, brightly lit fish market, with various fish charts on the wall. Around the corner is the restaurant. You won't go wrong with any of the soups here—seafood gumbo, shrimp bisque, and bouillabaisse, among others. And it'll be tough finding a better crab cake sandwich. A tasty summer treat: the smoked fish salad, with your choice of salmon, scrod, Chilean sea bass, or calamari over mesclun greens. There are a few tables outside.

Edible Arrangements, 219 Franklin Ave., Nutley; (973) 667-0700; www.ediblearrangements.com. The beautiful arrangements and centerpieces at Tariq Farid's burgeoning business are meant to be admired—and eaten. Fruits are washed, peeled, cleverly carved into floral-like shapes, tastefully arranged, beautifully gift-wrapped, and delivered fresh. Best seller: the Delicious Fruit

Design, overflowing with strawberries, cantaloupe, pineapple daisies, grapes, and honeydew. The Hearts and Berries arrangement features strawberries and pineapple hearts. From a single store in 1999, Farid now franchises 40-plus stores, not just in New Jersey but also in Massachusetts, Connecticut, Virginia, Florida, Georgia, California, and elsewhere.

Empire Coffee and Tea Company, 338 Bloomfield St., Hoboken; (201) 216-9625; www.empirecoffeetea.com. This is not, the owners are quick to point out, "a pretty little boutique shop." Empire is all about fresh ground coffee and special tea—and lots of it. Bags of freshly roasted gourmet coffee from around the world cover the floors; the aroma may knock you off your feet or transport you to someplace far away from cosmopolitan Hoboken. Unique coffees include Truckstop Fiesta, a rich, strong, exotic blend of Kenya AA and Brazilian French Roast; and Venezuela Tres Volcanos, a light, tangy brew. Teas range from chamomile, rose hips, and hibiscus to peach melba, lemongrass, and passion fruit. The original Empire Coffee and Tea, on 9th Avenue in New York City, is nearly 100 years old.

Greek Store, 612 Boulevard, Kenilworth; (908) 272-2550; www .eatgreek.com. An olive lover's vision of paradise? The olive bar at the Greek Store. There are 25 kinds of olives, including Gaeta olives from Italy, Turkish oil-cured olives, and, of course, Greek olives:

BIRTHPLACE OF THE SLOPPY JOE

The history of the Sloppy Joe, like the sandwich itself, can get a little messy. Jean Anderson, author of *The American Century Cookbook,* traces it to the 1930s in Sioux City, Iowa, where a greasy spoon started offering a ketchup-laced loose-meat sandwich. Sloppy Joe's, a popular bar in Key West, claims "the original Sloppy Joe Sandwich"—ground beef in a rich tomato sauce, with onions, peppers, and spices. The bar was once known as the Silver Slipper; Ernest Hemingway suggested it be renamed Sloppy Joe's after a Havana club he frequented. That bar got its name from the owner, Jose Garcia; patrons good-naturedly complained about the messy floors, thus "Sloppy Joe's."

Sometime around 1935, then–Maplewood, NJ, mayor Robert Sweeney asked Jack Burdorf, the owner of the **Town Hall Deli** in South Orange, to re-create the sandwich he used to enjoy at the Havana Sloppy Joe's. Jack came up with a sandwich layered with ham, tongue, and Swiss cheese topped with coleslaw and Russian dressing, tucked inside thinly sliced rye bread and cut into eight squares.

The Town Hall Deli (60 Valley St., South Orange; 973-762-4900; www.townhalldeli.com), which bills itself as "the birthplace of the Sloppy Joe," offers 9 kinds of Sloppy Joes, including ham, tongue, and Swiss; roast beef, turkey, and Swiss; and turkey, corned beef, and roast beef. Andrew Smith, editor in chief of *the Oxford Encyclopedia of Food and Drink,* says he has heard of a dozen or so different stories of the Sloppy Joe's beginnings. One thing, though, is beyond dispute: The Town Hall Deli's Sloppy Joe, the original Joe or not, is delicious.

green olives marinated in garlic and oil, almond-shaped kalamata olives, feta-stuffed olives, big olives, little olives. The Greek Store also offers cookies, wine, olive oil, bread, and Greek pasta. You can pick up moussaka, seasoned kebabs, pastitsio, Greek-style pork sausage, even squid and octopus in the refrigerated and frozen cases. Did we mention all the cheeses here? The store has its roots in Newark, where Nicholas Diamandas opened a Greek market, Liberty Food, in 1950. Customers got so used to calling it "the Greek store" that Nick changed the name.

London Food Company, 416 Bloomfield Ave., Montclair; (973) 783-6688; www.londonfoodco.com. Pining for some Taylor of Harrogate tea or Walker's shortbread? Pine no more. London Food Company specializes in English, Scottish, and Irish food. Owner Samantha Codlin, a native of Great Britain, and her husband, Rodney, a native of South Africa, have lived on four continents. The couple moved to Montclair in 1998; Samantha opened her well-stocked shop in October 2003. You can find 50-some kinds of loose and packaged tea; there are also chocolates and cookies, bread and scone mixes, preserves, steak and kidney pies, and many other items. Order some tea and biscuits, pull up a cozy chair, and you'll forget you're in New Jersey.

Mitsuwa Marketplace, 595 River Rd., Edgewater; (201) 941-9113; http://mitsuwa.com/english. Feel like turning Japanese? There's no better place than this mall-like complex of shops and

Island Food

One of the more welcome additions to the state's food scene is the influx of Caribbean restaurants, particularly Jamaican. Nearly all are simple, unfussy places; what they lack in fancy trappings they more than make up in quality—and value.

"Mother's Day" and "sharks" don't seem like they would ever belong together, but Stacy Baldeo, owner of **Leela's Trinidad Cuisine** (180 Bloomfield Ave., Montclair; 973-744-8118; www .leelastrinidadcuisine.com; $$) drives into New York to pick up shark, a special for Mother's Day in her handsome Trinidadian restaurant. Trinidad is a close cousin to Jamaican and other Caribbean food, with curries, roti, goat, oxtail, stewed meats, and fish sharing center stage. Portions are sizable; you'll like the stew beef and jerk chicken. For a refreshing, tangy taste of the tropics, try *mauby,* a tealike drink made with mauby tree bark, plus cinnamon, cloves, and other spices.

Munchie's (307 Irvington Ave., South Orange; 973-821-5471; Caribbean; $$) is one of my favorite restaurants (of any kind) in the state. Jamaican-born Sophia Taylor—her childhood nickname was Munchie—and husband Reid Taylor are the owners of this colorful little restaurant, where 45-rpm singles of Bob Marley, the Saints, and Roy Shirley under the glass-topped tables provide a quick intro to

stores. Inside the food market you can wander down aisles and aisles of Japanese food products and cookware. Here you'll find a candy counter and a food court where you can feast on sushi,

Jamaican music. All the meats here are cooked just right; the jerk chicken and jerk pork, packed with flavor and fire, are recommended. An absolute must: the homemade carrot juice, made with juiced carrots, sugar, orange juice, and limes.

If you can't find Andre Stone *inside* **Stone's Original Jerk Chicken** (506 Ellison St., Paterson; 973-668-0271; Caribbean; $$) check out back; he'll be grilling meats in a narrow alley behind the strip mall restaurant. The affable, Jamaican-born Stone once sold his jerk chicken in the backyard of a nearby bar. There are only a couple tables, so you might want to think takeout. Recommended: the jerk chicken, jerk pork, and oxtail.

Real Jamaican Jerk An' Ting (500 Hamilton St., Somerset; (732) 745-7300; www.realjamaicanjerk.com; Caribbean; $$) is a charming little restaurant, with green tropical walls and 5 tables. If you're a fan of jerk seasoning, as I am, you'll love the jerk wings here. You'll want to pick up a bottle of owner Iva Thompson's Jamaican jerk sauce, a super-spicy sauce made with Scotch bonnet peppers, ginger, garlic, scallions, and pepper. I have one in my fridge.

sashimi, and other Japanese specialties. The complex also includes a housewares outlet called Tajimi, and Kinokuniya bookstore, filled with Japanese books, magazines, and comics.

Nuts Online, 1201 E. Linden Ave., Linden; (800) 558-6887; www
.nutsonline.com. In 1930 Sol Braverman opened the Newark Nut Co.
in downtown Newark; today the business, now called Nuts Online,
is located in Linden and is owned by Braverman's grandsons, Jeff
and David. They sell 250,000 pounds of peanuts a year, but there
are plenty of other kinds of nuts: cashews, hazelnuts, pecans, pistachios, pignoli, Brazil nuts, almonds, and others. There is also a
selection of dates, figs, prunes, papayas, pretzels, and candied red
and green cherries.

Once Upon a Table, 105 Main St., Chester; (908) 879-2903;
www.onceuponatablenj.com/our-cafe. I love this place. It's part
decorative accessories and home furnishings shop, part cafe, all
wrapped up in an *Alice in Wonderland*–like warren of rooms. Salads
and sweets glisten behind a display case in the cafe, a space barely
big enough to turn sideways in. Once Upon a Table is owned by
Kimberly Carluccio-Wasser, a former fashion designer, and her
husband, Charles Wasser, a former securities lawyer. "I never liked
being a lawyer," Charles says. "I didn't want to go into corporate
America at all. I saw the light." Terrific sandwiches
here; my favorite is the roasted turkey breast
with cranberry chutney, walnuts, sliced Granny
Smith apples, and green leaf lettuce on
Tuscan-style bread. Not far behind is the
fresh mozzarella, prosciutto di Parma,
red ripe tomato, and basil pesto sandwich on herb focaccia. Great cookies and

GREEK

I love Greeks bearing gifts, especially if they're coming from the kitchen!

For a long time, when you said "Greek food" and "New York metropolitan area," you meant Astoria, Queens, with its great concentration of Greek restaurants and markets.

In recent years, though, Greek restaurants have popped up in New Jersey, and of the dozens I have tried, not one has disappointed. **Pithari Taverna** in Highland Park (p. 143) is the best in Central Jersey.

Best in Jersey? I would go with **Stamna Greek Taverna** (1045 Broad St., Bloomfield; www.stamnataverna.com; $$). The Bloomfield restaurant is located several doors down from Holsten's ice cream shop, where the last scene in *The Sopranos* was shot. Start with the grilled kalamari, or feta in Greek olive oil, then proceed to the lamb chops or Mediterranean sea bass. The lemon potatoes are a must side dish.

Forget its location—squeezed into a strip mall on ever-busy Route 17—or its nondescript name. **Greek City** (1300 Rte. 17, Ramsey; 201-760-2500: www.greekcityrestaurant.com; $$) is cool but casual in decor, and serves up some terrific dishes, especially the lamb porterhouse, a juicy, perfectly seasoned piece of meat. It's time to let octopus in your life, if you haven't already. The *octapodi*—grilled octopus drizzled with olive oil and vinegar—is highly recommended.

The *paidakia* or grilled spring lamb chops at **Taximi Greek Cuisine** (350 Bloomfield Ave., Caldwell; 973-287-6803; www .taximigreekcuisine.com; $$). approach $50, but they are so worth it. Don't worry—most of the other entrees are in the $10–$20 range. It's a lively, handsome restaurant—blue tiled walls, and bouzouki music as background. The saganaki (pan-seared cheese flamed in brandy); *horiatiki* salad; moussaka, and spanakopita are all first-rate.

brownies, too. There is no room to dine in the cafe. Take your food upstairs to the tables in the atmospheric sitting room. You'll feel like Alice wandering through the collection of tiny rooms. You'll have fun feeding your head and stomach at Once Upon a Table.

Shuga No Cream, 515 Leland Ave., Plainfield; (908) 222-1969. Debra Easter opened her coffee and tea "boutique" on Labor Day weekend in 1998 after deciding that 20-plus years as a medical technologist were enough. Her cute little shop—filled with the heady aroma of Colombian, ginger peach, punkin' spice, southern pecan, and dozens of other flavors—may cause you to swoon. Chocolates, animal crackers, imported cookies, muffins, and biscotti beckon at the front counter. Debra sells two dozen kinds of coffee beans,  from Irish cream, Sumatran, and white chocolate raspberry to southern peach. Specialties include Jamaican Me Crazy, a blend of vanilla, Kahlúa, and caramel; and Jamaican Blue Mountain, which she calls "the caviar of coffee." She prides herself on her selection of decaf coffees and teas. You can even get barbecue here, made by Debra's husband, Jim, and some of her great homemade coleslaw. There's a comfy lounge in a hardwood-floored back room. Don't try to start a conversation between 3 and 4 p.m., the regulars joke; that's when *General Hospital,* Debra's favorite show, is on.

Summit Cheese Shop, 75 Union Place, Summit; (908) 273-7700; www.summitcheeseshop.com. "The absolute most perfect cheeses in the world," says Brooke Tarabour, who writes the "Taste of New Jersey" column for the (Newark) *Star-Ledger*. About 120 kinds of cheese are on display, everything from brie and French beaufort d'été to English stilton, Danish esrom, and brandy-soaked, chestnut-leaf-wrapped goat cheese. The owners are Paul Pappas and his wife, Pam. "Try this," says Paul, shaving off samples with a formidable-looking knife. "You like that? Try this." There are wheels, bricks, and chunks of cheese in the case  and on counters; it almost looks like a minimuseum of cheese. Paul and Pam also sell 25 kinds of olives (my favorite: lemon and rosemary Moroccan olives), plus a selection of gourmet and specialty food items, pâtés, and terrines. Pam also makes soups. Looking for wild boar salami? You'll find it here.

Sussex County Food Co-Op, 30 Moran St., Newton; (973) 579-1882; www.sussexcountyfoods.org. "Good for You Food and Good to You Prices" is the slogan of the co-op, open since the early 1980s. It's dedicated to providing its members with high-quality products, with emphasis on organic and locally produced food suitable for a wide range of dietary needs. As with any co-op, members volunteer their time and energy to do the work necessary for the store to function. Members receive discounts and have a voice in co-op policy, but you don't have to be a member to shop here.

Swiss Pork Store, 24-10 Fair Lawn Ave., Fair Lawn; (201) 797-9779.; www.swissporkstoreoffairlawn.com. Despite the glut of

Diner Heaven

New Jersey is, for better or worse, the diner capital of the world, with 600-plus diners. You never have to go far to find one; they can be found in fully half of the state's 566 municipalities. Diners didn't start in New Jersey—that honor goes to Providence, Rhode Island—but here they have found an everlasting home. Give me a diner over a chain restaurant any day; the food is usually cheaper, and you can't beat the atmosphere—the stainless steel exterior, swivel stools, revolving cake displays, and waitresses who call you "Honey." I visited every diner in the state to write *Jersey Diners* (Rutgers University Press). For something different, visit **Nubian Flavor** (410 Springfield Ave., Newark; 973-242-2238). An old-time diner feel (wooden booths, coat racks) and plenty of good home cooking add up to a diner experience you won't forget. The owners, Pam and Rashid, don't serve pork products; their turkey sausage may have you swearing off your favorite bacon forever. Good waffles, french toast, and grits here. If I had to pick one Jersey diner to take a first-timer to, it would be the **Summit Diner** (Summit Avenue and Union Place, Summit; 908-277-3256). It's the state's only wood-paneled diner, and one of the oldest; Hemingway is said to have eaten here. You haven't lived, or died, until you've tried a Slider, the Summit's signature dish—Taylor ham, egg, and cheese on a roll. A few of my other favorites:

Bendix Diner, Route 17 and Williams Avenue, Hasbrouck Heights; (201) 288-0143. Plenty of commercials and movies (*Jersey Girl, Boys on the Side,* etc.) have been filmed here over the years. And the Bendix is home to the state's only blind diner waiter and stand-up comedian, John Diakakis, son of owner Tony Diakakis. John works late at night, and the jokes are free.

The Harris Diner, North Park and Washington Streets, East Orange; (973) 675-9703. If I need an eggs fix, I head straight to this striking L-shaped 1950s diner. All the Tums commercials you see on TV are filmed here; it's certainly no reflection on the food. Two eggs over, grits, bacon well done, wheat toast, and absolutely the hottest coffee in New Jersey: that's my breakfast of champions, available at the Harris.

White Mana, 470 Tonnele Ave. (Route 1), Jersey City; (201) 963-1441. Originally at the 1939 New York World's Fair, this flying saucer–shaped brick wonder is open daily, 24 hours a day. Hamburgers are cooked on a tiny grill; it's a great place to chill out in the early morning after a night in the big city.

White Manna, 358 River St., Hackensack; (201) 342-0914. This is the state's most photogenic diner, a tiny, red-and-white diner with 20 stools, two window nooks, and a grill that's even smaller than the White Mana's (both were originally owned by the same man, Webster Bridges, but no one seems to know why White Mana is missing an *n*).

supermarkets with their meat sections, old-time butcher shops still can be found throughout the Garden State, and their customers are not just seniors eager to hold on to a bit of the past. The Swiss Pork Store, which opened in 1950, is a lively, colorful place, a throwback to a time when grocers knew your first name. German salami, liverwurst, kielbasa, ham, veal loaf, steaks, Polish sauerkraut, warm

 German potato salad—the aromas alone may be enough to transport you back to the old country. The small, busy store also sells German, Austrian, and Polish cookies, preserves, candies, bread, teas, biscuits, and other items. There is no Swiss pork for sale; the name came from the original owners, one German, one Swiss. Worried about anti-German sentiment in the years after World War II, they called their business the Swiss Pork Store. You'll call it your favorite butcher shop.

T. M. Ward Coffee Co., 944 Broad St., Newark, (973) 623-1202; 7 S. Passaic Ave., Chatham, (973) 635-8929; www.tmwardcoffee .com. When Timothy Ward opened his shop on Broad Street across from Military Park in Newark, Ulysses S. Grant had just become the 18th president of the US. The store, now located farther up on Broad Street between City Hall and the Federal Building, is rich with the aroma of coffee, tea, and freshly roasted peanuts. It's a favorite haunt of downtown workers on lunch or snack breaks. Ward's grinds and packages 350,000 pounds of coffee beans a year; the beans come from Brazil, Colombia, Central America, Arabia, Yemen, and elsewhere. Bulk teas fill oaken bins. The shop makes its

JUST DESSERTS AND JUST D'SSERTS

It's not a typo. Just Desserts and Just D'sserts are two top-notch—and very different—bakers.

Grace Morello started making desserts in the basement of her home 20 years ago, opening a tiny shop, **Just Desserts** (718 Lafayette Ave., Hawthorne; 973-238-0307; www.justdessertsnj.com), in Totowa several years later. Ten years ago, she bought a purple-shuttered house in Hawthorne and converted an addition into a kitchen. Initially, she made desserts for country clubs and restaurants. Finally, she turned the cute purple house into a retail operation, and we're all the better for it. She offers 30-plus pies, cakes, tarts, and tortes, plus brownies, scones, cream puffs, muffins, and more. Call ahead to see what she's baking. My favorites: the banana cream tart, topped with chocolate shavings and whipped cream; and the chocolate espresso cake. "Life's too short for cheap dessert," Morello says.

Donna English also bakes in a house—the one she lives in. The accountant credits one of her two college-age daughters, Nicole, with giving her the push to start **Just D'sserts** (71 Rte. 46 West, Elmwood Park; 201-799-7717; www.jdbysparklc.com). It all started on Mother's Day, 2004, when English made a selection of desserts for her church. One sweet thing led to another—Wesley Snipes stopped by her table at an arts festival in Englewood and bought "one or two of everything"—and pretty soon English was busy in her kitchen, filling orders. What makes Just D'sserts different is that English delivers—actually, Nicole and English's other daughter, Jade, do the delivering. English (college friends nicknamed her Sparkle because she always seemed to be smiling) makes a dynamite sweet potato cheesecake. Other items include cupcakes, cookies, brownies, and fruit pizzas, the latter made with graham cracker crust, whipped cream, cream cheese, and a variety of fruit.

Gourmet Food Trucks

It took a while before the trucks ended up on this side of the Hudson River, but the past few years have seen an influx of trucks open in Newark, Hoboken, and Jersey City. Regulations and ordinances seem to be stricter in New Jersey than New York, so the gourmet food truck scene here may never been as lively as the Big Apple's, but there are several worthy trucks in the Garden State. Leave behind any preconceived notions about "grease trucks" or "roach coaches"— these trucks serve restaurant-quality food.

Cinnamon Snail (lunch and dinner in Hoboken and Red Bank; check Twitter and Facebook for times and locations; www.cinnamonsnail .com; $). The Snail is the country's first mobile vegan organic restaurant, according to owner Adam Sobel. The rail-thin Sobel is having way too much fun; his items include the Floating Telepathic Baba Salad (with arugula, sage-fennel pesto, and rosemary-smoked walnuts) and the Chocolate Cocoa Transvestite Party—a chocolate doughnut. Recommended dishes: the blue-corn spelt pancakes, the Korean barbecue seitan, and pretty much all the baked goods.

The Krave (lunch and dinner in downtown Jersey City; updates on Twitter and Facebook; www.kravetruck.com; $). Judging by the lines, this Korean barbecue truck may be the most popular food truck in Jersey City. I love the miniburgers—stuffed with meat and kimchi on a toasted brioche bun; the kimchidillas, a flour tortilla with choice of sesame chicken, short rib or tangy pork, plus shredded kimchi and Monterey jack) and the barbecue rice platters with either pork or chicken.

qba A Cuban Kitchen (lunch and dinner in Montclair and Jersey City; also storefront at 128 Watchung Ave., Montclair; 973-744-7221; $). For truck, check Twitter and Facebook for exact times and locations.

Lynna Martinez, owner of qba A Cuban Kitchen, is thinking big; she hopes to open a national chain of Cuban quick-service restaurants. The *lechon* (Cuban pulled pork braised in its own juices) and the chicken marinated in garlic *mojo* are standouts, as are her specialty sauces.

The Taco Truck (lunch and dinner in Hoboken, Jersey City, and Newark; also storefront at 62 Newark St., Hoboken; www.thetacotruck.com; $). For truck, check Twitter and Facebook page for exact times and locations. Chris Viola and Jason Scott's truck did so well on the street that they opened a storefront in high-rent Hoboken. Their *tortas* (Mexican sandwiches) are highly recommended, and good value besides.

Two Pitas in a Pod (lunch and dinner in Newark, Jersey City, and Hoboken; check Twitter and Facebook for exact times and locations; www.twopitasinapod.com; $). Athos Kyriakides and Scot Sherwood are longtime buddies—they both grew up in Wayne—who decided to take the lunch truck plunge in 2010. They do creative, nourishing takes on Middle Eastern and Asian food—besides falafel, you can find lemon coriander chicken souvlaki, Mediterranean braised pork, lamb *kefta* kebab, even the Vietnamese sandwiches known as *banh mi*.

Taqueria Autentica (various locations, downtown Newark; check Twitter and Facebook for updates; www.taqueriaautentica.com; $). Mike Natiello quit his job as an attorney to make tacos. His Taqueria Autentica truck can usually be found on Mulberry Street in downtown Newark, a block from the Prudential Center. Natiello uses prime beef for his *carne asada*; you can taste the difference. His *tortas* are first-rate; try the chicken and chorizo/black bean. One must: his Mexican pudding, with cayenne and chiles—smooth, spicy, sensational.

own tea blend, called Ward's Deluxe, packaged in brown paper bags. Chai—spiced tea, from the Hindi word for *tea*—is also available. Ward's coffee can be found in about 500 restaurants, luncheonettes, diners, country clubs, and offices throughout the state. It's a tiny, atmospheric, altogether irresistible shop.

Vitamia & Sons Ravioli Co., 206 Harrison Ave., Lodi; (973) 546-1140; www.pastaboy.com. Another misnomer for a name; Vitamia sells much more than ravioli. Italians make up New Jersey's largest ethnic or ancestral group, and Vitamia is one of the best—and liveliest—Italian food shops in the state. Owner Francesco Paul Vitamia always has a smile on his face and a joke to tell, whether in English or Italian. "I met you once, I met you twice, and then I focaccia," he'll say. This is pasta heaven; more than 100 kinds of pasta, including three-color gnocchi and heart-shaped ravioli, are featured. Most of them are made on the premises. Sunday mornings, this place is packed when church gets out across the street, but the line moves quickly. Make sure you pick up some sausage bread if you stop here.

Farmers' Markets

Many of the farmers' markets in North Jersey are part of the **New Jersey Council of Farmers and Communities** (NJCFC) markets. For up-to-date NJCFC farmers' market locations, days, and times, visit the council's website at www.njcfc.org. Also check the state

Department of Agriculture's **Jersey Fresh** site at http://jerseyfresh .nj.gov. Community market hours often change from year to year.

Blairstown Farmers' Market, Route 521 and Stillwater Road, Blairstown. **Sat from 2 to 7 p.m., early** June through late October.

Bloomfield Farmers' Market, Bloomfield Avenue at State Street, Bloomfield. **Thurs from 1 to 7 p.m., early July through late October.**

Boonton Farmers' Market, Upper Plane Street parking lot, Boonton. **Sat from 8:30 a.m. to 2 p.m., mid-June through late October.**

Caldwell Farmers' Market, municipal lot between Smull and Personette streets, Caldwell. **Fri from 2 p.m. to 7 p.m., late June through late October.**

Cedar Grove Farmers' Market, Morgan Farm and Museum, 903 Pompton Ave., Cedar Grove. **Wed from 2 to 7 p.m., late June through late September.**

Chatham Borough Farmers' Market, train station, Chatham. **Sat from 8 a.m. to 1 p.m., late June through mid-November.**

FOOD INSTITUTE

Want the latest food industry trends and news? The **Food Institute** (1 Broadway, 2nd Floor, Elmwood Park, 201-791-5570; www.foodinstitute.com), the best source of information on the food industry, is located in Elmwood Park. An annual membership costs $695, which entitles you to the weekly *Food Institute Report,* breaking news, daily updates, detailed studies, targeted reports, and access to the extensive archives, but you can read the latest industry news and developments on the institute's website for free. Learn about mergers and acquisitions, FTC approvals, big deals, little deals, recalls, press releases, and more.

Clifton Farmers' Market, 1st Street and Clifton Avenue, Clifton. Fri from 11 a.m. to 6 p.m., mid-June through early October.

Denville Farmers' Market, Bloomfield Avenue parking lot, Denville. Sun from 8:30 a.m. to 1 p.m., mid-June through mid-October.

East Hanover Farmers' Market, 609 Ridgedale Ave., East Hanover. Mon from noon to 6 p.m., mid-June through late October.

East Orange Farmers' Market, Halstedt Street and Central Avenue, East Orange. Tues from 9 a.m. to 5 p.m., early July through late October.

Elizabeth Farmers' Market, Union Square, between Elizabeth Avenue and High Street, Elizabeth. Tues from 11 a.m. to 6 p.m., mid-June through late November.

Emerson Farmers' Market, Linwood Avenue, Emerson. Sun from 10 a.m. to 3 p.m., late June through late October.

Englewood Farmers' Market, corner of N. Van Brunt and Demarest Avenue, Englewood. Fri from 11 a.m. to 6 p.m., mid-June through late October.

Fort Lee Farmers' Market, Fort Lee Community Center, 1355 Inwood Ter., Fort Lee. Sun from 8 a.m, to 2 p.m., mid-June through mid-November.

Friends of Van Vorst Park Farmers' Market, Jersey Avenue and Montgomery Street, Jersey City. Sat from 8 a.m. to 3 p.m., early May through November.

Hackettstown Farmers' Market, Main Street, Hackettstown. Mon from 2 to 7 p.m., early June through October.

Harvest Square Farmers' Market, 492 Bramhall Ave., Jersey City. Tues from 3 to 6 p.m., mid-July through late October.

Hasbrouck Heights Farmers' Market, Boulevard and Washington Place, Hasbrouck Heights. Tues from noon to 6 p.m., mid-June through late September.

Haworth Farmers' Market, Terrace Street parking lot, Haworth. Tues from 2 to 7 p.m., early June through late November.

Historic Downtown Special Improvement District Farmers' Market, Grove Street PATH station, Jersey City. Mon and Thurs from 4 to 8 p.m., early June through late December.

Hoboken Farmers' Market, Washington Street at Newark Street, Hoboken. Tues from 3 to 7:30 p.m., late June through early November.

Hoboken Uptown Farmers' Market, Hudson Street between 13th and 14th Streets, Hoboken. Tues from 3 to 7:30 p.m., late June through early November.

Jersey City Farmers' Market I, St. Patrick's Church, Bramhall and Ocean Avenues, Jersey City. Tues from 3:30 to 6:30 p.m., July through October.

Jersey City Farmers' Market II, Journal Square, Jersey City. Wed from 11 a.m. to 7 p.m., early July through mid-November.

Jersey City Farmers' Market III, Newport/Pavonia PATH station, Jersey City. Tues, Thurs, and Sat from 11 a.m. to 7 p.m., early June through late November.

Journal Square Farmers' Market, Kennedy Boulevard, Jersey City. Wed and Fri from 10 a.m. to 7 p.m., late June through late November.

Kearny Farmers' Market, Kearny Avenue between Bergen Avenue and Afton Street, Kearny. Thurs from noon to 6 p.m., mid-June through late October.

Linden Farmers' Market, Raymond Wood Bauer Promenade, Wood Avenue, Linden. Mon from noon to 6 p.m., early June through late October.

Livingston Farmers' Market, the Village at Livingston, 277 Eisenhower Ave., Livingston. Thurs from noon to 6 p.m., late June through late September.

Main Street South Orange Farmers' Market, 14 Sloan St., South Orange. Wed from 2 to 7 p.m., late June through late October,.

Madison Farmers' Market, Waverly Place, Madison. Thurs from 2 to 7 p.m., late June through late October.

Maplewood Farmers' Market, Indiana Street parking lot, 1 block west of Prospect Street, Maplewood. Mon from 2 to 7 p.m., mid-June through late October.

Market Square Farmers' Market, Bethany Baptist Church, 275 W. Market St., Newark. Thurs from 10 a.m. to 4 p.m., July through November.

Millburn Farmers' Market, Essex Street at the Main Street parking lot, Millburn. Tues from 8 a.m. to 2 p.m., mid-June through late October.

Montclair Farmers' Market, Walnut Street, Montclair. Sat from 8 a.m. to 2 p.m., early June through November.

Morris Plains Farmers' Market, Speedwell Avenue Extension, Morris Plains. Sat from 9 a.m. to 2 p.m., mid-June through late October.

Morristown Farmers' Market, parking lot between Morris Avenue and Dumont Place (behind the Morristown Diner), Morristown. Sun from 8:30 a.m. to 2 p.m., mid-June through late October.

Netcong Famers' Market, Main Street and Route 46, Netcong. Sat from 9 a.m. to 2 p.m., mid-June through early October.

Newark Farmers' Market I, Broad and Park Place, Newark. Thurs from 11 a.m. to 4 p.m., late July through late October.

Two Great Delis

The Millburn Deli, in Millburn, and the Evergreen Deli, in Springfield, couldn't be any more different, but they are both special. The **Millburn Deli** (328 Millburn Ave.; 973-379-5800; www.millburndeli.com) is a brightly lit, spacious shop with a dizzying array of sandwiches, subs, salads, soups, and fruit and cheese platters, and you absolutely must take a number. The **Evergreen Deli** (529 S. Springfield Ave.; 973-376-6095), with its screen door and faded tile floor, is a throwback to the 1920s, when the building housed a grocery store. The Millburn Deli's menu is much more expansive; you can get mesquite turkey with red onion, greens, smoked Gouda, and chipotle mayo on red onion focaccia. Its signature sandwich is the Gobbler—sliced turkey, turkey stuffing, and cranberry sauce. It's like Thanksgiving in a sandwich.

The Evergreen Deli, meanwhile, serves up maybe the state's best pastrami sandwich. Owner Tony Vascucci doesn't use top or bottom round for his pastrami, like many delis, but the plate of the brisket, a more expensive cut. Tony also offers weekday specials—chicken française, meat loaf, shrimp salad, and other items. His wife, Angel, makes the cheesecake, cookies, and brownies. Two different delis, two different experiences, two great stops.

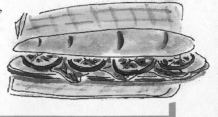

Newport Centre Farmers' Market, Newport Centre Mall. Tues from noon to 7 p.m., June through September.

New Providence Farmers' Market, Municipal Center, 360 Elkwood Ave., New Providence. Wed from 1 to 5 p.m., mid-June through late October.

Nutley Farmers' Market, municipal lot, William Street, Nutley. Sun from 9 a.m. to 1 p.m., early June through late Oct.

Old Lafayette Village Farmers' Market, Route 15, Lafayette. Sun from 10 a.m. to 3 p.m., late June through late October. The village itself is a colorful collection of shops and restaurants.

Paterson Farmers' Market, 449 E. Railway Ave., Paterson. Tues through Fri from 9 a.m. to 2 p.m.; Sat from 7 a.m. to 5 p.m., and Sun from 7 a.m. to 4 p.m., April 1 through December 31. . One of the bigger, and more colorful, farmers' markets in the state.

Pompton Lakes Farmers' Market, 247 Wanaque Ave., Pompton Lakes. Fri from 11 a.m. to 6 p.m., late June through mid-October.

Rahway Farmers' Market, E. Milton Avenue and Irving Street, Rahway. Thurs from 11 a.m. to 7 p.m., early May through mid-November.

Ramsey Farmers' Market, train station, Ramsey. Sun from 9 a.m. to 2 p.m., mid-June through mid-November.

Ridgewood Farmers' Market, train station, Ridgewood. Sun from 9 a.m. to 3 p.m., late June through late October.

Ringwood Farmers' Market, 30 Cannici Dr., Ringwood. Sat from 9 a.m. to 1 p.m., late May through late October.

Riverdale Farmers' Market, 211 Hamburg Tpke., Riverdale. Tues from 2:30 to 7 p.m., mid-June through mid-October.

River Vale Farmers' Market, Town Hall, 406 River Vale Rd., River Vale. Thurs from noon to 6 p.m., late June through late October.

Riverview Farmers' Market, Fisk Park, Jersey City. Sun from 9 a.m. to 3 p.m., mid-June through late October.

Roseland Farmers' Market, corner of Roseland and Harrison avenues, Roseland. Fri from noon to 7 p.m., mid-June through late October.

Roselle Park Farmers' Market, Chestnut Street and E. Grant Avenue, Roselle Park. Wed from 1 to 6 p.m., early July through late October.

CHEESE

Imagine a world without cheese. I can't, for one. No cheeseburgers. No grilled cheese sandwiches. And no—horror of horrors—pizza!

Sure, you can find a wide variety of cheese at your local supermarket, but the state's cheese shops offer the really good, one-of-a-kind stuff.

Here are three cheese shops—two in North Jersey, one down the Shore—that will fill all your cheese needs. Each makes quality sandwiches, too. In addition, there's a creamery that offers the ultimate cheese tour.

The Cheese Cave (14 Monmouth St., Red Bank; 732-842-0796; www.cheesecaveshop.com; $). Steve Catania, a former chef, has a wide-ranging knowledge of cheese and is only too willing to share it. He'll guide you from the milder goat and sheep's milk cheeses to the more assertive blue cheeses. Recommended cheeses here: Ossau-Iraty, a French sheep milk's cheese; Idiazabal, a sheep's milk cheese from Spain; and Prairie Breeze, a dry, crumbly cheddar from Iowa.

Cheese . . . Please! (26 Eastman St., Cranford; 908-272-4500; chzplz.com; $). There may be no more enthusiastic cheesemonger than Maria Tisdall, owner of Cheese . . . Please! She spent 22 years as

Rutherford Farmers' Market, Williams Plaza, downtown Rutherford. Wed from 11 a.m. to 6 p.m., early June through late Oct; Sat from 8 a.m. to 2 p.m., early July through late October.

a chef, including a stint cooking for 120 nuns. More than 100 cheeses are on display, and there are always a half dozen cheeses to sample at a side table near the front of the store. Excellent sandwiches, too—try the Matthew, with Firecracker chèvre and herb cream cheese, or the Erin, with sharp cheddar, chutney, and sweet apple.

Crane's Delicatessan & Cheese Shoppe (175 Maplewood Ave., Maplewood; 973-763-2050; cranesdeli.blogspot.com; $).

Steve Crane's shop in Maplewood Village is smaller than most, but no other cheese shop I know of offers breakfast, and great bread besides (from Balthazar's in New York). Recommended: Cypress Grove Lamb Chopper, a sheep milk's cheese, and Cahill's Irish whiskey cheese.

Valley Shepherd Creamery (50 Fairmount Rd., Long Valley; 908-876-3200; www.valleyshepherd.com; $). For something completely different, pay a visit to Valley Shepherd in the fall for a tour that includes the creamery's cheese "cave" (where cheese is kept in cold storage). Favorite cheeses here: the Nettlesome, Somerset, and Valley Thunder.

Scotch Plains Farmers' Market, municipal parking lot, Park Avenue, Scotch Plains. Sat from 8 a.m. to 2 p.m., early June through early November.

South Orange Farmers' Market, NJ Transit commuter parking lot, Sloan Street and W. Orange Avenue, South Orange. Wed from 2 to 7 p.m., June through October.

Sparta Farmers' Market, 65 Main St., Sparta. Sat from 10 a.m. to 2 p.m., mid-May through late October.

Summit Farmers' Market, Park and Shop Lot 2, Maple Street and DeForest Avenue, Summit. Sun from 8 a.m. to 1 p.m., early June through mid-November.

Springfield Farmers' Market, 101 Mountain Ave., Springfield. Mon from noon to 6 p.m., late June through late October.

Teaneck Farmers' Market, Garrison Road and Beverly Road, Teaneck. Thurs from noon to 6 p.m., late June through late October.

Tenafly Farmers' Market, Washington Street and Tenafly Road, Tenafly. Sun from 10 a.m. to 2 p.m., mid-May through late October.

University Hospital Auxiliary Farmers' Market, 150 Bergen St., Newark. Tues from 11 a.m. to 3 p.m., early June through late October.

Washington Borough (Warren County) Farmers' Market, Route 57, Washington Borough. Fri from 3 to 7 p.m., late June through late September.

Washington Township (Bergen County) Farmers' Market, 79 Pascack Rd., Washington. Sun from 9 a.m. to 1 p.m., mid-June through late September.

Westfield Farmers' Market, NJ Transit station, South Avenue parking lot, Westfield. Sat from 9:30 a.m. to 2 p.m., early July through late October.

West Milford Farmers' Market, 1911 Union Valley Rd., Hewitt section of town. Wed from 3 to 7 p.m., June through late Sept, and 2 to 6 p.m., late September through late October.

West Orange Farmers' Market, 66 Main St., behind town hall, West Orange. Fri from noon to 6 p.m., early July through late October.

Farms & Farm Stands

Abma's Farm & Market, 700 Lawlins Rd., Wyckoff; (201) 891-0278; www.abmasfarm.com. A family-run operation since 1935, Abma's is a roadside institution. More than 50 kinds of vegetables are grown here, and you can pick your own pumpkins in the fall. The market, housed in an 18th-century Dutch barn, offers produce, fruit, homemade pies and bread, condiments, homemade baskets, even toys. There is a kiddie zoo with goats, cows, llamas, rabbits, and other animals. Open year-round; closed Sun.

Alstede Farms, 84 Rte. 513, Chester; (908) 879-7189; www.alstede farms.com. This red-roofed farm market is a familiar sight along pic-

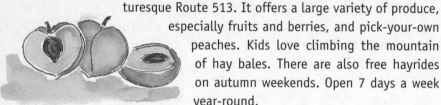

turesque Route 513. It offers a large variety of produce, especially fruits and berries, and pick-your-own peaches. Kids love climbing the mountain of hay bales. There are also free hayrides on autumn weekends. Open 7 days a week year-round.

Ashley Farms, 25 Hillsdale Ave., Flanders; (973) 584-7578; www.ashleyfarmsonline.com. This farm stand sells fresh fruit and vegetables and is known for its turkeys, both fresh and cooked. You'll also find freshly baked bread, apple cider, cider doughnuts, preserves and jellies, salad dressings, spices, homemade soup, and chili. Open year-round from 9 a.m. to 7 p.m. Mon through Fri, 9 a.m. to 6 p.m. Sat, and 9 a.m. to 5 p.m. Sun.

Best's Fruit Farm, 40 Rte. 46 West, Independence; (908) 852-3777. Best's gets the vote here for the best pies in North Jersey. This farm market, open year-round, is a post-and-beam building stocked with breads, cereals, snacks, soups, jellies—and pies.

Varieties include peach, apple, apple crumb, fruit berry, cherry, blueberry, and coconut custard. All feature thick, sugary crusts. My personal favorite is the blueberry, but you'll have your own.

Colin's Apple Pit, 222 Rte. 206 North, Branchville; (973) 948-3685. The low-slung, red, barnlike building that is Colin's is a roadside landmark in this part of Sussex County. Look here for produce, apples, cider, and especially the pies and other baked goods, including apple doughnuts, cinnamon twists and rolls, bear claws, and the biggest scones I've ever seen. Good, honest pies, especially the blueberry and apple. Other kinds include cherry, Dutch apple, and rhubarb. The mailing address is Branchville, but Colin's is actually located in Sandyston; the market is 5 miles north of the small town of Culver Lake. Open 7 a.m. to 6 p.m. year-round.

Demarest Farms, 244 Werimus Rd., Hillsdale; (201) 666-0472; www.demarestfarms.com. This place is known for its apples—Cortland, Empire, Gala, Golden Delicious, Winesap, and other varieties. It also offers a wide selection of fruits and vegetables. Open daily from April 1 through December 24.

Hacklebarney Farm Cider Mill, 104 State Park Rd., Chester; (908) 879-6593; www.njcidermill.com. This is apple heaven. Cortland, Empire, Gala, Golden Delicious, Jonagold, Red Delicious, Grimes Golden, Ida Red, Northern Spy,

THE JOYS OF DIM SUM

Dim sum is one of the great pleasures of Chinese food, and one relatively undiscovered by most Americans. Dim sum—Cantonese for "heart's delight"—is a collection of appetizers, snacks, and pastries that can include anything from steamed buns, shrimp dumplings, turnip cakes, and stuffed eggplant to spare ribs, stuffed crab claw, pepper corn squid, and sizzling veal with black pepper sauce. The items are wheeled on carts from table to table. You pick the dim sum you want; waiters keep track of what you've selected. Individual items cost just a few dollars, which means that two people can eat well for $20 or so. There's no need to traipse into Chinatown for first-rate dim sum; the following four restaurants in the Garden State (two in North Jersey and two in Central Jersey) have acquired a reputation for these tasty treats. Visit any of them and eat to your heart's delight. Dim sum is generally available from 11 a.m. to 3 p.m. Sat, Sun, and holidays only.

China Gourmet (468 Eagle Rock Ave., West Orange; 973-731-6411; www.chinagourmetnj.com) is a simple, tranquil place; you can watch your dim sum being cooked on a portable grill. Great dim sum here

and other varieties are all grown here. It all adds up to great cider—hot, mulled, and cold. The bakery offers cider doughnuts, raspberry logs (fruit-filled puff pastry), apple dumplings, apple cider puff pastry twists, double fudge chocolate brownies, and other treats. Pies include apple lattice, apple crumb, French apple, includes the pork triangle, a meat-filled puff pastry; baked pork buns, sweet and savory; and the shark fin dumpling.

Feeling brave? Try the cold jellyfish platter at **Joy Luck Chinese Pavilion** (555 Northfield Ave., West Orange; 973-243-9288). The very best sweet and pork buns can be found here; the roast pork and the Chinese broccoli with oyster sauce are also recommended.

The entrance to **Dynasty,** in Central Jersey (100 Rte. 22 West, Green Brook; 732-752-6363; www .dynastim.com), is fronted by stone lions; owner Timothy Kei owns both the Dynasty, which opened in the late 1990s, and Zen Central, which opened in London in the late 1980s. Standout dim sum here: the vegetarian dumpling, the shrimp dumpling, pork chops Peking style, and the bacon and shrimp roll.

Sunny Palace (1069 Rte. 18 South, East Brunswick; 732-651-8668; www.sunnypalace.com), housed in a former nightclub in Central Jersey, offers nearly 90 kinds of dim sum, from the outstanding pork and shrimp dumpling and shrimp wrapped in bacon to cheese-topped scallops and stuffed shrimp in bean curd skin.

and harvest—a mix of apple, blueberry, pear, and peach. You can even get cider dogs and baked beans, homemade jams, and soups. It's a popular fall destination; the corn maze gets bigger and better every year. Open Tues through Sun, generally from the first week of September through December 23.

Kash Farm, 181 Petersburg Rd., Hackettstown; (908) 852-0570. Among the offerings at this farm are eggplant, squash, peppers, beans, tomatoes, brussels sprouts, red cabbage, kale, basil, mint, and parsley. There's a petting zoo with goats and potbellied pigs. Open from 10 a.m. to 6 p.m. Thurs through Sun year-round.

Lucey's Berry Farm, 41 Beaver Run Rd., Lafayette; (973) 383-4309. Black raspberries, blueberries, and summer red raspberries are among the berries you'll find here, along with sweet corn and homemade jams and jellies. Open daily from 9 a.m. to 6 p.m., July through Oct.

Maxwell's Farm, 170 Changewater Rd., Changewater; (908) 797-3503. Bill Maxwell of Maxwell's Farm is known for his range of tomatoes, especially grape tomatoes, which have found increasing favor among farmers and consumers in recent years. In fact, the grape tomato market has overtaken the cherry tomato market in New Jersey. Grape tomatoes are smaller and sweeter than cherry tomatoes. Bill grows a wide variety of tomatoes for his roadside stand, the Westfield Farmers' Market, and three New York City greenmarkets. Open daily May through Oct; call for hours.

Nettie Ochs Cider Mill, 32 Old Short Hills Rd., Livingston; (973) 992-7753. This place is a local landmark, but it's not well known outside the immediate area. The tradition began in the 1870s, when Gottlieb Ochs (pronounced "ox") started making cider. Today his great-grandson, Bob Ochs, runs the business, which is named for

Gottlieb's daughter-in-law. Bob makes cider 7 days week from mid-September generally through February. "I want to keep it like it is, small and unique, so people have to come here to get it," Bob says. "It's the mixture of fruit, the quality of fruit, and the cleanliness of the equipment that makes good cider. If you use good fruit, you don't have to filter your cider because there's no junk left on the bottom." Top-quality apples are used. "There's something my father used to say: 'If you can't eat the apples, you shouldn't be drinking them.' I adhere to that same policy." Three thousand pounds of apples yield about 200 gallons of cider. Bob also sells apple cider doughnuts, honey, home-smoked cheese, jellies, and homemade pies. The mill is open daily from 9 a.m. to 5 p.m., Thurs to 8 p.m., from mid-September through February.

Stony Hill Farm Market, 15 North Rd., Chester; (908) 879-2908; www.stonyhillgardens.com. The draw here, beside the 18,000 square feet of greenhouses, is the Maize Quest, a maze adventure laid out on the 10-acre cornfield. Every year it has a different theme. A recent one centered on Egypt; your journey through the maze pathways taught you about the ancient Egyptians, the pharaohs, and the monuments they built. From the air, the maze looked like the Great Pyramid. Also available are hayrides and pick-your-own pumpkins. Open 7 days a week from 9 a.m. to 6 p.m., from May 1 through December 24.

Sun High Orchard, 19 Canfield Ave., Randolph; (973) 584-4734; www.sunhigh.com. Here you'll find vegetables, sweet corn, tomatoes, raspberries, peaches, apples, pick-your-own pumpkins, good pies, and apple cider and doughnuts. Open daily from 9 a.m. to 6 p.m., May through Nov.

Food Events

March
Annual Maple Sugaring Festival, New Jersey Audubon Society's Weis Ecology Center, 150 Snake Den Rd., Ringwood; (973) 835-2160. The festival, held since the late 1980s, is a fun, educational event for children and adults. You tour the grounds, participate in a tree-tapping, go into the kitchen for a tasting, and finish it off with a pancake breakfast using maple syrup made on-site. The center is also a popular field trip destination for area school and scout troops.

Late May
Garden State Wine Growers Association Blues and Wine Festival, Natirar Park, Peapack-Gladstone; (609) 588-0085; www .newjerseywines.com. Hundreds of New Jersey wines are available

for sampling, plus great blues music, crafters, kids' activities, carriage rides, classic cars, and gourmet food, everything from jambalaya and baby crab cakes to London broil sandwiches, chicken Caesar wraps, and gourmet desserts. Wineries represented at the festival include Alba Vineyard, Amalthea Cellars, Amwell Valley Vineyard, Balic Winery, Belleview Winery, Cream Ridge Winery, **Four Sisters Winery** (p. 100), Hopewell Valley Winery, Tomasello Winery, Unionville Vineyards, and Valenzano Winery. Admission fee includes wineglass, wine samples, music, parking, and entrance into Waterloo Village. The village is a National Historic Site and features a 1625 Lenape Indian village, an 1826 farm site, and an 1880 canal town. Admission without the wine samples is reduced for ages 16 to 20; free for under 16.

May or June

Crawfish Festival, Sussex County Fairgrounds, Augusta; www .crawfishfest.com. An annual event since 1989, the Crawfish Fest is a rousing, rollicking testament to good food and music. Founder Michael Arnone ships 10,000 pounds of live crawfish and a $30,000 crawfish cooking rig from Louisiana, where he lives, for this weekend event, one of the state's liveliest. Crawfish, crawfish pie, po'boys, jambalaya, étouffée, and other kinds of Cajun and Creole food are served, to the accompaniment of a dozen top Cajun, zydeco, and Delta blues bands. There are dancing tents, crafts, and plenty of activities for the kids.

June

Father's Day Pig Roast, Four Sisters Winery at Matarazzo Farms, 783 Rte. 519, Belvidere; (908) 475-3671; www.matarazzofarm.com/winery. Bring Dad to a good old-fashioned pig roast; he'll be happy you did. The highlight is a roasted suckling pig on a spit; you eat outside, under a party tent. Four Sisters also hosts a Hawaiian luau in mid-July, with tropical treats off the grill, a wine tasting and wine cellar tour, and the ever-popular and sidesplittingly funny limbo contest!

Late July

St. Ann's Feast, Church of St. Ann, 7th and Jefferson Streets, Hoboken; (201) 659-1114; www.st-annchurch.com. This big, popular, 10-day Italian street festival offers a mouthwatering array of food, games, kiddie rides, and nightly entertainment. The church was completed in 1906; the festival has been held since 1910. The biggest food draw: the outstanding *zeppoles* made by the women of St. Ann's Guild. One year a local newspaper published what it claimed were the ingredients to the secret recipe. The guild members quickly and angrily responded that the recipe published wasn't the real one.

August

New Jersey State Fair/Sussex County Farm and Horse Show, Sussex County Fairgrounds, Augusta; (973) 948-5500; www.njstatefair.org. The grandest of the state's county fairs, the Sussex County Farm and Horse Show has also served as the New Jersey

State Fair in recent years. It's a fun, enormously entertaining event, with flower shows, beauty contests, chainsaw wood carving, racing pigs, antique farm machinery, horse shows, and carnival rides, among the many attractions. Grandma's Favorite Cookie Contest, to which grandmothers from around the state submit their cookies for judging, is one of the most popular events. The food choices are nearly endless, from corn dogs and curly fries to pierogies and waffle ice-cream sandwiches. Must-tries: roast beef sandwiches from the Branchville Rotary Club, hand-rolled pretzels from Der Pretzel Haus, and fudge from Michael Koontz Candies.

Learn to Cook

Chef and Sommelier for a Day, Hilton Short Hills, 41 John F. Kennedy Pkwy., Short Hills; (973) 379-0100, ext. 7980. The hotel hosts Thursday programs for 1 or 2 persons who plan and help prepare dinner and wine selection, and then dine with up to 6 of their guests. The programs are held year-round in the restaurant kitchen of the Hilton Short Hills; the faculty includes the restaurant's executive chef and sommelier.

Chef Central, Paramus Town Center, 240 Rte. 17 North, Paramus; (201) 576-0100; www.chefcentral.com. The sprawling 15,000-square-foot store provides one-stop shopping for the serious and not-too-serious cook. There are 30 kinds of roasting pans,

50 different stockpots, 100-plus frying pans, 50 kinds of coffeemakers and espresso machines, cookbooks, wine and spirits, gifts, gourmet foods—and more than 365 cooking classes yearly. "The most amazing place—a Toys 'R' Us for cooks," says Alton Brown, host of Food TV's *Good Eats*. There's an even bigger Chef Central in Hartsdale, New York. Both stores host free demonstrations and cookbook signings and offer, for a fee, classes on everything from sushi making and cake decorating to cooking for one, cooking for kids, and father-daughter cooking.

Classic Thyme, 161 E. Broad St., Westfield; (908) 232-5445; www .classicthyme.com. Classic Thyme has expanded full-time, and then some, on the cooking-school front. It was once a storefront with a range of cookware, bakeware, accessories, and kitchen gadgets. Now owner David P. Martone is concentrating on his increasingly popular cooking school curriculum. Classes include Kids Cook on Their Day Off, Breakfast in Bed for Mom, preteen culinary workshops, and, for adults, Cooking with Beer; Holiday Cooking from Your Pressure Cooker, a 3-day dessert school, a master class on bread making, an 8-week wine school, a Friday night sushi workshop, and much, much more.

Cooktique, 9 W. Railroad Ave., Tenafly; (201) 568-7990; www .cooktique.com. This shop stocks a large selection of professional pots and pans, tools, gadgets, and molds, plus pastas, sauces, gourmet preserves and jams, salsas, marinades, and other items. But the main draw here is the dizzying variety of cooking classes, most held in the evening. Recent offerings have included Food of Naples; Beginners Cake Decorating; Sweet and Savory Crepes; Pizza Primer; Light, Quick, and Easy Summer Pastas; and Fabulously Fast and Fishy, among many others. Co-owner Cathy McCauley also gives Wednesday and Friday afternoon classes for children, from preschool to ages 10 and up. Adult classes are generally in the $40 to $75 range.

Gingercreek Cooking School, 304 Rte. 173, Stewartsville; (908) 479-6062. This is a cooking school with a difference: Owner-instructor Nancy Wyant offers 2.5-hour classes/demonstrations in a wide variety of American and European cuisines. Classes have included the cooking of Tuscany and Provence; grilling; English pub fare; Mexican food; and bread baking. Nancy uses the finest and freshest seasonal ingredients, and students gather around the table in her country home to sample the results. They also receive recipes for each dish prepared in class. There are classes for both adults and children. Class size is 12. Nancy started the school in 1987. See Nancy Wyant's recipe for **Fresh Raspberry Crostini** on p. 277.

Learn about Wine

Bacchus Winemaking Club, 1540 Rte. 37 West, Toms River; www.bacchusnj.com. Thousands of New Jerseyans make their own wine; a homemade wine competition held by the *Star-Ledger* attracted more than 400 entries. Many who make homemade wine do it at home; others prefer the convenience of a wine school, which provides grapes, barrels, and guidance. The state's first wine school was Bacchus, started by Dominick Chirichillo in 1997 and named after the Roman god of wine. Winemaking courses are broken into four 1-hour sessions. There's also an annual harvest kickoff party in the summer that is open to the public.

Landmark Eateries

After Athens, 19 Park Ave., Rutherford; (201) 729-0005; www .eroscafenj.com/after-athens; Greek; $$$. This is the best subterranean dining spot in the state, although admittedly it's not a big category. Upstairs is Eros Cafe, a cool, soothing spot with comfy chairs and sofas and delectable-looking desserts. Downstairs, though, is where things get really interesting. Owners Dimitri Valavanis and Maureen Frendak transformed a former hardware store into a cave, complete with faux columns, miniature friezes, and scalloped lights. Taverna? After Athens is a *kaverna*. Recommended: the Portabello After Athens; the cheese pie; the charcoal-grilled pork chops, meaty and monstrous; the pastitsio; and, for dessert, the peanut butter chocolate brownie cake and the blueberry pie. After Athens is a rarity: a one-of-a-kind dining experience with terrific food.

Andrew's Project, 737 Broadway, Bayonne; (201) 339-0033; http://andrewsproject.com; Healthy; $$. **Vasantha Perera, owner of Andrew's Project, which is named after his son, really gets around. There's photo of him with former president Bill Clinton on the wall, and the Sri Lankan–born Perera has cooked everywhere from Greece, Switzerland, and Monaco to Saudi Arabia, the United Arab Emirates, and Morocco. Don't be fooled by the cramped front of the store; there's a pleasant outdoor cafe out back. The menu offers healthy, creative fare from around the world—Mexican, Cuban, Jamaican, Middle Eastern, Russian, and more. Perera uses plants and herbs from his garden, and makes his own pasta.**

Benanti's, 16 W. 22nd St., Bayonne; (201) 437-5525; Italian Deli; $. I love the sandwich-ordering process at this old-fashioned Italian deli. You pick out a roll or loaf of bread from one of the cardboard boxes by the window, then walk to the counter and tell Charlie Benanti or one of his guys what you want in it. It's almost an insult to call the sandwiches here subs. Benanti's is old school, all right; even the breath mints at the counter are imported.

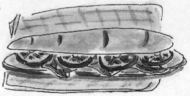

Boulevard Drinks, 48 Journal Sq., Jersey City; (201) 656-1855; Hot Dogs; $. The fitful, flickering sign above the marquee lets you know that you've arrived at Boulevard Drinks. If there were a National Register of Historic Food Places, then Boulevard Drinks, open since 1937, would be on it. The open-air stand doesn't look like much: yellow walls, bright-green menu board, a dozen stools, and characters right out of Damon Runyon. Hot dogs are priced in odd amounts—$1.13, $1.52, and so on, which seems appropriate. "People always talk about Rutt's Hut and places like that," says one regular. "They never talk about Boulevard Drinks." Pay one visit, and you won't stop talking about Boulevard Drinks.

Cafe Bello Ristorante, 1044 Ave. C, Bayonne; (201) 437-7538; Italian; $$. There are scant few restaurants in New Jersey that serve excellent pizza and Italian food; Cafe Bello is one of them. The pizzas, from a tiny brick oven near the bar, are uniformly excellent;

 try the Margherita, or the white pizza with prosciutto. The pasta dishes get the same loving care; go with the angel hair pasta in spicy vodka sauce, the *pappardelle ai porcini,* or the *rigatoni rossi verdi.* Bayonne is considered a pizza stronghold; Cafe Bello offers the city's best pizzas, and standout Italian food besides.

Cafe Matisse, 167 Park Ave., Rutherford; (201) 935-2995; www .cafematisse.com; American; $$$. Peter Loria's top-notch restaurant manages to be beautiful, elegant, and playful, all at the same time. Reproductions of Matisse paintings line the walls, which are done in a warm faux finish. The cuisine is contemporary American; appetizers include lightly peppered smoked salmon and baby arugula with dill

A Coffeehouse with Karma

In recent years coffeehouses have popped up quicker than fast-rising biscuits in New Jersey. Even the smallest town seems to have one or two latte-laden haunts. But one coffee shop in this part of the state stands out.

The decor at **Rockn' Joe,** formerly Cafe Rock (5 Eastman St., Cranford; 908-276-0595), is guaranteed to induce a little instant karma; the walls are lined with framed albums of the psychedelic and post-psychedelic era. Blind Faith. Black Sabbath. Jimi Hendrix. King Crimson. Peter Frampton. OK, so maybe some of owner Kevin Brennan's album choices are better than others. But there's no dispute over the coffee he serves; the cafe has earned the prestigious Golden Cup award (based on the quality of coffee beans and the coffee itself) from the Specialty Coffee Association of America every year since 2000, the only New Jersey shop to do so. The regular coffee, good and rich, will jump-start the groggiest of mornings. Good salads, sandwiches, and desserts are here, too. There are tables inside, and out on the sidewalk, but the prime sipping spots are the chic chairs and sofas in the front "parlor." There are also locations at 900 Green Ln., Union; (908) 354-0600; 339 Bloomfield Ave., Caldwell; (973) 226-1116; 3570 Rte. 27, Kendall Park; (732) 821-9500; 63 Main St., Millburn; (973) 376-6111; 1805 Ocean Ave., Point Pleasant Beach; (732) 899-1002; and 20 Prospect St., Westfield; (908) 232-1660.

lemon yogurt, spiced pistachio and toasted onion flatbread, and Parmesan-dusted shrimp with grilled marinated artichoke hearts, broccoli rabe goat cheese dumpling, lemon garlic crème, and lemon confit. Entrees include pan-grilled wild Pacific salmon fillet with currants and French lentils, topped with ginger-cumin-glazed carrot batons and spicy cucumber yogurt sauce. If your pocketbook allows you just one visit, make it in the summer, when you can dine in the restaurant's exquisite outdoor garden.

Chart House, Pier D-T, Lincoln Harbor, Harbor Boulevard, Weehawken; (201) 348-6628; www .chart-house.com; American; $$$. For pure dining drama, the Chart House may be unparalleled in New Jersey. This classy but convivial restaurant on the Hudson River offers an eye-popping panorama of the glittering Manhattan skyline. It's a great place for dinner or just drinks at the bar. They make a mean lobster bisque here. Try the coconut shrimp as an appetizer, and the Parmesan- and garlic-crusted Chilean sea bass, atop linguine with a terrific tomato basil sauce. There is also a Chart House at the Golden Nugget Hotel & Casino in Atlantic City—with a picturesque view of Farley Marina.

Cooper's, 594 Orange St., Newark; (973) 482-0316; $; www .coopersdeli.com; Deli; $. Low ceilings, nearly bare walls, two windows—one for lottery, one for liquor. No menus, or at least none in evidence. Walk up to the display case and tell the man what you want. He'll scribble some cryptic letters and symbols on a plastic bag, making it look like the sandwich-shop version of the Rosetta Stone. Is this any place to get a good pastrami on rye? You bet it is. A sandwich here will cost you five bucks, and it's unlikely you'll find a fatter sandwich, at that or any price. Place your order, and watch the sandwich makers slice and dice. Just when you think they've finished layering enough meat on the roll, they'll throw on what seems like another half pound or so. I counted no fewer than 34 slices of salami in each hulking half of the salami and provolone. My one quibble: The meat deserves a better roll than the slightly squishy hard roll here. Also at 567 S. Orange Ave., Newark; (973) 416-8930.

Dining Room at the Hilton Short Hills, 41 John F. Kennedy Pkwy., Short Hills; (973) 379-0100; American; $$$. This is New Jersey's only AAA five-diamond restaurant, located, appropriately, in Short Hills, one of the state's most exclusive enclaves. (Quickest way to start an argument with someone from Short Hills? Tell them they really live in Millburn, of which Short Hills is part.) In any event, the Dining Room is the place for a big event: closing a business deal, popping the question, celebrating a special occasion. Entrees include a slow-roasted rack of lamb with niçoise olives and roasted red peppers; Australian prawns with homemade tagliatelle; and Peking duck breast. The hotel has two casual dining options: the Terrace, which offers informal American cuisine, plus a popular

Chengdu 23: Best Authentic Chinese

Outside of Italian, Chinese restaurants are the most common in New Jersey. Most offer the usual Chinese-American standards— egg drop soup, fried rice, General Tso's chicken—you know the routine. Several restaurants are more authentic, and it's no surprise their clientele is largely Chinese. **Chengdu 23** (8 Willowbrook Rd., Wayne, 973-812-2800; www.chengdu23.com; $$) is the best of the bunch. The names of the dishes alone are enticing. Ants Climbing a Tree does not involve ants or a tree; it's minced pork in cellophane noodles, and a delicious side dish. Chicken with Jingling Bells? Gets its name from the sound the crispy dumplings are said to make when the chicken, snow peas, mushrooms, and water chestnuts hit them.

The best dishes can be found on the menu under "Chef's Specialties" and "Authentic Szechuan Cuisine." Prawns with minced pork and picked vegetables and scallion, Spicy Volcano Chicken, Sichuan Seafood Delight, and Tea-Smoked Duck are all highly recommended.

You could order General Tso's, moo shu pork, and chicken with broccoli at Chengdu 23, but why would you, when the authentic dishes pack all the flavor, spice and excitement?

Sunday brunch, in a garden setting; and the Patio Bar and Grill, open in the summer and overlooking the hotel's lagoon pool.

Divina Ristorante, 461 Bloomfield Ave., Caldwell; (973) 228-5228; www.divinaristorante.com; Italian; $$. The food at Divina is close to divine. There's nothing fancy about the decor or surroundings; all the attention at Mario Carlino's casual restaurant is put in the food. I love gnocchi—there's something about the texture and taste of those plump dumplings—and one of the best anywhere is the homemade spinach and ricotta gnocchi with marinara and basil here. The lobster ravioli, penne alla calabrese, and the orecchiette with fresh Jersey tomato sauce and shaved Parmigiano Reggiano cheese are all tops. If all that weren't enough, Carlino makes a mean cheesecake.

Four Seasons Kebab House, 594 Valley Rd., Upper Montclair; (973) 707-7651; www.fourseasonskebabhouse.com; Turkish; $$. Turkish food has long taken a back seat to Greek and other Mediterranean cuisine—good luck convincing your food-savvy friends that filo, kebabs, and pilaf or rice dishes are all of Turkish origin. But Turkish restaurants are finally getting their due in Jersey. Four Seasons, with tables on the sidewalk, an indoor dining room, and a cute leafy outdoor cafe in back, is one of the better ones. The roll pastry feta cheese—crispy, feta-filled pastries—makes for a standout appetizer. The baba ghanoush, chicken kebabs, and lamb burger all rock. For dessert, the baklava (light, not overly sweet) and Turkish flan or *kazandibi,* a cinnamon-dusted pudding, are musts.

Freshwaters, 1442 South Ave., Plainfield; (908) 561-9099; www .myfreshwaters.com; Southern/Soul Food; $$. Yes, there really is a Freshwater behind Freshwater's. Clifton Freshwater and his wife, Sharon, run this soul food and southern-style restaurant. It's the latest chapter in the couple's Plainfield restaurant odyssey; they opened a take-out place on Belvidere and South in 1987, moved to Watchung and 4th, and then bought an old house on South Avenue. The former bedroom is now the kitchen, and the former kitchen is now the ladies' room. You'll find great fried chicken, fillet of catfish, and barbecue pork baby back ribs here. And the sides—collard greens, okra, black-eyed peas, mac and cheese, potato salad, rice and gravy—are first-rate. You'll love the homemade ice tea, flavored with ginger, lemon, and honey. Customers have included Queen Latifah and Wesley Snipes. "What you see here is a lot of trials and tribulations, mistakes and errors, 12 years of hard work, burning up food, tastes right, doesn't taste right," Clifton Freshwater explains. "It all adds up to Freshwaters." It all adds up to a special place.

Hobby's, 32 Branford Place, Newark; (973) 623-0410; www.hobbys deli.com; Deli; $. At one time, a dozen Jewish delis dotted downtown Newark. Hobby's, run by the inimitable Sam Brummer and his sons, Marc and Michael, is the only one left. This old-time deli and luncheonette feeds hundreds of downtown workers—from judges to office workers to sanitation men—every day. Corned beef, lox, tongue, knishes, triple-decker clubs, matzo ball soup, cream soda—it's all here. "We have pastrami flowing through our veins," says Marc Brummer, who forsook a career as an attorney to work in the family business. Finding a parking spot in downtown Newark is a challenge, but you'll be rewarded by your visit to the city's last true Jewish deli.

Inn at Millrace Pond, Route 519, Hope; (908) 459-4884; www .innatmillracepond.com; American; $$$. Consistently rated among New Jersey's top restaurants, this former Moravian gristmill offers first-rate food in a cozy, romantic setting. The inn has 17 distinctive guest rooms and a tavern with a fireplace. Popular entrees include herb- and peppercorn-breaded loin of lamb seared and then baked to perfection, served with port wine demi-glace, roasted finger potatoes, and spaghetti squash; a bouillabaisse with shrimp, scallops, clams, lobsters, and fennel served in a tomato saffron stock over fettuccine; and seared venison tournedos served with a cranberry demi-glace, mashed roasted sweet potatoes, and patty pan and spaghetti squash. You could make it an evening, a night, even a weekend at the 100-year-old inn.

Jeremiah's, 44 N. Beverwyck Rd., Lake Hiawatha; (973) 334-2004; www.jeremiahsdeli.com; Healthy; $. Jeremiah was a bullfrog, and frogs—frolicking on lily pads, flying through the air—decorate the walls and ceiling at Jeremiah's. The cafe is named after Jeremy Giordano, one of two pizza deliverymen murdered in Sussex County in 1997. His sister, Theresa Navarro, and her husband, Jose, are the owners. Theresa, an earnest woman with piercing blue eyes, offers 15 different sandwiches and a half-dozen kinds of pinwheels (rolled flatbread with alfalfa sprouts cut into 6 pieces and made with tuna, ham, roast beef, turkey, grilled veggies, and fresh mozzarella and tomato). There are daily specials: A typical offering might include cool cucumber dill soup; arugula, sliced tomato, and breaded-chicken and feta cheese salad; chicken, artichokes, fresh mozzarella, tomato, and penne; and a steak, bacon, and cheddar wrap. But you'll keep coming back for her salads. Salad Theresa is a sweet, summery mix of candied walnuts, grilled onions, mixed greens, tomatoes, and tender chicken. Salad Valerie combines strips of delicious grilled prosciutto, chicken, and Parmesan over greens. And the peppercorn Parmesan and honey mustard dressings are first-rate.

Je's, 34 William St., Newark; (973) 623-8848; Southern/Soul Food; $. This is the heart of the New Jersey soul food universe: a family-style cafeteria and luncheonette that has served the likes of Shaquille O'Neal and Patti LaBelle. Je's, named after founder Laszlo Jezierski, is run by Harry Sutton. Popular dishes here include liver, catfish, short ribs, and smothered chicken. Sides include yams, lima beans, black-eyed peas, collard greens, okra, string beans, potato salad, corn, and pickled beets. "What we do here is strictly southern cooking," Harry's late wife, Diane, once said. "It doesn't belong to one ethnic group. It's southern, it's tradition, it's America."

Jimmy Buff's, 60 Washington St., West Orange; (973) 325-9897; www.jimmybuff.com; Hot Dogs; $. This sturdy shrine to the Italian hot dog—hot dog, potatoes, onions, peppers, and enough cholesterol to give your doctor a heart attack—was opened by Jimmy "Buff" Racioppi at the corner of 14th Avenue and 9th Street in Newark in 1932. He died in 1950; his grandson, Jimmy "Big Dog" Racioppi, runs the Jimmy Buff's in West Orange and East Hanover, while Jimmy's uncle Mike owns a store on Route 22 in Scotch Plains. "I have made more Italian hot dogs than anyone in the world," Mike Racioppi boasts. Each week Jimmy Buff's goes through 300 pounds of hot dogs, 2,000 pounds of potatoes, 250 pounds of sausage, and 700 pounds of onions. This is the first place you'd go for a genuine Italian hot dog and the last place you'd take the calorie counter in your family. There are also Jimmy Buff's at 354 Rte. 10 West, East Hanover, (973) 463-0099; Route 22 West, Scotch Plains, (908) 233-BUFF; 506 Boulevard, Kenilworth, (908) 276-2833; and 1594 Sussex Tpke., Randolph, (973) 584-3339.

OTHER LEGENDARY HOT DOG HANGOUTS

Hiram's, 1345 Palisades Ave., Fort Lee; (201) 592-9602.

Hot Grill, 669 Lexington Ave., Clifton; (973) 772-6000;
www.hotgrill.org.

Libby's, 98 McBride Ave., Paterson; (973) 278-8718.

Rutt's Hut, 417 River Rd., Clifton; (973) 779-8615;
www.ruttshut.com.

Tony's Specialized Hot Dogs, Lake Street and Park Avenue,
Newark (there is no phone).

Madame Claude Cafe, 364½ 4th St., Jersey City; (201) 876-8800; www.madameclaudecafe.com; French Cafe; $. Parental advisory: Madame Claude Cafe, a slice of French country in downtown Jersey City, is named after a woman who ran a legendary escort service in Paris in the 1960s. Culinary advisory: You're going to love this place. Madame Claude doesn't look like much from the outside—squat, brick-walled—but the interior is small and cozy, with hardwood floors, sunshiny-yellow walls, and 13 tables, many of them lined against a mirrored wall. The overall effect is that of a cute French country diner, if such a thing exists. The owners are Mattias Gustafsson and his wife, Alice Troietto. The waitresses speak English, but it's a great place to dust off your high school French. Recommended: the big, puffy omelets; the crepes; pain perdu (french toast); and poulet ratatouille (roasted chicken and ratatouille on toasted baguette, with mesclun salad), among other dishes. Daily specials might include blanquette de veau (veal stew served with coconut rice) and *lapin aux pruneaux* (rabbit stew in a prune sauce). The chicken soup is a hearty, carrot- and tomato-tinged broth that exudes country goodness.

The Manor, 111 Prospect Ave., West Orange; (973) 731-2360; www.themanorrestaurant.com; American; $$$. The Manor is like stepping into another world, albeit one where men are always required to wear jackets. The classical-themed architecture, fountains, and greenery will make you wonder whether you're really in the middle of the country's most densely populated state. Winner of many dining awards, including *New Jersey Monthly*'s Best of the Best, North Jersey, The Manor is the place for that business-account dinner. There is also an a la carte luncheon on Thursday and Friday. The overall menu is European and American; when you've finished dinner, you can dance off the calories in Le Dome, The Manor's rooftop nightclub. See The Manor's recipe for **Roasted Butternut Squash Soup** on p. 280.

Mi Gente Cafe, 7 Central Ave., Newark; (973) 621-9000; Cuban; $. Downtown Newark, fueled by the new Prudential Center sports arena, is suddenly awash in new restaurants, cafes, and bars. The best deal downtown is the lunch special at this tiny Cuban cafe just off Broad Street; $5.99 gets your choice of ample-size entree, plus veggies and rice. The Cubano sandwich and *pan con lechon* are great lunch, or dinner, choices. There are just 5 tables, so if you see an empty one, grab it.

Ocha, 403 Bloomfield Ave., Caldwell; (973) 228-8856; Japanese; $$. It seems as though every time you turn around, a new sushi restaurant is opening somewhere in New Jersey. Ocha, run by a young couple, Neal and Joyce, is easily one of the better ones. Several of the dishes seem more special effects than serious food; the yellowtail seviche is served in a dish resting atop flashing red and blue lights. But make no mistake: The quality of the food here is top-notch. One must-try: the scallops carpaccio, razor-thin-sliced scallop strips enlivened with truffle oil, sea salt, and *yuzo,* a Japanese citrus. Another: the sushi pizza, a tasty combination of seaweed, scallion, onion, tomato, and a spicy barbecue sauce. It's a good bet you won't find it at Domino's anytime soon.

Perona Farms, 350 Andover-Sparta Rd., Andover; (973) 729-6161; www.peronafarms.com; American; $$. Sunday brunches are a New Jersey tradition, and one of the more lavish, in terms of food and surroundings, is offered at Perona Farms. Emil and Angiolina Perona opened a 200-acre farm here in 1917; the grounds soon became a country getaway for the likes of swashbuckling actor

Errol Flynn and baseball star Joe DiMaggio. "I swam with Ethel Merman, Jimmy Durante, Zsa Zsa Gabor, all these people," says Mark Avondoglio, grandson of the founders. Today brunch is served in a grand room, complete with silver service and revolving ice sculptures. Brunch items include chilled shrimp and oysters on the half shell, eggs Benedict, banana pancakes, prosciutto sliced on an antique Berkel prosciutto slicer, and lobster, cucumber, and red potato salads. And salmon. Perona Farms smokes its own salmon, about 10 tons a week; it is available in gourmet shops statewide. After filling up on brunch, take a walk, like Joe DiMaggio once did, around the picturesque grounds.

Rebecca's, 236 Old River Rd., Edgewater; (201) 768-3420; www.rebeccascubanrestaurant.com; Cuban; $$. Folk music whispers overhead. Blue votive candles flicker at the tables. Rosa Ledo, whom everyone calls Mama Rosa, is in the middle of it all, making sure everything's running smoothly at Rebecca's. The Cuban-Caribbean restaurant is owned by her daughter, Rebecca Chernalis, a flight attendant. It's cozy (indoor capacity: 40) and romantic, with attentive but not overbearing service. The menu combines Caribbean spices and salsas with more traditional Cuban dishes, such as Mama Rosa's black bean soup and *lechon asado,* roast pork marinated in a garlic *mojo* and served with rice and plantains. Recommended: the salad of avocado and hearts of palm, with mesclun greens and a red wine vinaigrette; the fresh cranberry and goat cheese salad with baby greens, walnuts,

and a balsamic vinaigrette; red pepper snapper with five kinds of pepper; and the coconut mashed yams. The outdoor cafe, a stunning grotto, makes for a perfect retreat from the outside world.

Red Wolfe Inn, 130 Rte. 519, White Township (Warren County); (908) 475-4772; American; $$$. It looks more like a roadhouse than a steak house, but don't be fooled—or get jittery when you see real wolves out back. Actually, they're wolf hybrids belonging to owner Rudy Walz. Kept in an enclosure behind the restaurant, they're as tame as can be, even if one is named Chaos. The best steak here— the Loki—is named after one of Walz's pets. It's a 24-ounce New York strip, juicy, tender, and perfectly cooked. Other menu items include fajitas, steak quesadillas, beer-battered frog legs, and an outstanding rack of lamb. Stand outside the Red Wolfe Inn and you can see Pennsylvania, but this one-of-a-kind restaurant is an easy ride down Route 78 or Route 80 from just about anywhere.

Runway Cafe, Blairstown Airport, 36 Lambert Rd., Blairstown; (908) 362-9170; American; $. There are two ways to get to Jeanne Anderson's cozy cafe and her delicious homemade pies—you can either drive or fly. The cafe, located at little Blairstown Airport, also serves breakfast, burgers, and sandwiches. The floor is striped like an airport runway, the clock is shaped like a propeller, and the walls are filled with such homespun messages as "Some day my ship will come in, and with any luck I'll be at the airport." It is not unusual for regulars to fly in for a cup of coffee and a slice of pie; Harrison Ford is a sometime customer. Jeanne makes a good apple pie, with layers of Granny Smith apples, and a great coconut custard pie. "Life is uncertain," reads another message. "Eat dessert first."

Ruth's Chris Steakhouse, Hilton Parsippany, 1 Hilton Ct., Parsippany; (973) 889-1400; www.ruthschris.com; American; $$$. Also 1000 Harbor Blvd., Weehawken; (201) 863-5100; 2020 Atlantic Ave., Atlantic City; (609) 344-5833, and 2 Village Blvd., Forrestal Village, Plainsboro; (609) 452-0041. On a mission for the best steaks in New Jersey? Start—or end—your journey at Ruth's Chris. In 1965 Ruth Fertel, then a medical assistant at Tulane University, was searching for extra money to raise her two sons. Searching the classified ads, she came upon a restaurant named Chris Steak House, which she bought for $18,000. Today there are more than 80 Ruth's Chris worldwide, including three in New Jersey. The steaks are top-grade US prime. You may expect the restaurant to be a stuffy place, given the Hilton name and Ruth's Chris reputation. Not so; the waiters and waitresses are informative, patient, even funny at times. Both the filet mignon and T-bone are terrific. Surprisingly good desserts, too—try the crème brûlée and cheesecake.

Sawadee, 137 Newark Ave., Jersey City; (201) 433-0888; http://sawadeejc.com; Thai; $$. The best Thai food in Jersey City can be found in this gorgeous-looking restaurant, with subdued lighting,

Good Barbecue North of the Mason-Dixon Line

There's some good barbecue in South Jersey (see "Roadside Barbecue," p. 195). Finding it in North Jersey, though, is a considerable challenge. My top pick is **Shack's BBQ** (1160 E. Grand St., Elizabeth; 908-436-0005; $). It offers good southern cooking and barbecue in a plain-Jane storefront. Owner Vonda McPherson picked the right spot, across the street from the county courthouse and right next door to a bail bondsman—her dad, James McPherson. Vonda's cook is Neria Harrison, who grew up in Burnt Core, Alabama. Vonda describes her fare as "healthy soul food"—little or no grease, easy on the butter and salt. Her ribs are four hefty, tender ribs in a mildly fiery, somewhat sweet sauce. Her southern fried chicken is near perfect—crisp, crunchy, juicy. She also makes good sides, especially the yams and potato salad. And you may not find a better chopped barbecue sandwich anywhere in New Jersey.

Buddhas in backlit nooks, and fresh orchids at each table. You'll never guess this was a former shoe store. Sawadee—it means "hello" in Thai—brings the heat. Most dishes marked "hot" are just that—a refreshing change from most Thai restaurants in the state, which tone down the spice and fire for American palates. The *tom yum* hot pot, a bewitching blend of seafood in a lemongrass broth, is a great appetizer. Other favorites: the steamed Thai dumplings, spicy lemongrass with choice of meat or fish, jungle curry with chicken, and the seafood spring rolls.

Soram Restaurant, 545 Livingston St., Norwood; (201) 768-0878; Korean; $$. Korean restaurants abound in Bergen County, especially in Cliffside Park. Soram, in tiny Norwood, is on the short list of the state's best Korean restaurants. The menu is easy-to-digest, with dishes listed in Korean and English. *Duk bok eum* (stir-fried rice cakes with vegetables in a soy house sauce) make for an auspicious appetizer; the *duk kai bi* (charbroiled marinated beef cakes with king oyster mushrooms), for an entrancing entree. *Bin dae duk* (ground mung bean pancake with pork slices and bean sprouts) engages a variety of flavors and textures—soft, crispy, fried, crunchy, meaty. and more.

The Southern Belle, 615 Bloomfield Ave., Montclair; (973) 746-2233; www.southernbelle montclair.com; Southern/Soul Food; $$. Lauren Browning, the owner of Southern Belle, is a Jersey girl by birth, but she received her southern/soul food "education" at the University of Richmond, which she attended. Browning, who invites customers to submit their favorite recipes, serves up tasty Southern standards—Belle's Backyard Fried Chicken, country-style meat loaf, Alabama blackened catfish, and seafood gumbo, among others.

Soul Food

Je's in Newark (p. 80) has long been the center of the Jersey soul food scene. **Freshwaters** (p. 78) is another long-standing landmark. But newer soul food joints have opened in recent years. They may be short on decor, but they're big on flavor and value.

Holley's Gourmet to Go (392 Central Ave., East Orange; 973-678-0415; $) is modest in look, but its owner is anything but. Fish, Keith Holley says, will make him famous. "You laugh; when you see me on TV, you won't be laughing anymore." He hasn't hit the big time yet, which is a good thing for the rest of us because it means you can enjoy his food. Fish is indeed the star here; his whiting sandwich—masterfully seasoned, expertly cooked—is just about perfect.

Guy Longchamp, co-owner of the **Soul Food Factory** (683 Springfield Ave., Newark; 973-991-0156: www.thesoulfoodfactory .com; $) was once manager of the hip-hop group the Outsidaz. You'll be singing the praises of the uncomplicated food here; the sides, including the yams, potato salad, and mac and cheese, are especially noteworthy.

Stage House Restaurant and Wine Bar, 366 Park Ave., Scotch Plains; (908) 322-4224; www.stagehouserestaurant.com; American; $$$. One of the state's top dining spots, the Stage House, located in an 18th-century inn, continues to entrance and dazzle. Fireplaces, wood floors, and candlelight distinguish the intimate dining rooms. Appetizers? Fruitwood-smoked salmon, with spoonbill caviar, crème fraîche, shaved fennel, and herbs; and tuna tartare, with sweet

Another no-frills restaurant that delivers in the taste department is **Two Fish Five Loaves** (2264 Rte. 22 West, Union, 973-624-1444; 113 Watchung Ave., Plainfield, 908-222-2000; 693 Lyons Ave., Irvington, 973-399-1100; www.twofishfiveloaves.com; $). "We're not real fancy here," says owner Kevin Smallwood. "You're not going to come in, see fancy tablecloths." Or fancy anything—the Irvington location is takeout only. Smallwood makes excellent fried chicken and a fried porgie sandwich; anything fried is fine here.

The owner of **Sisters of Soul Southern Cuisine** (1314 St. Georges Ave., Linden; 908-587-0100; www.sistersofsoul.biz; $$), Cynthia Johnson, is a retired county police officer. It's a simple, spare place, but you'll lose yourself in Johnson's fine, soulful fare. Start with a glass or pitcher of Uptown, the traditional southern half-lemonade, half–ice tea drink. Must-tries: the smothered turkey wings; the southern shrimp, in a delightful pink cream sauce; and the oh-so-yummy yams. Good homemade desserts, too.

Japanese rice, scallions, and black sesame seeds. A la carte items, available Sunday through Thursday, include Peking duck, with lentil and hickory bacon salad and butternut squash. Prix-fixe and tasting menus are available only on Friday and Saturday. Desserts are a marvel—chilled papaya bisque, warm Belgian chocolate tart, and poached apricots are among the selections. "Contemporary American cuisine is rich and exciting these days, with a wide variety of culinary influences from across the globe," says Executive Chef Michael Clampffer, who once served as sous chef here.

Star Tavern, 400 High St., Orange; (973) 675-3336; www.star tavern.net; Pizza; $. If you polled North Jerseyans about their favorite thin-crust pizza, you'd get hundreds of different recommendations, but the Star Tavern just might end up on top. This local institution, run by a series of Italian families until Aristotelis Vayianos bought it in 1980, exudes camp and cool. It has a long bar, American flags on the wall, and a poster of a maniacally grinning Jack Nicholson from *The Shining*. The cheese pie is glorious but not overly greasy, with the crust slightly—and nicely—burned at the edges. Any mission to find the state's best thin-crust pie must include the Star.

The Waiting Room, 66 E. Cherry St., Rahway; (732) 382-0900; www.thewaitingroom.us; American; $$. A former McCrory's may not sound like a promising dining destination, but The Waiting Room delivers on all counts. The restaurant, so named because its original location served as an unofficial waiting room for the nearby train station, may look like a sports bar, but the food coming out of owner Chris Wenson's kitchen is anything but. The garlic pork chops are excellent; the baby lamb chops, somehow even better. Wenson is a wit; directions on the website advise "from the north, go south; from the south, go north." Go to Rahway, you'll be happy.

Walpack Inn, Route 615, Walpack Center; (973) 948-3890; www
.walpackinn.com; American; $$$. Don't go looking for green veg-
gies as side dishes here; there are none (your choices: potatoes
and rice). This country restaurant is a shrine to meat—prime rib,
steak, ribs, rack of lamb, and chicken, all impeccably prepared. Fill
up on your greens at the salad bar, and get that knife ready. Prices
may seem high, but portions are huge. The interior is a literal wild
kingdom—there are mounted deer, bear, sheep, buffalo, and other
animals along the walls. Outside is an unparalleled view—meadow,
woods, hills. The Walpack Inn is not easy to find, but the trip down
twisty country roads is worth it.

Ziegler's Town Tavern Country Inn, 673 Macopin Rd., West
Milford; (973) 697-8990; American; $$. There are several reasons
to visit this rambling, out-of-the-way restaurant, nestled in the
hills of Passaic County north of the town of Newfoundland. One is
the decor—Christmas tree lights strung around the bar and dried
wasps' nests hanging from the ceiling. Seems as though a friend of
co-owner Bruce Ziegler dropped a wasps' nest off at the restaurant
one day, thinking it might add something to the atmosphere. Bruce
liked it and hung it up, and pretty soon friends and neighbors were
dropping off their nests. But forget the odd choice of furnishings.
The main reason you should go here (other than the combination
of high-quality food at budget prices) is the king's cut prime rib. It
is a monstrous, joyously juicy piece of meat. I haven't run across a
better one anywhere in the state.

Cricket Hill Brewery, 24 Kulick Rd., Fairfield; (973) 276-9415; www.crickethillbrewery.com. Cricket Hill is one of the state's smaller breweries but owner Rick Reed is a proud—and hopeful—brewmaster. "This is the finest beer in America," he says of his East Coast Lager, an amber brew with the words *Jersey Shore Pour* on the label. Fairfield is a long way from the Shore, but Reed's heart is in the right place. "Curious beer drinkers are stepping out from under the mind-numbing barrage of large brewery advertising and deciding for themselves what they like," he says. His Cricket Hill IPA and Cricket Hill American Ale are both highly recommended. Others include Jersey Summer Breakfast Ale, Nocturne, and Paymaster's Porter Ale.

Gaslight Brewery & Restaurant, 15 S. Orange Ave., South Orange; (973) 762-7077; www.gaslightbrewery.net. Essex County's first brewpub has a relaxed atmosphere, with dartboard, shuffleboard, and live entertainment twice a week. Eight of its beers are on tap at any one time; selections include Bison Brown Ale, a Northern English brown ale; Perfect Stout, a rich, dry, extra-dark ale; and Eliminator, a honey double Maibock made with German pilsner, Canadian honey malt, and New Jersey clover honey. Many menu selections are made with beer, including the beer cheese soup, fish-and-chips, barbecued ribs, and roast beef. Not-so-ordinary brewpub fare includes Roquefort and roasted pear salad;

three-chile chicken; asparagus and goat cheese pizza; grilled ostrich steak; and sauerbraten.

High Point Wheat Beer Co., 22 Park Place, Butler; (973) 838-7400; www.ramsteinbeer.com. The first exclusive wheat beer brewer in the US, High Point brews the award-winning Ramstein beers, which can be found on draft and in bottles throughout New Jersey, New York, and Pennsylvania. High Point's Oktoberfest beers can be found in several of the state's best-known German restaurants. Brewery tours are available on the second Sat of each month from 2 to 4 p.m.; free samples are given to those ages 21 and over.

Krogh's Restaurant & Brew Pub, 23 White Deer Plaza, Sparta; (973) 729-8428; www.kroghs.com. Since 1927 Krogh's has provided good food and drink in a country atmosphere. Seven brews are available, including Alpine Glow Red Ale, Log Cabin Nut Brown, and Three Sisters Golden Wheat. Krogh's offers an extensive lunch and dinner menu, with everything from burgers and pasta to Mexican and Cajun.

Long Valley Pub and Brewery, Routes 513/24 and 517, Long Valley; (908) 876-1122; www.restaurantvillageatlongvalley.com. Housed in a restored 250-year-old barn in scenic Long Valley, this pub offers 2 bars, a diverse menu, and a broad range of beer styles. There's outdoor dining in season. Long Valley is the winner of the 1999 Great American Beer Festival bronze medal for its Robust Porter; its other brews include Lazy Jake Porter, German Valley Amber Ale, and Black River Brown Ale.

The Ironbound

The Ironbound—which apparently derived its name from the coming of the railroad in the 1930s—is Newark's most colorful neighborhood, and a paradise for food lovers. It is home to most of the state's best Spanish and Portuguese restaurants and is also the location of many Brazilian, Central American, and Italian restaurants. You could eat every day for a month here and barely scratch the surface of the variety of food available.

Where to begin? Probably the best-known, though not necessarily the best, Ironbound restaurant is **Iberia Tavern & Restaurant** (80–84 Ferry St.; 973-344-7603). Across the street is **Iberia Peninsula** (63–69 Ferry St.; 973-344-5611); both are owned by Jorge Fernandes and João Loureiro. In many Ironbound restaurants, the line between Spanish and Portuguese food often blurs. "Portuguese is more fried, Spanish is more sauce; beyond that, I can't tell you the difference," one restaurant server said, laughing.

Rodizio, a Brazilian specialty, is a nonstop meat orgy; skewers of chicken, sirloin steak, filet mignon, pork tenderloin, pork ribs, sausage, even exotic fare like chicken hearts and ostrich are brought to the table and slid onto your plate. The skewers keep coming until

New Jersey Beer Co., 4201 Tonnele Ave., North Bergen; (201) 758-8342; www.njbeerco.com. This Hudson County microbrewery started production in May 2010. Beers include Hudson Pale Ale; Garden State Stout, and 1787 Abbey Single, a Belgian-style session ale.

you tell the waiter to stop. One of the better ones is at **Brasilia** (132-A Ferry St.; 973-465-1227).

Casa Vasca (141 Elm St.; 973-465-1350) offers Spanish/Basque cuisine in charming surroundings. **Tony Da Caneca** (72 Elm Rd.; 973-589-6882) doles out hearty portions of good Portuguese food in a big dining room. **Titanic** (486 Market St.; 973-589-6166) lays on the kitsch—a life preserver, mast, and furled sail in the dining room; a movie poster of Leonardo DiCaprio and Kate Winslet in the foyer—but there's plenty of good food to be found, especially the mussels marinara and the seafood combination in red sauce.

Many Ironbound habitués call **Forno's** (47 Ferry St.; 973-589-4767) their favorite restaurant. It can get a bit noisy if not boisterous, but the food is uniformly excellent.

For more informal dining, my best bet is **Casa do Pao de Queijo** (220 Ferry St., Newark; 973-344-3145). "House of Cheese Bread" will roll off the tongue easier than the Portuguese name for this Brazilian restaurant. It's part of a 400-plus chain in Brazil; this is the only one in New Jersey. The cheese buns are delicious—big and puffy, and begging to be warmed up in the oven. There are good sandwiches and salads, too, and it's a great place to watch that next World Cup—or any—soccer match.

Trap Rock Restaurant & Brewery, 279 Springfield Ave., Berkeley Heights; (908) 665-1755; www.traprockrestaurant.net. Opened in 1997, Trap Rock, on 2 floors, allows you to experience an English country inn atmosphere minutes from the interstate. Beers on hand include the smooth, sweet Steam Engine Ale; the fine,

full-bodied Ghost Pony Helles Lager; the colorful, and colorfully named, Dave's Commitment Ale; and Hathor Red Lager, named for the Egyptian goddess credited with the invention of beer. The menu is expansive and creative. Appetizers run from warm mozzarella in a *rustica* bread crisp and a warm goat cheese roasted tomato tart to mixed grill satays and sautéed spicy squid. Recommended entrees: the grilled basil-marinated loin pork chop, the pan-roasted beef tenderloin, and the spice-rubbed tuna served rare. Good homemade

FIVE-STAR BURGERS

Every summer I head up the *Star-Ledger's* popular **Munchmobile** (p. 99) series, in which a crew—myself, a photographer, and several readers—roams the state searching for the best steak, seafood, Italian, Mexican, Thai, french fries, ice cream, and other food. We'll hit more than 100 places throughout the summer and, yes, eat at every single one. When the Munchmobile is in hibernation, I write a weekly restaurant column called "Eat with Pete."

One of my meatier solo missions was to find the state's best burger. Thirteen burgers in 6 days, which must be some sort of record. That was just for one story; my quest for the perfect burger is ongoing. Two of the state's best burgers can be found in its capital city and its biggest city.

Rossi's Bar & Grill (501 Morris Ave., Trenton; 609-394-9089; www.rossiburger.com; $) is in Trenton's Chambersburg section. Rossi's basic burger is a Gulliver-size product in a land of often Lilliputian burgers. Good kaiser roll, too.

Don't be put off by the dive-bar atmosphere of **Krug's Tavern** (118 Wilson Ave., Newark; 973-465-9795; www.krugstavern .com; $). This is easily Newark's best burger—fat, juicy mounds of meat cooked on a grill not much bigger than an unfolded newspaper. Don't go expecting fancy craft beers, either; Bud and Coors are the norm. Krug's (pronounced "Kroogs") is within walking distance of Newark Penn Station, in case you're coming in by train.

desserts, too; try the crème brûlée, the cream cheese and Maine blueberry–filled napoleon, and the passion fruit sorbet.

Wine Trail

Four Sisters Winery at Matarazzo Farms, 783 Rte. 519, Belvidere; (908) 475-3671; www.foursisterswinery.com. The vineyard is just part of the agricultural business run by Matty and Laurie Matarazzo on their 392-acre farm. In 1981 they started planting wine grapes amid the fruits and vegetables; to date, Four Sisters has won more than 20 medals in regional, national, and international wine competitions. The winery hosts many special events, including Mardi Gras celebrations, barefoot grape-stomping parties, murder mystery luncheons, a Mother's Day luncheon, a Father's Day pig roast (p. 66), and the Family Harvest Festival in October, with pumpkin and apple picking, hayrides, a corn maze, and more. White wines include Cayuga, a semidry wine for salads and light main dishes; Seyval Reserve, an oak-aged wine with a very dry finish; and Warren Hills White, a semisweet wine. Reds include Papa's Red, a dry table wine; and Leon Millot, a dry, robust red that's good with pastas and roasts. The mailing address says Belvidere, but Four Sisters is actually located in White Township, 2.5 miles north of the intersection of Routes 46 and 519.

Westfall Winery, 141 Clove Rd., Montague; (973) 293-3428; www
.westfallwinery.com. The state's northernmost winery, launched
in 2003, is located in Sussex County. Owners Georgene and Loren
Mortimer met in college and soon were making wine together. Their
wines won six medals at the state wine competition. "Not bad for
a first-year winery," Loren says. Wines include a white Zinfandel;
Cabernet Sauvignon; a midsummer white table wine; Spanish
Passion, Westfall's take on Sangria; and Peach Chardonnay. The
Mortimers also run a winemaking school at their winery. Tastings
are available Thursday through Sunday from April through December.

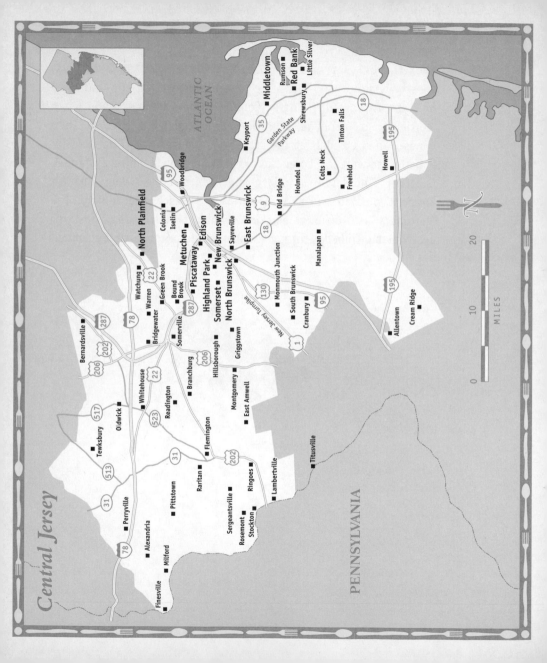

Central Jersey

ATLANTIC OCEAN

PENNSYLVANIA

Middletown
Rumson
Red Bank
Little Silver
Shrewsbury
Tinton Falls
Keyport
Garden State Parkway
Colts Neck
Freehold
Holmdel
Howell
Old Bridge
East Brunswick
Sayreville
Manalapan
Monmouth Junction
South Brunswick
Cranbury
Allentown
Cream Ridge

Woodbridge
Colonia
Iselin
North Plainfield
Metuchen
Edison
New Brunswick
Piscataway
Highland Park
Somerset
North Brunswick
Watchung
Warren
Green Brook
Bound Brook
Bridgewater
Somerville
Branchburg
Griggstown
Bernardsville
Whitehouse
Readington
Hillsborough
Montgomery
East Amwell
Oldwick
Tewksbury
Flemington
Titusville
Perryville
Pittstown
Raritan
Ringees
Lambertville
Alexandria
Sergeantsville
Stockton
Rosemont
Milford
Finesville

New Jersey Turnpike

95
35
18
195
9
18
130
22
287
78
206
202
287
22
206
517
523
31
31
513
202
78
31

N

MILES

0   10   20

Central Jersey

Where Central Jersey actually begins and ends is the source of endless disagreement. For the purposes of this book, it means the counties in the state's midsection—blue-collar Middlesex, blue-blooded Somerset, retiree-haven Monmouth, and rural Hunterdon. But, like the rest of New Jersey, generalizations come cheap; you can just as easily find traffic-clogged roads in Hunterdon County as you can hip young couples in Red Bank or Asbury Park in Monmouth County.

Family farms are still being worked in Cranbury and East Brunswick, minutes from warehouses and industrial complexes. One of my favorite, fun juxtapositions is in Woodbridge: J. J. Bitting, a brewpub and restaurant, is located practically next door to the local police headquarters. The Main Streets of most Central Jersey towns are filled with a wide-ranging array of food shops and restaurants, reflecting the area's diverse population mix. Indian? Head to Woodbridge and Edison. Asian? One of the area's most *colorful* seafood markets is in Watchung. Thai? Somerville has one of the state's best Thai restaurants. Hunterdon County is dotted with general stores, farm markets, and picturesque small towns, and the rolling countryside makes for a great one-day or weekend getaway.

In this chapter you'll find Farmer Steve and his organic popcorn, a log cabin devoted to honey, several high-end restaurants, the World's Best Peanut Brittle, and the state's biggest sandwiches. How could you resist?

Made Here

Bent Spoon, 35 Palmer Sq. West, Princeton; (609) 924-BENT; www .thebentspoon.com. Dark chocolate habañero ice cream? Grapefruit Campari? Wild Turkey chocolate bourbon pecan? Is this a science experiment or an ice-cream shop? A little of both, and totally delicious. The Bent Spoon, named after an object in *The Matrix,* has been wowing ice-cream lovers with its cool, creative flavors of ice cream and gelato since it opened in May 2004. The owners, Gabrielle Carbone and Matthew Errico, pride themselves on using the freshest, most natural ingredients possible. All their dairy products are hormone-free. Pretty much all of their ice cream is wonderful. The flavors change constantly; Carbone and Errico have made 400-plus favors to date. *Inside Jersey* magazine sampled ice-cream shops around the state in 2011 and named Bent Spoon the best overall.

Birnn Chocolates, Cleveland and Madison Avenues, Highland Park; (732) 545-4400; www.birnnchocolates.com. "The Finest

Chocolates on the Face of the Earth" is the motto at Birnn Chocolates, which began in 1932, when Charles Henry Birnn opened Regina Sweets in Highland Park. The company's chocolates, especially its French chocolate truffles, can be found in 300-plus shops around the country.
Birnn's makes more than 200 kinds of chocolates, everything from caramels, clusters, and cream-filled sandwiches to nonpareils, raspberry jellies, and peppermint patties. There is also a wide variety of gift boxes and heart-shaped Valentine's Day assortments.

The Blue Rooster Bakery & Cafe, 17 N. Main St., Cranbury; (609) 235-7539; www.blueroosterbakery.com. Perfect place to while away—or forget—a rainy day? I'd choose the Blue Rooster in one of the state's most picturesque small towns. It's both a bakery (self-serve coffee at the front counter, excellent scones) and a breakfast/lunch/dinner spot, located in a charming Victorian home. Dinner is where the Blue Rooster especially shines—Moroccan rack of lamb; pan-roasted breast of duck and pissaladière (flaky tart topped with caramelized onion, anchovy, kalamata olive, and tomato) are among the not-so-ordinary choices.

Brownie Express, PO Box 49, Pittstown, 08867; (908) 735-2178; www.thebrownieexpress.com. Gail Fernando makes flat-out great brownies. They're thick, rich, and fudgy and are available in a dozen flavors. I particularly love the no-nut (just chocolate), mixed nut, and almond ones. One difference: She doesn't use cocoa powder or chips. Instead, she starts with bonbon-quality chocolate, adding fresh eggs, unbleached flour, sweet butter, sugar, and a little baking powder. The brownies have no preservatives, salt, or extra sweetener. Internet and mail orders only.

Cross Country Nurseries, 199 Kingwood-Locktown Rd., Rosemont; (908) 996-4646; www.chiliplants.com. Sometimes a great notion begins with a seed of an idea, or in Janie Lamson's case, a package of seeds. In 1993 her brother handed Janie, then growing perennials and ornamental grasses and ferns, six packages of hot pepper seeds and asked her to grow them for him. From the simple request grew a thriving business. Cross Country Nurseries offers the world's largest selection of chile and sweet pepper plants, nearly 500 in all, everything from Afghan, Aji Colorado, and Anaheim M to Vietnamese Multi-Color, Wild Sanibel, and Zimbabwe Bird. Live plants are available from April through June; fresh chiles are available from September through frost. Janie and her husband, Fernando Villegas, ship anywhere in the US. Chiles come in all shapes, sizes, colors, and flavors, from sweet or mildly spicy to fiery hot.

The Dessert Plate, 34 E. Main St., Somerville; (908) 722-9881; www.thedessertplate.com. A bakery in an old movie theater may not sound like a recipe for success, but owners Megyn Craine and Kevin Gora are onto something at their business, which opened in

2001. Ignore the spartan, white-walled decor and head straight for the display case. First-rate scones are really hard to find in New Jersey—don't ask me why—but the scones here are terrific, softer and fluffier than the norm. There are some atypical flavors, like ginger. The cheesecake is incredibly creamy, almost brie-like, and they make an amazing flourless chocolate cake. You can even order a "customized" cake, choosing your preferred cake flavor, icing, and filling. Craine and Gora pride themselves on using no preservatives, mixes, or substitutes—fresh fruit, milk, eggs, butter, and cream are their principal ingredients. I miss the old Cort Theater, where the bakery is located, but I'd miss this place a whole lot more if it ever moved. One note: The Dessert Plate does not take credit cards.

Farmer Steve's Popcorn, Amwell Valley Organic Grains, PO Box 411, Ringoes 08551; www.farmersteve.com. Steve Spayd is the state's biggest popcorn grower, a statement that may take some time to swallow. Yes, popcorn is grown, not made. It's the only variety of corn that pops. Popcorn cornstalks look like other cornstalks, but the kernels and diameter of the ear are a bit smaller. A hydrogeologist with the state Department of Environmental Protection, Steve started farming part-time in 1989. He and his wife, Debi, changed the name from Harrowed Farm to Amwell Valley Organic Grains to better reflect their organic farming operation. About 1997 they began selling their popcorn in microwavable bags. It is lightly salted with a natural mineral salt and has no oil added, and "absolutely no partially hydrogenated oils." The popcorn comes in 2-box trial packs, 5-box snack packs, and 12-box cases. The popcorn is available by mail order, on their Internet site, and in select natural foods markets around the state.

Griggstown Quail Farm, 989 Griggstown Rd., Griggstown; (908) 359-5375; www.griggstownquailfarm.com. Joan and George Rude started in 1975 with 12 bobwhite quail breeders. Today they raise thousands of game birds not only for food but also for sport; their clients range from New York City restaurants to hunters and hunting-dog trainers. Birds available include *pouisson* (tender, juicy chickens processed at the plant here at 24 days old); mallard ducks (they fly around freely, which makes their meat a rich, dark red in color); Japanese or Coturnix quail (the couple's choice over the bobwhite quail because it is juicier and tastier); and turkey (free-range turkeys available for Thanksgiving). The birds are sold in many quality food markets around the state and can be purchased at Griggstown Quail Farm's market. Griggstown, part of Franklin Township, is just north of Princeton in Somerset County.

Mr. Tod's Pies, 1760 Easton Ave., Somerset; (732) 356-8900; www.whybake.com. That's Tod Wilson, not Sweeney Todd, so there won't be any surprises in your pies. Wilson started out selling his sweet potato pies to restaurants, eventually opening a store in an otherwise-unremarkable strip mall along Easton Avenue. His banana cream pie is outstanding; the Key lime is one of the best you'll find anywhere. Cherry pie was always my childhood favorite, and Mr. Tod's cherry pie is a fruity success.

Good Country Brunch

Flemington, with its Main Street charm and scores of shopping outlets on the fringes of downtown, makes for a great weekend drive from anywhere in the state. If it's Sunday, get thee to the **Market Roost** (65 Main St., Flemington; 908-788-4949; $), a country store and cafe with a brunch that is miles away from the usual assembly-line operation. There's no buffet line here; you order from a 14-item menu. There are tasty twists on old standards; the English muffin, with ham, asparagus, and tomato slices, is topped with a beef cheddar sauce and bacon pieces. The Kahlúa french toast is thick-sliced, pan-cooked, topped with toasted almonds, and served with Vermont maple syrup. Great sticky buns are topped with raisins and pecans. The pièce de résistance, though, may be the eggs Benedict, with a memorable hollandaise sauce and choice of fresh asparagus, maple sugar–cured ham, or turkey breast. If you can, save room for dessert, especially the seven-layer chocolate cake and the Key lime tartlet.

Muirhead of Ringoes, 43 Rte. 202, Ringoes; (800) 782-7803; www.muirheadfoods.com. Ed and Doris Simpson operated an acclaimed restaurant, Muirhead, in Hunterdon County for 20 years. Customers kept asking Ed for jars of his salad dressing, so he started making it available retail. The couple eventually closed the restaurant to concentrate on a line of specialty foods—mustards, salad dressings, sauces, marmalades, chutneys, jellies, and butters. You can find them in Williams-Sonoma and gourmet shops around the state, or you can order by mail. The Simpsons are especially proud of their Pecan Pumpkin Butter, a recent finalist in the new product category at the New York Fancy Food Show. Spread it on bread, rolls, and bagels; mix it into your baking batters; or use it to create a pecan or pumpkin pie. Some personal favorites: Muirhead Dijon Mustard, Muirhead Cinnamon Apple Butter, and Muirhead Balsamic Vinaigrette. See Muirhead of Ringoes's recipe for **Cinnamon Apple Butter Cheesecake** on p. 306.

Old Monmouth Candies, 627 Park Ave. (old Route 33), Freehold; (732) 462-1311; www.oldmonmouthcandies.com. A sign outside Old Monmouth says world's best peanut brittle, and who's to argue? It's been made here since 1910 of select natural ingredients, including choice, large Virginia peanuts. Old Monmouth does much of its business through mail order, although you can make arrangements to pick up your order at the factory. They also make good candy bars—roasted almond, crisp rice, peanut butter, and creamy caramel. Open every day.

Papa Ganache, 25 Church St., Keyport; (732) 217-1750; Bakery. Papa Ganache is a couple things—a bakery where "organic" and

"vegan" don't have to mean "boring" or "tasteless," and a school of sorts, where children with behavioral challenges learn about conflict resolution, coping, and other skills. The owner is Lisa Siroti, a psychotherapist. There's so much good stuff here—a Key lime–raspberry cheesecake cup, coconut cream tarts, the Almond Joyous (a chocolate cupcake topped with soy "butter cream" and blended with coconut)—that you forget you're eating healthy. My favorite thing: the apple galette, a rustic tart with a near-perfect combination of crumb, crust, and fruit.

Readington River Buffalo Co., 937 Rte. 523, Readington; (908) 806-0030; www.njbison.com. The owners of the Readington River Buffalo Co. say they're the state's largest buffalo farm. Make that the only buffalo farm! American bison are raised on the 230-acre farm outside Flemington. Bison meat is juicy and tender but lower in calories, fat, and cholesterol than pork, beef, or even skinless chicken. You can get everything from ground bison, bison franks, and strip steaks to bison ravioli, bison jerky, and bison back ribs. In May the business holds its annual Buffalo Watch: Walkways between the grazing pastures are opened for better viewing of the herds; parking and farm tours are free; and proceeds from food sales go to the local first aid squad. The store is open from 9 a.m. to 4 p.m. Sat and Sun and weekdays by appointment. See Readington River Buffalo Co.'s recipe for **Bison Chili** on p. 293.

BEST JELLY DOUGHNUT IN THE STATE

The doughnut may be Jersey's favorite sweet treat—our expanding waistlines are proof—and the state's best jelly doughnut can be found in the unlikeliest of places—in a tiny doughnut shop in Plainfield called, naturally, the **Plainfield Donut Shop** (131 Watchung Ave., Plainfield; 908-756-4033; bakery/luncheonette; It's really more luncheonette than doughnut shop, with a long counter and eight stools; the doughnuts almost seem an afterthought. But the jelly doughnut is jammin' with a dark, thick, not-too-sugary filling. Fancier, more modern bakeries may get the billing, but this little fluorescent-lit shop in downtown Plainfield outdoes them all, at least when it comes to the all-American jelly doughnut.

Ye Olde Pie Shoppe, 74 Oceanport Ave., Little Silver; (732) 530-3337; www.yeoldepieshoppe.com. Pie shells made from scratch, plus fresh fruits and filling: It all adds up to pie perfection at this bustling shop. Tom and Eileen Caruso are the owners. "People know us because we put a lot of meringue [beaten egg whites and granulated sugar] in our [lemon meringue] pies," Tom says. "We just pack it with egg whites and a sweet tart lemon pudding that we make." Their banana cream pie is outstanding—a soft, fluffy, pillowy pie, jammed with bananas. Pop it in the fridge and drape a do not disturb sign around it; it's that good. The French apple and Key lime pies also are highly recommended.

Baker's Treat, 156 Main St., Flemington, (908) 782-9449; www .bakerstreat.com. "We're not just an ordinary bakery," says Nancy Baron, owner of Baker's Treat. No kidding. What's going on in the kitchen is only part of the story here. Nancy, a former psychiatric social worker, donates 100 percent of her profits to women in early recovery from alcohol and substance abuse. A year or two after its opening in 1999, Baker's Treat had become the premier gourmet cafe and pastry shop in the Flemington area. The pastry chef is Janine Harrison; her cakes and cookies are highly recommended. The shop's trademark item is its Rugie, a hand-rolled spiral of sour cream pastry with one of three fillings: pecan/apricot, walnut/golden raisin, or cranberry. The salads here are terrific, too. The Adirondack chairs on the shaded lawn outside the series of shops at Turntable Junction make for a perfect summer retreat. There is another location at 415 Amwell Rd., Hillsborough (908-829-3361), a small take-out bakery/cafe at 9B Church St. in Lambertville (609-397-2272) and a cafe in the Somerset County Courthouse (40 N. Bridge St., Somerville; 908-526-5050).

Bee Happy Honey House, 50 Mine St., Flemington; (908) 788-6004. Bee Happy is odds-on the most peculiar—and most charming—shop in upscale, outlet-happy Flemington. This log cabin shrine to honey from around the world is run by Lisa and Harry Schrag, who treat their business with an eye for detail and a sense of humor. "If your honey wants some honey / let your honey spend some money / just to buy himself some honey," begins one of Harry's corny little poems above the cash register. The cabin dates to the 1940s, when it was used as a stoneware pottery studio. Lisa Schrag is a sweet, tiny woman with a tiny voice, but don't be fooled; she's a good saleswoman. She'll first ask you whether you like light or dark honey, immediately offer you samples, and sweetly try to convince you to buy a jar of fancy French honey. Maybe she's just trying to make things easier; there are hundreds of jars on display—acacia, alfalfa, and buckwheat; sunflower, sun thistle, and wildflower; and everything in between. The Schrags also sell teas, jams, jellies, cookie and pancake mixes, even honey-based hair- and skin-care products. "Be happy," Lisa says on my way out the door. A delightful, time-warp kind of place.

Captain Fresh Seafood Supermarket, 1569 Rte. 22, Watchung; (908) 668-8131. Amid the commercial clutter of Route 22 is this dimly lit, cramped seafood market that feels like it belongs to another time and place. Captain Fresh has been open since 1996. Sandy Lin and Danny Shu's market remains a secret to the population at large, but not to members of the Asian community, who find good, fresh, and above all cheap fish here. Scallops, lobster, shrimp, tuna, crab claws, salmon, flounder: If it swims, you'll probably find it here. They'll boil, broil, fry, or steam your fish at no extra charge while you wait. There are prepared seafood dishes, plus salads and sandwiches; try the grilled crab cake. The rest of the market is devoted to groceries—snacks, seasonings, sauces, noodles, and the like. Asian markets are the one place where I can always find my favorite first-aid ointment—Tiger Balm, absolutely the best remedy for mosquito bites.

Dearborn Farms, 2170 Rte. 35, Holmdel; (732) 264-0256; www.dearbornfarms.com. A marvel of a store: a farm market with the freshest produce, plus a full-scale deli and butcher shop. There are fruits and vegetables; homemade pies; bread (Dearborn's gets its from 15 bakers); a selection of heat-and-serve dinners (grilled lemon chicken, lasagna, shrimp and roasted vegetables, etc.); 20 kinds of soup; and some great salads, everything from cherry tomato, calamari, and chicken pasta to Italian tuna, octopus, and Sicilian olive. Interestingly enough, the market is located on one of the more heavily commercialized stretches of highway in New Jersey.

Delicious Orchards, 36 Rte. 34 South, Colts Neck; (732) 462-1989; www.deliciousorchardsnj.com. This megamarket is no secret, not with two million visitors a year. Its size may deter millions more; what could possibly be good, they might wonder, at a place this big? Well, just about everything. Spread out over a Home Depot–size space are produce, meats, cheeses, salads, doughnuts, pastries, muffins, bread, cakes, cookies, prepared foods, salads, pastas, and sauces. It's not easy finding trolley buns—long, narrow, glazed cinnamon buns—north of Trenton. You can find them here, and they're terrific. If there's one thing Delicious Orchards is known for, it's the pies; they make 500 a day here. The apple, bulging with fresh, sweet fruit, is excellent. About 3.5 pounds of apples, which cook down to about 2 pounds, are used in each one. Other pies include peach, blueberry crumb, pecan, coconut custard, and pumpkin. Wander the aisles, and see if you can resist. Open every day but Mon. Delicious Orchards celebrated its 100th anniversary as a business in 2011. See Delicious Orchards's recipe for **Mrs. Barclay's Baked Apples** on p. 307.

Dutch Country Farmers' Market, 19 Commerce St., Raritan Township (Hunterdon County); (908) 806-8476. Want to sample Pennsylvania Dutch cooking without driving all the way to Lancaster County, PA? Just head over to Dutch Country Farmers' Market. It's a supermarket of tasty treats, everything from doughnuts, pastries, and bread to salads, butcher meats, rotisserie chickens, and more. Get a fresh-baked pretzel right out of the oven. The market is broken down into a dozen shops and counters. Melvin Beiler's cheese shop, with 50-plus kinds of cheese, is a good place to start. Next door is a wonderful candy store run by his wife, Martha; chocolate, fudge, licorice sticks, and hundreds of other kinds of sweets are there. Over at Fisher's Seafood and Salads, there is a too-tempting array of traditional Pennsylvania Dutch food—shepherd's pie, baked lima beans, broccoli and cauliflower casserole, blueberry cheese delight, and dirt pudding, a black-and-white pudding generally made from vanilla cream cheese, Cool Whip, and Oreos. King's Fresh and BBQ Poultry specializes in farm-fresh chickens; it also has the biggest stuffed pork chops you may ever see. I've saved the best for last: the still-hot cinnamon buns at JR's Bakery. Terrific, and just $1 each. The market, located behind the Shoprite on Route 202 just south of the Flemington Circle, is open Thurs, Fri, and Sat only.

Gary's Wine & Marketplace, 100 Rte. 202 (Morristown Road), Bernardsville; (908) 766-6699; www.garyswine.com. Clearly, this is not your neighborhood wine store. Thousands of bottles in aisle upon aisle, wine accessories, a gourmet shop, even a cafe—Gary's is one-stop shopping for all your wine, and epicurean, needs. Owner Gary Fisch doesn't look a day over 20, but he has established a reputation as a savvy, enthusiastic wine buyer and collector. The staff will steer you to the best buys under $15—say a bottle of Two Brothers Big Tattoo Red 2002—or to something pricier if money is no object, such as a bottle of Château Haut Brion Graves 2000 for $370. The cafe offers first-rate sandwiches and salads; 150 varieties of cheese; and cakes, tarts, and pastries from specialty bakers in the area. There are regular demonstrations  and book signings. It's a fun place whether you know everything about wine or nothing. There are other stores at 121 Main St., Madison, (973) 822-0200; and 1308 Rte. 23 North, Wayne, (973) 633-3900.

George Street Co-op, 89 Morris St., New Brunswick; (732) 247-8280; www.georgestreetcoop.com. This venerable downtown New Brunswick institution has been around forever, or so it seems. It started in 1973, when some students from the Vegetarian Club at Rutgers University opened a buying club in a garage off George Street. They soon moved to a small storefront on George Street. The co-op is now located in even bigger quarters on nearby Morris Street. The co-op's aim is to sell vegetarian foods with the least amount of processing and contaminants but with the greatest nutritional value possible. Anyone can shop at the store, which is stocked with organic produce, organic whole grains, breads and cereals, low-carb foods, chips and natural treats, juices and juicers, ready-to-eat sandwiches and entrees, and many other items. Membership is $24 a year. If you work 2 hours a month at the co-op, you get a 6 percent discount. If you work 2 hours a week, you get 15 percent off. And the co-op offers a 5 percent everyday discount to those 65 and over. The co-op is open daily.

Sickles Market, 1 Harrison Ave., Little Silver; (732) 741-9563; www.sicklesmarket.com. Every town should have a place like Sickles, a spacious, brightly lit, neatly laid-out market. The owners pride themselves on fresh produce and unique, high-quality gourmet and specialty items. You'll find hot cereals like McCann's Irish Oatmeal; real maple syrup from Brown Family Farm; jams and preserves from Sarabeth, Earth and Vine, and Bonne Maman; Blue Crab Bay Company chowders; the best artisanal goat's-, cow's-, and sheep's-milk cheeses from around the country; and fresh fruits and vegetables.

At least 10 soups are available daily; favorites include chicken potpie, potato leek, and triple onion. There are first-rate salads and slaws, too—whole wheat berries; orzo, pumpkin seeds, and dried cranberries; artichoke hearts with fresh thyme and lemon; and Asian coleslaw, with sunflower seeds, sesame seeds, and rice-wine vinaigrelle, among others. Boston cream pie, chocolate cheesecake, and other baked goods can be found in the pastry case. And don't forget to check out the baked ziti; I guarantee it's the tallest baked ziti you'll find anywhere. "I hate this place," a customer told me, smiling. "You can't stop buying things." She's right. See Sickles Market's recipe for **Mrs. Sickles's French Silk Chocolate Pie** on p. 308.

Verducci's, 176 Rte. 202 North, Raritan Township (Hunterdon County); (908) 788-7750; www.verduccis.com. This is a big, beautiful, bustling gourmet store. The neat trick here is prying yourself away from the bakery, just inside the front door. Chocolate caramel pyramids, chocolate truffle mousse, and chocolate espresso cookies are only a few of the tempting treats. Excellent breads, 100-plus kinds of cheeses, fresh seafood, pastas, wraps, sandwiches, soups, sides, and salads are available. Verducci's hosts a variety of special events, including a strawberry festival, a Southwestern Labor Day party, and a "Mediterranean cruise," where foods from Greece, Egypt, Spain, Morocco, and Italy are sampled. In the warmer months you can enjoy your lunch at the tables outside the main store. They overlook the parking lot, but with food this good and fresh, you won't care about the scenery.

Wegmans, 724 Rte. 202 South, Branchburg, (908) 243-9600; see additional locations, below; www.wegmans.com. From its humble beginnings—John Wegman opened his Rochester Fruit and Vegetable Co. in New York in 1916—Wegmans, with stores in New Jersey, New York, Pennsylvania, and Virginia, has emerged as a leader in good, fresh supermarket food. Buy artisanal breads at the European Breads bakery; fresh salads and sandwiches at the Deli and Market Cafe; California rolls at the Sushi Bar; and delicious pastry and sweets at the Patisserie (don't you dare put a box of Wegmans minibrownies in front of me; they'll be gone before you know it). Gift baskets, bulk foods, international foods, organic produce, homemade pizza—it's all here. They even host cooking classes. Locations: 15 Woodbridge Center Dr., Woodbridge, (732) 596-3200; 55 Rte. 9 South, Manalapan, (732) 625-4100; 2100 Rte. 790 West, Cherry Hill, (856) 488-2700; 220 Nassau Park Blvd., West Windsor, (609) 919-9300; and 1104 Rte. 35, Ocean Township, (732) 695-7000.

Farmers' Markets

Many of the farmers' markets in Central Jersey are part of the **New Jersey Council of Farmers and Communities** (NJCFC) markets. For up-to-date NJCFC farmers' market locations, days, and times, visit the council's website at www.njcfc.org. Community market hours often change from year to year.

Bernardsville Farmers' Market, NJ Transit railroad station, Route 202 and Claremont Road, Bernardsville. Sat from 9 a.m. to 2 p.m., mid-June through mid-November.

Bound Brook Farmers' Market, E. Main Street commuter parking lot, Bound Brook. Sat from 9 a.m. to 2 p.m., mid-June through early October.

Clinton Farmers' Market, 1 New St., Clinton. Sun from 10 a.m. to 2 p.m., mid-July through late October.

Downtown Freehold Farmers' Market, Hall of Records Plaza, Freehold. Fri from 11 a.m. to 3 p.m., early July through mid-October.

Edison Farmers' Market, 925 Amboy Ave., Edison. Sun from 8 a.m. to 2 p.m., late June through late September.

Flemington Farmers' Market, Liberty Village, 1 Church St., Flemington. Sun from 10 a.m. to 6 p.m., June through late November.

A Special Farmers' Market

Any place that calls itself the **Garden State Farmer's Market** (2549 Rte. 1 South, North Brunswick; 732-940-9877) has a lot to live up to. But the Garden State Farmer's Market proves itself more than worthy. Forget the unlikely location—right on Route 1—and step inside the giant shedlike building. There are rows and rows of farm-fresh fruits and vegetables, at prices certainly cheaper than your local supermarket. Tomatoes, peppers, cucumbers, oranges, grapefruit, berries, grapes— that's only a small sample. Specials abound—a quart of strawberries for 99 cents, for example. But wait, there's more. A deli offers salads and cold cuts, and dozens of varieties of fish glisten atop ice in the fish market. There's even a selection of sauces, spices, and condiments.

Franklin Township Farmers' Market, 921 Hamilton St., Franklin. Sat from 9 a.m. to 2 p.m., early July through late October.

Galleria Red Bank Farmers' Market, 2 Bridge Ave., Red Bank. Sun from 9 a.m. to 2 p.m., early May through mid-November.

Highland Park Farmers' Market, senior recreation center parking lot between 2nd and 3rd Avenues, Highland Park. Fri from 11 a.m. to 5:30 p.m., mid-June through mid-November.

Hunterdon Land Trust Farmers' Market, 111 Mine St., Flemington. Sun from 9 a.m. to 1 p.m. mid-May through late November.

Keyport Farmers' Market, 70 W. Front St., Keyport. Thurs from 1 p.m. to close, July through October.

Metuchen Farmers' Market, Pearl Street parking lot, Metuchen. Sat from 9 a.m. to 2 p.m., mid-June through early October.

Middlesex Borough Farmers' Market, Union Avenue, Middlesex. Fri from 11 a.m. to 5:30 p.m., mid-June through mid-November.

Montgomery Farmers' Market, Village Shopper, Routes 206 and 518, Montgomery. Sat from 9 a.m. to 1 p.m., mid-June through late October.

New Brunswick Community Farmers' Market, 178 Jones Ave., New Brunswick. Thurs from 11 a.m. to 3 p.m., and Sat from 11 a.m. to 5 p.m., mid-June through mid-October.

North Plainfield Farmers' Market, Somerset Street and Race Street, North Plainfield. Sat from 9 a.m. to 2 p.m., July through September.

Old Bridge Farmers' Market, Municipal Complex, Route 516 and Cottrell Road, Old Bridge. Wed from 11 a.m. to 7 p.m., early June through late October.

Best Cupcake in the State

Sugar + Sunshine (6 Market St., Plainsboro; 609-936-3777; www.sugarandsunshinebakery.com; $). My all-time weakness here is the chocolate cupcake, and nobody makes them better than Sugar + Sunshine in Plainsboro. Gigi Burton's spacious, brightly lit shop offers scones and muffins and other baked goods, but head straight to the cupcakes; there are usually about a dozen available at any one time. The chocolate/chocolate is my favorite, but the coconut/lemon buttercream, vanilla/chocolate, and carrot/cream cheese are not far behind. "We wanted to focus on nostalgic American desserts," Burton said. "We didn't want to do these fancy little French pastries."

Other worthy cupcake makers:

Mr. Cupcakes (1216 Van Houten Ave., Clifton; 973-859-0180). Offering 40 cupcake flavors, their ingredients are baked inside rather than stuffed or filled. Other locations in Hackensack, Oradell, and Red Bank.

The Stuffed Cupcake Place (231 Franklin Ave., Nutley; 973-667-7778). Nearly 100 kinds of stuffed cupcakes are available at Maureen and Keith Jaret's bakery, formerly known as the Petite Cafe.

North Plainfield Farmers' Market, Somerset Street opposite Borough Hall, North Plainfield. **Sat from 9 a.m. to 2 p.m., July through October.**

Pottersville Farmers' Market, 2090 Black River Rd., Pottersville. **Every other Sat 9 a.m. to 1 p.m., from late May through early September.**

Rutgers Garden Farm Market, 112 Ryders Ln., New Brunswick. **Fri from noon to 5 p.m., early May through mid-November.**

Sergeantsville Farmers' Market, Route 604, Sergeantsville. **Sat from 8:30 a.m. to noon, early May through late September.**

Somerville Farmers' Market, Grove Street and E. Main Street, Somerville. **Thurs from noon to 5 p.m., early June through late September.**

West Amwell Farmers' Market, 150 Rocktown-Lambertville Rd., West Amwell. **Sat from 9 a.m. to noon, mid-June through early October.**

Woodbridge Farmers' Market, 1 Main St., Woodbridge. **Wed from 3 to 7:30 p.m., late June through late October.**

Bardy Farms and Greenhouses, 149 Washington Valley Rd., Warren; (732) 356-4244; www.bardyfarms.com. Here's a farm stand with history. Abraham Bardy, who emigrated from Russia in 1904, was a poor farmer who started vegetable farming in Union. He and his wife, Gussie, and their eight children later operated a market in Elizabeth and a grocery store and supermarket in Union. Today Phillip Bardy, grandson of Abraham, continues the family farmstand tradition with his wife, Donna. They sell a variety of fruits and vegetables and make their own pies and breads. The market is open daily year-round from 8 a.m. to 6 p.m.

Battleview Orchards, 91 Wemrock Rd., Freehold; (732) 462-0756; www.battlevieworchards.com. This is a country store, with baked goods, pies, cider, jellies, jams, dips, and fruits and vegetables in season. Pick-your-own strawberries are available around late May. Special events here include an Easter egg hunt, with more than 4,000 eggs to search for, and behind-the-scenes farm tours. Open year-round.

Cheesequake Farms, 191 Rte. 34 South, Old Bridge; (732) 583-6780; www.cheesequakefarms.com. This is a good source for Jersey peaches, beans, and sweet corn, as well as peppers, tomatoes, squash, cucumbers, pumpkins, and sweet potatoes grown right here. Open daily from 9 a.m. to 6 p.m., Palm Sunday through Christmas Eve.

Giamarese Farm, 155 Fresh Pond Rd., East Brunswick; (732) 821-9494; www.giamaresefarm.com. Jim and Sue Giamarese are a young, hardworking couple who bought the family farm from his parents, aunts, and uncles in 1986. Their efforts paid off in 1989, when they won the national Outstanding Young Farmer Award. They feature pick-your-own strawberries, raspberries, peaches, tomatoes, peppers, and other fruit and produce. Their farm market is open from 9 a.m. to 7 p.m. Mon through Sat and 1 to 7 p.m. Sun from May 1 through December 23. Free hayrides on weekends in October.

Melick's Town Farm, 19 King St., Oldwick; (908) 439-3888; www .melickstownfarm.com. Talk about a family farm history. "All my ancestors in this country were born, baptized, married, and buried within 5 miles of Oldwick," says George Melick, owner, with his wife, Norma, of Melick's Town Farm, the largest fruit grower in North or Central Jersey. Their children, Peter, John, and Rebecca, are the 10th generation of Melicks to work the family farm. They sell their produce at farm stands in Oldwick (part of Tewksbury Township) and nearby Califon (472 Rte. 513; 908-832-2905). Buy fresh apple cider in September and October at the family's cider mill in Oldwick. The Oldwick farm stand is open daily from Apr through Nov; the Califon farm stand is open daily from July through Sept. See Melick's Town Farms's recipe for **Corn Slaw** on p. 300.

Mysty Mountain Farm, 2 Boulder Hill Rd., Tewksbury; (908) 832-6088. Maple syrup farms are so rare in New Jersey that the state Department of Agriculture doesn't keep statistics on production. Charlie Garrett, owner of Mysty Mountain Farm, in Hunterdon County, makes maple syrup in a five- or six-week period that generally runs from mid-February to the end of March. He can tap from among 400 sugar, red, and black maple trees on his 19-acre farm. Charlie makes a light syrup, best for waffles and pancakes, and a dark, thicker syrup, great for cooking or ladling over ice cream. The syrup, which comes in attractive maple leaf–shaped bottles, is available at the farm year-round (call ahead) and at local stores. Charlie gives tours in season; the nominal admission charge includes a small bottle of syrup. Tour hours are from 1 to 4 p.m., Sat and Sun in season.

Peaceful Valley Orchards, 441 Pittstown Rd., Pittstown; (908) 713-1705; www.peacefulvalleyorchards.com. In 2001 Meredith and Jeremy Compton—they met at a Rutgers University research farm—took over the former Hodulik Brothers farm in Pittstown, which had been inactive for five years. The young couple has since transformed the farm into a warm, friendly operation. They grow 18

kinds of apples, several varieties of peaches, and 5 varieties of pears. Their farm market is open from May through Nov. You can pick your own apples and pumpkins in the fall.

Phillips Farms, 290 Church Rd., Holland Township; (908) 995-0022; www.phillipsfarms.com. This is a good source for fruits and vegetables in the rolling, picturesque countryside of western Hunterdon County. Marc Phillips also sells his fruits and produce at Greenmarket locations at Union Square, Manhattan, and Brooklyn Borough Hall. Try the preserves and fruit spreads, including apricot, blackberry, blueberry, red raspberry, and strawberry-rhubarb. Open daily, 9 a.m. to 6 p.m., from April 1 through October 31. The website says Milford, but the farm is located in Holland Township.

Schaefer Farms, 1051 Rte. 523, Readington; (908) 782-2705; www.schaeferfarms.com. Here's a fun, kid-friendly farm with a large zoo of barnyard animals, and the one-and-only Schaefer Frightfest, a trilogy of terror—a haunted hayride, a haunted house, and the Mass-Acre Maize. Not recommended for children under age 10. It's held every Friday, Saturday, and Sunday in October and the first Saturday in November. Admission is $15 per person for all three events. The farm market is open from 9 a.m. to 6 p.m. daily.

Stults Farm, 62 John White Rd., Cranbury; (609) 799-2523; farm stand at 146 Cranbury Neck Rd.; www.stultsfarm.com. Four generations of the Stults family have worked the fields along Cranbury Neck, John White, and George Davison Roads in Cranbury. Kip Stults is the current owner; his son, Brian, and daughter, Amy, help him

The Official State Sandwich

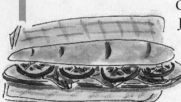

Call it what you want—"sub" (in North Jersey) or "hoagie" (in South Jersey), this cold-cut-laden lunch—or dinner— staple is Jersey's favorite sandwich. Delis and sub shops are a dime a dozen in this state; these (in addition to the **White House Subs** shop in Atlantic City, which is listed separately in the Shore section, p. 268) stand out.

Carmen's Deli (42 E. Browning Rd., Bellmawr; 856-931-7203). Unprepossessing store with the best hoagies in South Jersey, and that includes the much-hyped White House Subs shop. Great chicken salad hoagie. Also recommended: the Rose's Special, with hot capocollo, provolone, soppressata, prosciutto, roasted peppers, tomato, and onions.

Primo Hoagies (various locations in South Jersey; www .primohoagies.com). I always stay well away from chains, but I'll make an exception with Primo Hoagies, with 23 locations in all. All subs are loaded with meat, and the bread's top-notch.

Tastee Sub Shop (267 Plainfield Ave., Edison; 732-985-5423). President Obama paid Tastee a visit in 2010 for a roundtable discussion with small business owners. But this no-frills sub joint had been on the map well before the Secret Service got there. There are no fancy ingredients or condiments; choices include tomatoes, lettuce, onions, and hot peppers. That's it.

and his wife, Jill. They grow peaches, corn, tomatoes, cucumbers, beans, eggplant, peppers, and other fruits and vegetables. You can pick your own strawberries, raspberries, blackberries, blueberries, peas, peppers, tomatoes, beans, melons, and eggplant. Open daily June 1 through October 31; call for hours.

Von Thun's Country Farm Market, 519 Ridge Rd. (Route 522), Monmouth Junction; (732) 329-8656; www.vonthunfarms.com. Von Thun's, which celebrates its 100th anniversary in 2013, is well known for its ripe, juicy strawberries. Pick-your-own fields are available for strawberries, raspberries, blackberries, pumpkins, peas, and string beans. The farm market is open daily, from Apr through Oct.

Food Events

Late April

Shad Festival, Lambertville Area Chamber of Commerce, 239 N. Union St., Lambertville; (609) 397-0055; www.lambertville.org. This popular, long-running festival marks the arrival of spring and the return of the shad, a bony seagoing fish born in freshwater. Fred Lewis, who managed the Lewis Fishery from 1963 to 1999, was the inspiration behind the festival. The Lewis family, who have lived in the area for more than 100 years, is credited with helping clean up the Delaware River and restoring the greenish-blue shad to Lambertville. Fred Lewis died in early 2004 at the age of 88, but the Shad Festival continues on in his memory. The 2-day festival features plenty of good food, from the likes of **Triumph Brewing** (pp. 203, 294) in Princeton (try their India Pale Ale pulled-pork sandwiches), **Baker's Treat** (p. 113) in Flemington, and the Chocolate Box in Lambertville, among others. On Sunday a traditional riverside shad dinner is held, with 3 seatings. The menu includes grilled shad, fish chowder, baked potato, and coleslaw. The weekend also includes entertainment, shad-hauling demonstrations, and rides and amusements for kids.

Mid-May

Greek Festival, St. George Greek Orthodox Church, 1101 River Rd., Piscataway; (732) 463-1642; www.stgeorgepiscataway.org. Church fairs are a popular summertime happening around the state, and this weekend event is one of the best, especially for the food. It's been held since 1973 and seems to get more popular every year. Gyros, dolmas, moussaka, and more can be found at the food tables. Try to get to the grounds early; the traffic jams along River Road attest to the festival's popularity.

July 4

All-American Barbecue, Sergeantsville Inn, 600 Rosemont-Ringoes Rd., Sergeantsville; (609) 397-3700. This annual festival, held in the rolling countryside of Hunterdon County, is an unabashed celebration of Americana—an all-you-can-eat feast of chicken, ribs, hamburgers, hot dogs, chili, salads, and desserts; plus live music and fireworks. An added, fun feature is the Great Crate Race, when families and children compete in homemade, Soapbox Derby–like cars. It begins at 9 a.m. The barbecue runs from noon to 8 p.m. The barbecued chicken alone is worth the trip. The inn stays open that day for lunch and dinner. Just down the road is the Green Sergeants bridge, the state's only covered bridge.

Early August

Annual Bluegrass Music Festival, Cream Ridge Winery, 145 Rte. 539, Cream Ridge; (609) 259-9797. Bluegrass and wine seem like perfect partners, and Cream Ridge Winery's annual festival is one of the more enjoyable events on the summer calendar. There are wine tastings and tours, food (burgers, barbecued chicken, and Italian specialties), and bluegrass bands playing all day. Admission fee. Held rain or shine.

Middlesex County Fair, Cranbury and Fern Roads, East Brunswick; (732) 257-8858; www.middlesexcountyfair.org. One of the state's top county fairs, the Middlesex County Fair features an array of agricultural, crafts, and food competitions; rides; exhibits; costume parades for both children and animals—and food. Burgers, hot dogs, barbecue, pizza, ice cream, funnel cakes—all the county fair standards are represented. The highlight is the barbecued chicken, served under the "Chicken Pavilion." The fair itself runs for a week, and it's always fun.

Mid-September

Fruit Crush and Pig Roast Festival, Cream Ridge Winery, 145 Rte. 539, Cream Ridge; (609) 259-9797; www.creamridgewinery.com. See fruit crushed before it is made into wine. Take a winery tour and sample some of the wines, including the just-released cranberry or cherry wines. Best yet, buy roasted pork sandwiches right from that roasted pig! Admission fee. Held rain or shine.

Late September

Gourmet Food & Gift Show, Garden State Convention & Exhibit Center, 50 Atrium Dr., Somerset; (609) 398-4450; www.gourmet shows.com. There's no better place to sample the latest in gourmet and specialty food products than this big, bustling show, held at the Garden State Convention Center in late September and at the Atlantic City Convention Center in late October. There are scores of tables and booths devoted to gourmet and specialty foods, wine, cookbooks, kitchen appliances, and much more. Watch celebrity chefs give cooking demonstrations and others compete in cooking contests. Past exhibitors have included, among many others, Alba Vineyards, Jersey Devil Chili, La Fleur de Lis, Canada Dry, Stella Artois beer, and the Food Network.

Early October

Country Jamboree and Chili Cook-Off, Front Street, Keyport; (732) 946-2711; www.keyportonline.com. Kick up your heels to lively country music at this two-day event featuring line dancing, crafters, a good variety of food, and a chili cook-off. Chili contest winners are eligible to participate in the International Chili Society's world championship cook-off. Held since 1997, the Country Jamboree offers free admission.

Garden State Wine Growers Harvest Festival, Alba Vineyard, 260 Rte. 627, Finesville; (908) 588-0085; www.newjerseywines .com. This festival offers wines from about 20 New Jersey vineyards, plus wine cellar tours, live music, kids' activities, classic cars, and a hot-air balloon launch. Admission charge; children free. Food includes the usual burgers and hot dogs, but try the roast pork sandwiches, deep-fried turkey, and Italian specialties. No pets are allowed on the grounds.

Learn to Cook

L'École des Chefs Relais & Châteaux, 11 E. 44th St., #707, New York, NY; (877) 334-6464; www.ecoledeschefs.com. Here is a unique culinary internship enabling amateur cooks to enter the kitchens of Michelin- and Mobil-starred Relais Gourmands restaurants. Stir, chop, and mix your way through the various kitchen stations as you learn the secrets behind some of the world's most exciting menus. Interns learn about the rigorous standards involved in choosing ingredients, creating flavors, and pairing wines with foods. Internships are available for 2 or 5 days at select restaurants around the country; since the Ryland Inn closed, there is no participating New Jersey restaurant, but the Hotel Fauchere, which is in the program, is in Milford, PA, just over the bridge from Montague, Sussex County. Sessions run from morning to evening and include staff meals.

Mumford's, 33 Apple St., Tinton Falls; (732) 747-7646; www .mumfords.com. Chris Mumford operated a celebrated restaurant, Mumford's Unique American Cuisine in Long Branch, for nearly 10 years, but time away from his family led him to close the restaurant and open Mumford's, a combination cooking school, gourmet shop, and housewares store. Cooking classes are offered year-round; recent courses included In the Heart of Tuscany, What Goes with Sake, and It's All About Chocolate. In addition to the prepared curriculum, Mumford's offers private classes on dates of your choice. The cafe features such tempting sandwiches as a Caribbean club, turkey and Vermont cheddar, bruschetta chicken, and One Serious Hamburger, with grilled red onions, beefsteak tomatoes, baby greens, chipotle aioli, and choice of cheese.

Verducci's, 176 Rte. 202 North, Raritan Township (Hunterdon County); (908) 788-7750; www.verduccis.com. This gourmet store (see entry in Specialty Stores & Markets, p. 119) hosts cooking classes year-round. Recent offerings included Smokin' Soups, Stews, and Ragouts; Beer, Not Just a Beverage; Essence of Italy; and Marinades and Grilling Sauces. There are classes for singles and for special events, too. The classes, which include a 3-course meal you help prepare, generally run 2 hours.

Learn about Wine

Grape Expectations, 25E Kearny St., Bridgewater; (732) 764-WINE; www.grapeexpectationsnj.com. Grape Expectations, housed in a former warehouse, is one of about a dozen winemaking facilities around the state. Members—everyone from dentists and doctors to well drillers and garbagemen—crush and press the grapes under the watchful eye of owner Jim Lowney, savoring the fruits of their labor months later. Forget about crushing grapes with your feet; a fire-engine-red crusher/destemmer, which looks like a mulcher you'd use in the yard, does the job. Members pay anywhere from $300 to $400 per quarter barrel of wine, enough for 60 bottles of wine. Barrel renting is an additional charge, or you can buy your own.

Landmark Eateries

Anton's at the Swan, 43 S. Main St., Lambertville; (609) 397-1960; www.antons-at-the-swan.com; American; $$$. There is a world of dining opportunities in artsy Lambertville, everything from coffeehouses and vegetarian to Thai and Italian. Anton's at the Swan—named for the stately old Swan Hotel—is the most tranquil if not romantic restaurant in this lively little town. The restaurant, with its dark-wood-and-antiques decor, is on the hotel's ground floor. Chef-Owner Chris Connors focuses on using as many local and indigenous ingredients as possible, while infusing them with a  "global outlook." He and his wife, Ursula, grow tomatoes, chile peppers, and other vegetables used in the restaurant in a garden at their Baptistown home. Perennial menu favorites include curried corn and coconut soup with crab in the summer, brown butter and roasted tomato risotto in early fall, and braised duck and wild mushroom shepherd's pie in the winter.

Burrito Royale, 4049 Rte. 1 South, South Brunswick; (732) 297-6148; Mexican; $. Nestled in the trees along Route 1 in South Brunswick, Burrito Royale is one of those places that has been around forever yet remains relatively unknown. The brick-front burrito and taco joint is innocuous inside and out but serves up huge, good, and cheap food. Eileen and Samuel Scott opened it in 1977; their son, Jim, runs it now. Try the California burrito, jammed with beef, cheese, and lettuce in a soft, moist tortilla doused in red sauce, or the enchilada, a huge, soft corn tortilla bulging with beans and chili, covered with gooey cheese, and swimming in a tangy red sauce. The tostada is the size of a small hubcap, but a lot more nutritious, with beans, beef, cheese, and lettuce melted together in a corn tortilla.

Cafe Bua, 1353 Stelton Rd., Piscataway; (732) 819-3900; www .cafebua.com; Asian Fusion; $. No two words on a restaurant menu make me cringe more than "Asian fusion," which often translates to "menu disaster"—restaurants trying to re-create dishes from a half dozen or more countries instead of concentrating on just one. Forget what I just said, though, and head immediately to Cafe Bua, whose menu is all over the Asian map but consistently focused, and wonderful. The owner is Thai-born Oat Chorphaka. Skip the Philly cheesesteak, grilled Reuben, and other American standards on the menu and proceed directly to the outstanding hot-and-sour soup, the winning wonton soup, the superior spicy beef salad, or the red curry meatballs. For a memorable—if quickly melting—dessert, order the shaved ice, a multicolored mountain of fresh fruit, vanilla ice cream, chopped ice, and red bean paste, topped with condensed milk and syrup.

David Burke Fromagerie, 26 Ridge Rd., Rumson; (732) 842-8088; www.fromagerierestaurant.com; American; $$$$. Since 1972 Fromagerie has represented class and elegance. Renowned chef David Burke took over the restaurant in 2006, turning the emphasis from classic French to American cooking. Dishes range from Hot and Angry Lobster Cocktail and prime beef carpaccio to Red Bank roasted organic chicken, handmade cavatelli, and braised short rib.

Fine china, candlelight, and a fireplace make for a singular dining experience, minutes from and yet worlds away from the typical Jersey Shore burger joint and seafood shack. Fromagerie is not for the frugal—entrees are in the $30 to $50 range—but you can keep things somewhat reasonable by forgoing a bottle of high-priced wine. And, given the restaurant's name, don't forget to try some cheese; samplers are available.

Jo-Sho, 120 Cedar Grove Ln., Somerset; (732) 469-8969; Japanese; $$. Some of Jersey's best dining can be found in unremarkable-looking strip malls, and Jo-Sho, squeezed between a Chinese restaurant and a health club, is proof. It's a tranquil, soothing space, with a dining room and the req-

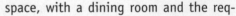

uisite sushi bar. The co-owner is Yoko Shinohara, who is only too happy to tell you where her fish comes from and that the residents of Yokohama live long lives because they eat seaweed. You can tell right from the start Jo-Sho is not cookie-cutter Japanese; the miso soup, which can often be characterless, is surprisingly flavorful. The deluxe sashimi, with yellowtail, big-eyed tuna, scallops, fluke, and more, is recommended.

Luca's Ristorante, 2019 Rte. 27, Franklin; (732) 297-7676; www .lucasristorante.com; Italian; $$. Andrea Di Meglio opened Luca's

Biggest Sandwich in the State

New Jersey is home to some pretty big eaters. Diners, all-you-can-eat buffets, Sunday brunches—all of them seem to encourage second and third and fourth helpings. There are plenty of Jewish delis around the state that like to load up the sandwiches, but one carries it to extravagant extreme. That's **Harold's New York Deli Restaurant** (3050 Woodbridge Ave.; Edison; 732-661-9100; www.haroldsfamousdeli.com; $$). This is Jewish deli as big-budget Broadway spectacular; you can look right into the kitchen, and the sandwiches, salads, cakes, knishes, and other items are supersize and then some. Softball-size matzos and hubcap-size pancakes. Ten-inch-long apple turnovers and 2-pound éclairs. Lampshade-size, 40-pound carrot cakes. The triple-decker sandwiches, piled nearly a foot high with meat, will set you back about $25, but they also will feed 4 to 6 people comfortably. Fortunately, you also can buy "normal-size" sandwiches. The owner is Harold Jaffe, who was once part-owner of the famed Carnegie Deli in New York City. Harold's, located in the Ramada Inn, boasts "the world's best pastrami," "the world's best corned beef," "the world's best cheesecake," and "the world's largest pickle bar." This is what is known in the business as chutzpah.

when he was 18; he's still in the kitchen 20 years later. Tired of the same old Italian standards? Luca's pastas include *agnolotti di cacao,* a cocoa ravioli stuffed with roasted butternut squash, and organic whole wheat penne *piedimonte* with artichokes, asparagus, shiitake mushrooms, broccoli, yellow squash, cherry tomatoes, and topped with fontina.

Origin, 25 Division St., Somerville; (908) 685-1344; www.origin thai.com; Thai; $$. Somerville has reinvented itself in recent years, going from a pizzeria-dominated town to one in which there are now 50-plus restaurants, from classic American and Italian to Cuban, Japanese, and Thai. Origin is considered among the state's best Thai restaurants, and don't hold its origin against it. The restaurant is located in a former laundry, although you'd never know it. Chef Manop Sutipayakul's fare is Thai-French fusion. All the tried-and-true Thai standards are here and done well: chicken satay, pad thai, vegetarian roll, green papaya salad, and soft-shell crab. More adventurous dishes include Muscovy duck breast, ostrich fillet, escargots, broiled striped bass with ginger and leeks, and a squid salad with mango, baby greens, tomatoes, and shallots. There are both Thai and French desserts.

Perryville Inn, 167 Perryville Rd., Perryville; (908) 730-9500; www.theperryvilleinn.com; American; $$$. Elegant dining in a relaxed country setting, minutes from Route 78. The inn has quite a history. Cornelius Carhart, a second major in the Colonial Army, had the inn built; as news of Commodore Perry's dramatic victory at

Lake Erie in the War of 1812 reached the area, the carpenters, swept away by patriotic zeal, nailed the last post beam into place, doused it with whiskey, and, according to local lore, christened the area Perryville. The inn was scheduled to be demolished in the late 1950s due to the construction of Route 78, but the then-owners agreed to move it 100 feet. Today the inn includes a cozy lounge, a small dining room, and the main dining room, which looks out on the woods. The chef is Paul Ingenito; his wife, Lorraine, often serves as the hostess. Original dishes include Griggstown rabbit potpie with herbed dumplings, black truffle, and pearl onions; and herb-roasted rack and sliced sirloin of Colorado lamb, with a creamy potato gratin and summer vegetable ratatouille. What's for dessert? How about a Retro Ring Ding, layers of devil's food cake and white and dark chocolate mousse covered with a chocolate ganache?

Pithari Taverna, 28 Woodbridge Ave., Highland Park; (732) 572-0616; www.thepithari.com; Greek; $$. Greek restaurants often get overlooked in the rich culinary diversity of New Jersey. Pithari Taverna is one of the state's newest Greek restaurants, and it's already among the best. Proprietor Tassos Stefanopoulos also owns New Athens Corner, the Greek bakery/grocery next door. Pithari is a colorful, casual place; a video shows scenes from the Greek countryside. Authentic? The Greek salad, enlivened by an excellent oil-and-vinegar dressing, is without greens; you don't find lettuce in real Greek salads, Stefanopoulos says. Don't know here to begin? Try the grandly titled Ultimate Greek Spreads, with dolmades (grape leaves), tzatziki (yogurt-based sauce), taramosalata (caviar dip), and melitzanosalata (eggplant).

Polar Cub, Route 22 West, Whitehouse; (908) 534-4401; Ice Cream; $. Pick a hot summer night—make that any summer night—and you'll find a line of people waiting at the windows of this legendary ice-cream stand. The Polar Cub, with its circular roof and bygone-past feel, has been serving good ice cream since the mid-1950s. Mario Monaco, from nearby Branchburg, liked the place so much he bought it in 1998. Mario uses Welsh Farms ice cream, which he says is creamier than other brands. A surefire kid pleaser here: the purplish-red-blue neon ice cream. Goes down like ice cream, tastes like bubble gum.

Restaurant Nicholas, 160 Rte. 35, Middletown; (732) 345-9977; www.restaurantnicholas.com; American; $$$. Nicholas Harary, proprietor of Restaurant Nicholas, is among the new breed of New Jersey restaurant owners: young, enthusiastic, and very exacting. Nicholas, former sommelier at Jean Georges in New York (well before that, he washed dishes in an Italian restaurant in East Brunswick), has created a stylish, elegant, but not stuffy restaurant;

GEMÜTLICHKEIT IN THE GARDEN STATE

Gemütlichkeit is a German word encompassing conviviality, hospitality, good food, lively music, and maybe a stein or two of good German beer. Fritzy's in Howell and the Black Forest in Allentown, two of the state's best German restaurants, have since closed, but two other restaurants—one long-established, the other the new kid on the bloc—offer distinctive experience and atmosphere.

The **Black Forest Inn** (249 Rte. 206, Stanhope; 973-347-3344; www.blackforestinn.com; $$$). is Jersey's best-known German restaurant, with several wood-beamed dining rooms and such house specialties as house-made bratwurst and wild boar braised in Riesling. There's also good selection of German beers, including Spaten Dunkel and Weihenstephaner.

You wouldn't normally think Wrightstown when it comes to German food—the town is best known as the location of the Fort Dix army base—but the Burlington County town has become a draw for lovers of sauerbraten, bratwurst, and other German standards because of **Sebastian's Schnitzelhaus** (43 Fort Dix St., Wrightstown; 609-724-9609; www.enjoysebastians.com; $$). The surroundings aren't fancy, but the food is the real deal—*schweine schnitzel* (boneless pork), *kalbs schnitzel natur* (breaded veal cutlets), and more. The restaurant is BYOB.

dishes are uncovered tableside with gusto, and Nicholas and his wife, Melissa, make the rounds of the two dining rooms. It comes as no surprise that 300-plus bottles of wine—they start at $30—are available. It's strictly prix fixe here; the 6-course tasting menu is $85, while a 3-course menu is $65. The 6-course menu might include marinated Long Island oysters, seared *foie gras*, wild Alaskan salmon, braised short ribs, artisanal cheese, and dessert.

Sigiri, 52 Rte. 27, Edison; (732) 744-9667; www.sigirinyc.com; Sri Lankan; $$. Sigiri, within walking distance of the Metropark train station, is the state's best Sri Lankan restaurant. OK, so it's the state's only Sri Lankan restaurant, but no matter; the food at this small restaurant is consistently good. Sri Lankan and Indian food use the same lineup of spices—cumin, coriander, cardamom, cloves, and ginger, among others—but in different grinds and mixtures. You'll find curries, soups, stews, and rice dishes here, along with such Sri Lankan staples as string hopper—strings of rice-flour dough squeezed through a sieve and then steamed. My absolute favorite dish here: the lamb black curry—tender, juicy, peppery.

Stage Left, 5 Livingston Ave., New Brunswick; (732) 828-4444; www.stageleft.com; American; $$$. Francis Schott, owner of Stage Left, rides a Harley, but don't expect to see it parked in front of his four-star restaurant or any vestige of biker culture inside. The food is exemplary, but what separates Stage Left from most fine restaurants is the extraordinary wine selection. The service is expert and polished, but Francis—must be that Harley—likes to have a little fun, at least with his menu. The bar menu features what the restaurant calls the Best Cheeseburger in the World (wood-grilled Angus beef with two-year-aged Vermont cheddar, tomato, and red onion). In a showdown of burgers around the state, *Inside Jersey* magazine named it Jersey's best burger.

Stockton Inn, 1 Main St., Stockton; (609) 397-1250; www .stocktoninn.com; American; $$. There are few spots as romantic or charming as the Stockton Inn, in the center of this quiet Hunterdon County community. Fireplaces, 1930s-vintage murals of fox hunts and church meetings, several cozy dining rooms, and lovely gardens out back add up to an unforgettable dining destination. The hotel and its wishing well inspired the Rodgers and Hart tune "There's a Small Hotel," which first appeared in the 1936 Broadway hit *On Your Toes* and was later reprised in *Pal Joey*. A corner table favored by F. Scott Fitzgerald, Damon Runyon, Dorothy Parker, and friends was named the Algonquin Roundtable in honor of their New York City hangout. The Stockton Inn is no stuffy country inn; dress is casual, and the bar is a lively gathering spot for locals and those in the know. Lunch is served until 2:30 p.m. Mon through Sat, but you can order anytime from the inn's extensive tavern menu and sit either in the bar or at one of the outside tables.

Brewpubs & Microbreweries

Basil T's Brewery Pub & Italian Grill, 183 Riverside Ave., Red Bank; (732) 842-5990; www.basilt.com. Basil T's put itself on

LITTLE INDIA

One of the more atmospheric neighborhoods in New Jersey is Little India, a colorful collection of jewelry and clothing shops, restaurants, sweetshops, and grocery stores along Oak Tree Road in Woodbridge and neighboring Edison. More than 50,000 Asian Indians live in Central Jersey alone, and the streets of Little India are packed with sari-clad shoppers, especially on the weekend.

The best-known restaurant is **Moghul** (1655 Oak Tree Rd., Edison; 732-549-5050; www.moghul.com; $$). Behind a glass partition, cooks tend to the tandoor, the Indian clay oven. Moghul leans toward North Indian cuisine, known for its rich sauces flavored with aromatic ground and whole spices, and is famous for its soups, tandoori chicken, curries, kebabs, and other traditional dishes. The weekend brunches are legendary, offering a full range of appetizers, soups, salads, meat and seafood dishes, and desserts, and they're reasonably priced.

Across the road is the pink-and-green neon-lit **Moghul Express** (1670 Oak Tree Rd., Edison; 732-549-6222; $). Ornamental balls, figures, and mobiles hang from the ceiling, and there is both a sweets counter and a fast-food restaurant. Moghul and Moghul Express are

the beer map when its Maxwell's Dry Stout won a gold medal at the 2002 Great American Beer Festival. Always on tap are Basil T's "Famous Five"—Ms. Lucy's Weimaraner Wheat, Rosie's Tale-Waggin' Pale Ale, Basil's Rocket Red Ale, Big Vic's Short Order Porter, and Maxwell's Dry Stout. The restaurant offers authentic and first-rate owned by Satish Mehtani, who came to this country in 1969. Satish gets around; the take-out stand's walls are decorated with photos of him with Mother Teresa, Hillary Clinton, and other notables. Sweets are very popular, and Moghul Express stocks more than 50 kinds, most made of milk and sugar, with added ingredients. The most popular are *rasmali,* made of cottage cheese and pistachios, and *kaju katli,* a marzipan-like confection made of cashews.

Another celebrated sweetshop is **Chowpatty** (1349 Oak Tree Rd., Iselin [a section of Woodbridge]; 732-283-9020; www.chowpattyfoods .com; $). The owners are Chandrakant and Sushila Patel, who also operate a southern Indian, vegetarian restaurant of the same name next door. How popular are sweets in Indian food and culture? The Patels sell about $1 million worth a year.

For an unforgettable introduction to Bombay cuisine and Indian culture in general, visit **Dimple's Bombay Talk** (1358 Oak Tree Rd., Iselin; 732-283-0066; www .bombaytalkusa.com; $). Bollywood hits play on a television, the conversation is lively and animated, and the atmosphere is casual. It is one of three area restaurants owned by Dilip Mehta, who emigrated from Bombay in 1987.

Italian dishes—pasta fagioli, perciatelli amatraciana, and orec-chiette rapini, among others. Basil T's claims the country's largest mug club. For an annual fee of $35, you get a beautiful 23-ounce ceramic mug that is kept at the bar, and beers served in it are just $3.25 each. Memberships run from August 15 through the following

August 14; each year you get to take the previous year's mug home. You can also buy a growler—a glass to-go jug—for $24 and refill it for $12.

Harvest Moon Brewery and Cafe, 392 George St., New Brunswick; (732) 249-6666; www.harvestmoonbrewery.com. Conveniently located in downtown New Brunswick, Harvest Moon offers good brew, dependable food, and a lively atmosphere. The brew tanks are located behind glass just inside the entrance. About 10 beers are available at any one time. Recommended: Crazy Golden Girl, a light-colored, medium-bodied ale; British Nut Brown, a brown ale; Prince William's Mild Manor, a mild ale; and the Siberian Express, an imperial stout.

J. J. Bitting, 33 Main St., Woodbridge; (732) 634-2929; www .njbrewpubs.com. J. J. Bitting manages to be a fun and atmospheric spot, with giant copper kettles in the center of the spacious brick-walled dining room. And it's located, interestingly enough, almost next door to township police headquarters. The town wanted to tear down the former coal and grain depot building when it was rebuilding the town hall, but now-owner Mike Cerami stepped in and worked out a deal. Cerami, who has run several area restaurants, opened J. J. Bitting in 1997. For an appetizer try the Blackjack Chili, slow-simmered black beans in Black Jack Stout with andouille sausage, ground beef, and bell peppers in a bread boule. Brews include Victoria's Golden Ale; Avenel Amber, a medium-hopped, light-bodied amber lager and my favorite; Duff Beer, an American-style lager ("mmm Duff's," as Homer would say); and Black Jack Stout, a creamy-smooth, unfiltered stout. In 2003 BeerAdvocate.com named Bitting the second-best brewpub in America.

Pizzeria Uno Chicago Grill & Brewery, 61 Rte. 1, Edison; (732) 548-7979; www.pizzeriauno.com. How many pizzerias can boast of a brewery inside? The Pizzeria Uno in Edison, located on Route 1 South between Woodbridge Center and Menlo Park Mall, can. It's part of the nationwide 200-restaurant chain. Brewmaster Chris Percello brews all the restaurant's beer on the premises, using a custom-built brewing system.

River Horse Brewing Company, 80 Lambert Ln., Lambertville; (609) 397-7776; www.riverhorse.com. River Horse is a 20-barrel microbrewery located in the scenic small town of Lambertville, just across the Delaware River from New Hope, PA. River Horse has been making good beer since 1996; its River Horse Lager, a personal favorite, is available at Trenton Thunder ball games and other venues. Other beers include River Horse Special Ale, a copper-colored ale with a slightly malty taste; River Horse Dark Harvest Ale, a dark, robust, deep red ale; and River Horse Hop Hazard Pale Ale, a full-bodied American pale ale brewed with five hops varieties. The brewery and gift shop are open from noon to 5 p.m. Fri, Sat, and Sun.

Best Bars in New Jersey

Nobody knows Jersey's bars better than Ray Foley. The Wall resident and former Marine is founder and editor of *Bartender* magazine, and author of *Bartending for Dummies, The Ultimate Cocktail Book, Bartender Magazine's Ultimate Bartender's Guide,* and other books. He's the guy who came up with the Fuzzy Navel, among other drinks. I asked Foley, a former bartender and assistant general manager at **The Manor** (p. 83) in West Orange, to list his favorite bars in Jersey. Here they are, in no particular order:

Bamboo Grille (185 Madisonville Rd., Basking Ridge; 908-766-9499; www.bamboo-grille.com). Spectacular view of the golf course, terrific happy hour, fun crowd.

Roots Steak House (40 W. Park Place, Morristown; 973-326-1800; rootssteakhouse.com). The bar is first-class, and so are the bartenders.

The Porch (810 Rte. 71, Spring Lake Heights; 732-449-5880; www.porchpub.com). Great fun, lots of TVs and games, and run for years by a wonderful manager (Nancy Lewis) and experienced bartenders.

St. Stephen's Green Publick House (2031 Rte. 71, Spring Lake Heights; 732-449-2626; www.ststephensgreenpub.com). A real Irish bar with Irish food and the best selection of Irish whiskey.

The Terrace Lounge at The Manor (111 Prospect Ave., West Orange; 973-731-2360; www.themanorrestaurant.com). A classic, and I have to mention it—I worked there for 10 years!

90 Acres at Natirar (2 Main St., Peapack-Gladstone; 908-901-9500; www.natirar.com). A sanctuary of luxury and tranquility where bartenders serve drinks infused with herbs from the local garden.

Union Landing Restaurant (622 Green Ave., Brielle; 732-528-6665; www.unionlanding.com). Great view, seafood, and cocktails on the water. Local and summer crowd.

Martell's Tiki Bar (Boardwalk, Point Pleasant Beach; 732-892-0131; www.tiki bar.com). Thirst-quenching tropical drinks on the famous Jersey boardwalk and the best people watching.

Avenue Restaurant (23 Ocean Ave., Long Branch; 732-759-2900; www.leclubavenue.com). Enjoy freshly prepared cocktails while looking over the beautiful Atlantic Ocean in a first-class atmosphere.

The Lady Secret Cafe at Monmouth Park (175 Oceanport Ave., Oceanport; 732-222-5100; www.monmouthpark.com). Named for a famous horse. Wonderful bartenders, impressive service, real horse people, great tips!

Ship Inn, 61 Bridge St., Milford; (908) 995-0188; www.shipinn
.com. On January 3, 1995, the Ship Inn became the first business
in New Jersey to brew beer for public consumption on the premises since the days of Prohibition. The original 1880s Victorian
building, which once housed an ice-cream parlor, bakery, and
speakeasy, underwent extensive renovation in the 1980s. The
brewer is Tim Hall, son of the inn's founders, David Hall, a native
of Liverpool, and his wife, Ann. The Ship Inn is a bridge, food-
and beer-wise, between Great Britain and the Garden State. Brews
include Cromwell's Demise, English Best Bitter, Golden Wheat Light,
Paddlewheel Pale Ale, Olde Pheasant Plucker, and Hop Monster IPA.
"All our ales are served with England in mind," Tim says. The menu
hails from both sides of the big pond—fish-and-chips; seafood
scampi; roast beef and Yorkshire pudding; Eastern Shore crab cakes;
shepherd's pie; Tiddy Oggie and Ships, the Royal Navy's version of a
Cornish pasty; and the good old-fashioned burger and fries. All the
major British holidays are celebrated here, including Boxing Day,
December 26, and Robbie Burns Day, January 24, in honor of the
Scottish poet.

Wine Trail

Alba Vineyard, 269 Rte. 627, Milford; (908) 995-7800; www
.albavineyard.com. Consistently rated among New Jersey's top
wineries, Alba has been producing first-rate wines since the early

1980s. It is located in an 1805 converted stone barn in the beautiful Musconetcong Valley, just 2 miles east of the Delaware River. Alba has won many wine competition awards; its Red Raspberry received the highest score for a fruit wine in history from the Beverage Testing Institute of Chicago, which evaluates wines for such magazines as the *Wine Enthusiast, Wine & Spirits,* and *The New Yorker*. Alba hosts a range of special events, including Wine and Chocolate Weekend in February, Summerfest in July, and the Garden State Wine Growers Harvest Festival in October (p. 135). Open from noon to 5 p.m. Wed, Thurs, and Fri; 11 a.m. to 6 p.m. Sat; and noon to 5 p.m. Sun. The winery has a Milford mailing address but is actually located in the village of Finesville, which is part of Holland Township.

Amwell Valley Vineyard, 80 Old York Rd., Ringoes; (908) 788-5852; www.amwellvalleyvineyard.com. In 1982 Amwell Valley Vineyard became the first New Jersey winery licensed under the Farm Winery Act, but it took some doing. Michael Fisher, founder of Amwell Valley Vineyard, helped overturn the archaic wine laws of New Jersey with the help of three associates and Congresswoman Barbara McConnell. Michael, a senior scientist at Merck, the pharmacological giant headquartered in Rahway, runs the vineyard with his son, Jeffrey, and Jeffrey's wife, Debra. Amwell Valley makes about 20 kinds of wines, made from French vinifera and French-American hybrids and fruit trees grown on 15 acres.

Open for tours and tastings from 1 to 5 p.m. Sat and Sun; other times by appointment.

Cream Ridge Winery, 145 Rte. 539, Cream Ridge; (609) 259-9797; www.creamridgewinery.com. Cream Ridge, located along twisting Route 539 (the summer shortcut to the Jersey Shore for those wishing to avoid the perpetually clogged Garden State Parkway), is especially known for its fruit wines—cherry, plum, and cranberry. The vineyard, opened in 1988, is run by the Amabile family; the cherry wine is called, naturally, Ciliegia (Cherry) Amabile. Other wines include sangria, Cabernet Franc, Syrah, plum, and a holiday spice wine released in November. The winery hosts many events, including a benefit for the Foundation for the Assistance of Abandoned Children; the organization runs an orphanage from which two of the winemakers' grandchildren were adopted. And at the winery's annual open house in April, you can listen to Italian music while sampling wine and Italian gourmet food. Open from 11 a.m. to 6 p.m. Mon through Sat and 11 a.m. to 5 p.m. Sun.

Unionville Vineyards, 9 Rocktown Rd., Ringoes; (908) 788-0400; www.unionvillevineyards.com. Unionville bills itself as "New Jersey's Finest Winery." Although other vineyards, and their customers, might beg to differ, Unionville has racked up a long line of awards and acclaim. The *New York Times* has called it the state's top winery, and Hugh Johnson's annual *Pocket Wine Book* has listed Unionville as New Jersey's top winery since 1997. In 1998 owners Kris Nielsen and Pat Galloway planted their first vines on what had originally been the nation's largest peach orchard. Wines include Merlot Reserve, Hunter's Red Reserve Meritage, Chambourcin, Fields of Fire, and Cool Foxy Lady, a dessert wine. Like many of the state's bigger vineyards, Unionville hosts a variety of fun events, including Spring Fling, Summerfest, and cooking-with-wine demonstrations. Open year-round from 11 a.m. to 4 p.m. Thurs through Sun. Note: The vineyard is actually located in East Amwell Township.

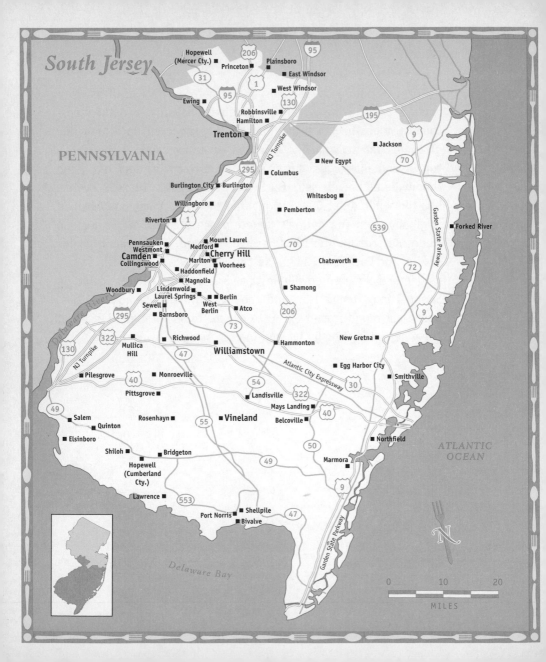

South Jersey

South Jersey is the state's breadbasket. New Jersey is among the leading growers of blueberries and cranberries in the US. As evidence of that, Hammonton is called the nation's blueberry capital, and Chatsworth, the center of the Pine Barrens, holds an annual cranberry festival. Deep in Salem County, muskrat trappers continue century-old traditions, and the local firehouse hosts an annual muskrat dinner. Bivalve, Shellpile, and Sea Breeze, along Delaware Bay, are some of the quietest—and most remote—towns in the state, but there is at least one restaurant down there that's well worth the trip to the end of the road. Country roads here reward the wanderer and adventurer, and, contrary to appearances, they always lead somewhere. Open-air barbecue stands line Route 40, also known as the Black Horse Pike. Many of the state's vineyards have found fertile ground in South Jersey's sandy-loamed, clay-bottomed earth. Top dining destination: Cherry Hill, where you can find any food imaginable.

In this chapter we'll visit Cheesecake World and the Kibitz Room, Tomasello Winery and the British Connection. We'll learn about everything from dandelion pesto to elegant French food and discover where to find the state's best cheesesteaks, sticky buns, and blueberry pies.

Made Here

Andreas Bros. Chile Pepper Co., 36 Arctic Pkwy., Ewing; (609) 209-0625; www.abcpepperco.com. Twin brothers Tom and Chris Andreas planted a few habañero pepper seeds in their father's garden in the early 1990s, but it was not until 2000, when they bought the former Jones' Greenhouse in Ewing, outside Trenton, that they got serious about chile peppers. They started with a few varieties, and today they offer about two dozen kinds. But the brothers are making a name in specialty food circles for their Andreas Bros. Oyster and Seafood Sauce. Disappointed by the sauces they sampled at seafood markets and restaurants around the country, Tom and Chris decided to create their own. The sauce— great not only for oysters but also for clams, shellfish, and broiled or grilled fish steaks—comes in mild and hot versions. It is available by phone or Internet order.

Cedar Run Farms, 105 Porchtown Rd., Pittsgrove; (856) 358-1318; www.walkersfarmmarket.com. The Walker family, owners of Cedar Run Farms, knows a little something about asparagus; they grow asparagus spears for fresh market consumption and are the exclusive seed producer for all of the New Jersey male hybrid asparagus varieties. Can't say I knew there were male and female asparagus, but one thing I do know is that Cedar Run's asparagus salsa and asparagus guacamole are good. Unlike guacamole made from avocados, asparagus guacamole contains no fat and no cholesterol and is high in vitamins A, B, and C. The salsa is full of chunks of asparagus and tomatoes mixed with jalapeños, chiles, and onions. Both products are available by phone and Internet orders.

Cheesecake World, 228 Rte. 9 South, Marmora; (609) 390-2468. You'd think, with a name like Cheesecake World, there'd be a lavish showroom and fancy website. The interior is plain-Jane, and the most lavish furnishing is the giant fiberglass cow outside. The father-daughter team of Ed and Katie Whatley make about 15,000 cheesecakes a year. Most popular flavors: the raspberry swirl and the Awesome Cheesecake, which is half chocolate, half plain, with a chocolate glaze on top. Others flavors include pecan turtle, chocolate swirl, orange creamsicle, chocolate chip, almond amaretto, Key lime, and seven kinds of low-carb, sugar-free cheesecake. One interesting feature about the cheesecakes: None have crusts. It's cheesecake, pure and simple. They take phone orders and serve walk-in customers. They also make stuffed bread; the pepperoni-and-mozzarella-stuffed bread, with its crusty, chewy exterior, is terrific. Cheesecake World is open 7 days a week, except for Christmas Day and the first 3 weeks of January.

Fruitwood Orchards Honey Farm, 419 Elk Rd., Monroeville; (856) 881-7748; www.fruitwoodorchardshoney.com. The Wright family has been farming in the Delaware Valley since the 1800s and has been making honey since the early 1950s. From locations in New Jersey and Florida, millions of bees in thousands of hives are shipped to pollinate crops and produce honey across the country. You can buy 20 varieties of honey by mail order—clover, orange blossom, tupelo, wildflower, alfalfa, eucalyptus, blueberry, and others—in sizes ranging from an 8-ounce bottle to a 60-pound pail. No artificial preservatives or colorings are used. Fruitwood also sells apple butter, old-fashioned blackstrap molasses, 100 percent natural maple syrup, and pure bee pollen, a high-protein food. You can also order by phone or over the Internet.

Lee Turkey Farm, 201 Hickory Corner Rd., East Windsor; (609) 448-0629; www.leeturkeyfarm.com. The Lee family has farmed the same land for six generations, since 1868. You'll find fresh produce at the farm market, and pick-your-own fruits and vegetables in season, but the main draw is, as the name says, turkeys. More than 5,000 turkeys are raised annually. Fresh turkeys are available from October through January 2; frozen turkeys and turkey parts are sold year-round. The farm is also popular for its walking, hayride, harvest, and strawberry tours.

Lucy's Ravioli Kitchen & Market, 830 Rte. 206, Princeton Township; (609) 924-6881; www.lucysravioli.com. The store's namesake was a colorful New York City sandwich shop owner who appeared as the fortune-teller in Woody Allen's 1984 film *Broadway Danny Rose* (part of which was filmed in New Jersey). Lucy's offers 20-plus kinds of ravioli, from ricotta, four-cheese, and pesto to Cajun, chicken  black bean, and porcini and goat cheese.

There's plenty to like here: pastas, homemade sauces, cheese, a dozen kinds of sandwiches, salads, and daily soups (Tuscan white bean, chicken and andouille gumbo, Asian ginger noodle, and Cuban black bean chili, among others). Pasta fillings are made with fresh vegetables, eggs, cheese, seafood, and herbs and spices; no preservatives, filler bases, or processed food substitutes are used. "Everything you see," reads a quote from Sophia Loren on the menu, "I owe to spaghetti." Open every day but Sun.

Monkey Joe's Big Nut Co., 205 N. White Horse Pike, Laurel Springs; (877) 944-NUTS or (856) 627-4600; www.jbec.com. Joe Bush, owner of Monkey Joe's Big Nut Co., is a nut. Monkey Joe, who owns a 1904 antique organ, is one of only six "genuine organ grinders" in the country. He has performed, with George the Inimitable Monkey, at street fairs, company picnics, advertising promotions, TV shows, and other events, even at the White House for presidents Ronald Reagan and George H. W. Bush. "No relation," Bush says of the latter. But nuts are his main business. He sells jumbo cashews, jumbo peanuts, butter toasted peanuts, macadamias, pistachios, almonds, and mixed nuts. The company has actually been around since 1967; it was started by Joe and Alice Mora. Bush took over the operation from the second owner, John Robertson. "Fine-quality gourmet nuts unlike any other in this part of the country," Bush says of his products. "Everything is natural, fresh cooked, and homemade every day." The nuts are available online and in select shops and markets around the state.

Smithville Bakery, Route 9 and Moss Mill Road, Smithville; (609) 652-6471. It always amazes me how many New Jerseyans have never visited or even heard of Smithville, a village of charming shops, stores, and restaurants just minutes off exit 48 on the Garden State Parkway. It's a beautiful setting, with a lake, ducks, and ample benches and tables. Smithville Bakery is a great breakfast spot—the country breakfasts here are highly recommended—but I love the bakery part, in front. Good sticky buns, sugar twists, and other doughnuts. A must-try: the blueberry cheese crumb cake. Smithville is actually two connected villages: Historic Smithville and the Village Greene. For more information, visit www.smithville nj.com.

Specialty Stores & Markets

B. F. Mazzeo, 601 New Rd., Northfield; (609) 641-6608; www .bfmazzeo.com. Ben Mazzeo started selling fruit and vegetables from his truck, going from store to store and restaurant to restaurant, in 1957. Today the business includes a retail store well stocked with produce, prepared foods, baked goods, party trays, gourmet cheeses, preserves, cookies, nuts, and other items. Mazzeo's prides itself on its fruit and gourmet gift baskets, which can be sent anywhere in the US.

Bon Appetit, Princeton Shopping Center, 301 N. Harrison St., Princeton; (609) 924-7755; www.bonappetitfinefoods.com. Princeton is the state's blue-blood center, a town where BMWs and Jaguars are the ride of choice, and an Ivy League atmosphere prevails. Bon Appetit is a gourmet food store, but you won't need to take out a second mortgage to shop here. Jams, preserves, cookies, scores of cheeses, sauces, spices, bricks of Belgian chocolate, coffees, teas— it's all here. The deli offers an array of

salads, including curried chicken salad, apple slaw, pasta primavera, couscous with golden raisins, and wild rice with dried berries. There are more than 30 kinds of reasonably priced specialty sandwiches and wraps; sit in the adjoining cafe. Up at the counter are plum brandy chocolates with the sign SORRY, 21 AND OVER ONLY. The owner is Michel Lemmerling, who earned the prestigious title Taste-Fromage, awarded to those with expertise in cheese. The Lemmerling family is from Belgium, where they run what is considered the country's premier gourmet shop.

British Connection, 130 New Jersey Ave., Absecon; (609) 404-4444; www.yourbritishconnection.com. Yearning for some Cornish pasties or pork pie? Dying for a Penguin bar or a package of Elton's Tea Cakes? You could hop on the next plane to Great Britain, or you can head down to Absecon and the British Connection. The shop, open year-round, features a selection of British gourmet and frozen foods, groceries, tea, and candy, plus Australian foods and tea. British Connection ships anywhere in the US. Absecon is just west of Atlantic City.

Forked River Butcher Shop, 109 Lacey Rd., Forked River; (609) 693-7100. Great wurst is hard to find, and the Forked River Butcher Shop, which opened in 1970, may make the state's best. Wolfgang Barsch's operation includes a bustling deli/butcher shop, with a smokehouse next door. They roast entire pigs to order here. You can pick the pig up, or it can be delivered to your door or backyard. There is a dazzling array of cold cuts, butcher meats, salads, sandwiches, and prepared foods. The many German specialties include rouladen and schnitzel. Start with the liverwurst, thick, juicy, and wonderful, and some of the shop's excellent homemade rye. The bakery offers many cakes, breads, and pies, but the standout is the fruity and flaky apple strudel.

Haars Health Food Center, 1437 S. Delsea Dr. (Route 47), Vineland; (866) 268-2414; www.haarshealthfoodcenter.com. Kelly Haars runs an expansive, neatly arranged store stocked with vitamins and supplements; natural, low- and no-sugar and low-carb items; cheeses, yogurts, cold cuts, drinks, candies, snacks, and 25 kinds of coffee beans. Looking for a bottle of Reed's Ginger Beer? You can find it here, in the refrigerated cases at the back of the store. Love cheesecake but feel guilty about eating a slice? Kelly makes a good low-carb cheesecake.

Miel Patisserie, 1990 Rte. 70 East, Cherry Hill; (856) 424-6435. What's an elegant pastry shop doing on kitschy Route 70? Owner Robert Bennett's business partner owns the Village Walk Shopping Center, where Miel (French for "honey") is located. Bennett served as pastry chef at Le Bec-Fin in Philadelphia and was guest pastry chef at Ronald Reagan's second inaugural celebration. He has even represented the US in the World Cup Pastry Championship. Everything looks so delicately constructed and exquisitely shaped that his shop resembles a fine arts museum of sweets. The selection ranges from croissants, Danish, turnovers, and brownies to pear almond fig tarts, sour cream pecan cheesecake, crème brûlée, and a variety of breads. Chocolate in particular is done proud here; the chocolate éclair is coated with a terrific chocolate glaze. The fruit tart, topped with pieces of strawberry, peach, blueberry, and kiwi, is an ideal summer treat. Note: Miel's address is Route 70 East, but it's actually located on Route 70 West.

Napoleon's Cremepuffery, 947 E. Gibbsboro Rd., Lindenwold; (856) PUF-PUFF; http://napoleonscremepuffery.com. Charlene Napoleon ditched her job as a beauty products saleswoman to open this one-of-a-kind shop. Good news for the rest of us. Napoleon—an appropriate name—makes cream puffs, and that's it. The shop is housed in a rambling yellow house across the street from a middle school in this Camden County community. You can order puffs in quantities of one, four, a dozen, or more. There is a mountain of empty puffs on a tray; tell the girl behind the counter what flavor you want—generally vanilla, chocolate, coconut, or pistachio, although the selection varies—and she'll use a bellowslike device to squeeze the appropriate cream into the puff. Mix and match flavors any way you want. "You won't find better cream puffs anywhere," Charlene says. I'm not in any position to disagree. The Cremepuffery is a bit off the beaten path but well worth the detour.

Porfirio's, 320 Anderson St., Trenton; (609) 393-4116; www.por firios.com. There are many Italian specialty shops in Chambersburg, Trenton's Italian section, but Porfirio's stands out for its selection and variety. John Porfirio opened the shop, then on Clinton Avenue, in 1964. Now Bobby Calabro, the third-generation owner, runs the sprawling market, filled with homemade pasta and sauce, plus prosciutto, olives, imported candies, bread, cheese, biscotti, cannoli, and other items. Porfirio's makes about 4,000 pounds of pasta every week; the top-selling kind is not spaghetti, lasagna, or ravioli, as one might think, but gnocchi, made with fresh Idaho potatoes. There's also a cafe inside. There is another Porfirio's at 1600 Rte. 33, Hamilton; (609) 689-6620.

Small World Coffee, 14 Witherspoon St., Princeton, (609) 924-4377; 254 Nassau St., Princeton, (609) 921-8011; www.small worldcoffee.com. Surest sign of a coffee shop's popularity: a 90-degree day and there's a line out the door. Small World Coffee is a popular hangout for Princeton University students, but you'll find coffee lovers of all ages here. Small World uses what it calls "East Coast Roast"—darker than a full-city, lighter than a French roast, a deliberate attempt to differentiate itself from the style of roasting common to the West Coast, where very dark roasted coffees are the rage. A personal favorite: the organic Sumatran. The food here is more than just brownies and cookies: Offerings include slow-cooked steel-cut Irish oats, served with organic maple syrup, organic banana, nutty granola, or brown sugar; herbal vegetable chowder, sweet potato with cilantro, and other soups; and a variety of healthy, hearty sandwiches. No time to sit down? Get a coffee to go, a handful of Small World's oatmeal raisin cookies, and you'll go away convinced what a wonderful world it can be.

Zena's Patisserie, 308 Broad St., Riverton; (856) 303-8700; www .zenaspatisserie.blogspot.com. Owner Zena Demirceviren, a native of Turkey, was a pastry chef at a five-star Istanbul hotel before emigrating to America. Her bakery-cafe is a cute, cozy space, with hardwood floors, two tables, chairs along the window, and delicious baked goods. Her apple turnovers—the fruit sandwiched between two flaky shells—are huge. She makes a mean cheesecake, available as an entire cake or perfect-for-one servings. Good strudel, too, cinnamon-topped and oozing fruit, and blueberry pie. Zena also makes salads, sandwiches, panini, soups (served with homemade bread), and grilled wraps.

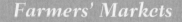

Farmers' Markets

The best source of up-to-date information about dates and times for roadside markets, pick-your-own farms, and community markets in South Jersey is the state Department of Agriculture's **Jersey Fresh** website, www.jerseyfresh.nj.gov. Community market hours often change from year to year.

Barnegat Farmers' Market, East Bay Avenue and Route 9, Barnegat. Thurs from noon to 5 p.m., late June through early September.

Berlin Farmers' Market, 41 Clementon Rd., Berlin. Thurs through Sat from 10 a.m. to 9 p.m., Sun from 10 a.m. to 6 p.m., year-round.

Bordentown City Community Farmers' Market, Farnsworth Avenue, Bordentown City. Wed from 4 p.m. until dusk, early June through late October.

Bridgeton Farmers' Market, Riverfront parking lot, between Bridge and Commerce Streets, Bridgeton. Fri from 10 a.m. to 2 p.m., mid-June through late August.

Burlington County Farmers' Market, 500 Centerton Rd., Moorestown. Sat from 8:30 a.m. to 1 p.m., mid-May through late October.

Camden Community Farmers' Market, 1600 Haddon Ave., Camden. Fri from 10 a.m. to 4 p.m., mid-June through late October.

Capitol City Farmers' Market, E. State Street, Trenton. Thurs from 11 a.m. to 2 p.m., early July through late October.

Collingswood Farmers' Market, between Collings and Irvin Avenues, Collingswood. Sat 8 a.m. to noon, early May through mid-November.

Columbus Farmers' Market, Route 206, Columbus. Thurs and Sun from 7:30 a.m. to 3 p.m., May through November.

Cowtown Farmers' Market, 780 Rte. 40, Pilesgrove. Tues and Sat from 8 a.m. to 4 p.m., year-round. This is also the location of New Jersey's only professional rodeo; see www.cowtownrodeo.com.

Fairview Farmers' Market, Yorkshire Square, near Collins and Alabama, Camden. Wed from 9 a.m. to 1 p.m., July through early November.

Farmers' Market at Jackson Crossing, 21 South Hope Chapel Rd., Jackson. Thurs from noon to 6 p.m., early July through late October.

Forked River Farmers' Market, Route 9 and Lacey Road, Forked River. Fri from noon to 5 p.m., early July through mid-September.

Greening Princeton Farmers' Market, Firestone Library, Princeton University. Tues from 11 a.m. to 3 p.m., mid-April through mid-May.

Haddonfield Farmers' Market, Chestnut Street, Haddonfield. Sat from 8 a.m. to noon, late May through early October.

Hammonton Farmers' Market, Central and Bellevue Avenues, Hammonton. Fri from 4 to 8 p.m., mid-June through early September.

Healthier Heart Farmers' Market at Trinity Cathedral, 801 W. State St., Trenton. Thurs from 11 a.m. to 5 p.m., mid-June through early September.

Hightstown Farmers Market, Memorial Park, Hightstown. Fri from 4 to 8 p.m., early June through late September.

Hopewell Community Farmers' Market, Greenwood Avenue, Hopewell. Wed from 2 to 7 p.m., year-round.

Jersey Fresh Farmers' Market at Smithville, Smithville on the Village Green, Route 9, Smithville. Fri from 11 a.m. to 4 p.m., early July through late September.

Lawrenceville Farmers' Market, 16 Gordon Ave., Lawrenceville. Sat from 10 a.m. to 2 p.m., early June through late October.

Medford Lakes Farmers' Market, Trading Post Way and Aetna Way, Medford Lakes. Sat from 8:30 a.m. to 12:30 p.m., mid-June through mid-October.

Merchantville Farmers' Market, 9 S. Centre St., Merchantville. First and third Fri of each month from late May through early November.

Our Lady of Lourdes Community Farmers' Market, 1600 Haddon Ave., Camden. Wed from 2 to 5 p.m., late June through late October.

Pennington Farmers' Market, 101 Rte. 31 South, Pennington. Sat from 9 a.m. to 1 p.m., early June through late October.

Princeton Farmers' Market, 55 Witherspoon St., Princeton. Thurs from 11 a.m. to 4 p.m., mid-May through mid-November.

Robbinsville Farmers' Market, Routes 536 and 33, Robbinsville. Mon from 3 to 8 p.m., late June through late September.

Salem Farmers' Market, W. Broadway, Salem. Thurs from 10 a.m. to 2 p.m., late May through August.

Trenton Farmers' Market, 960 Spruce St., Trenton. Tues through Sat from 9 a.m. to 6 p.m., May through October; Thurs through Sat from 9 a.m. to 6 p.m., November through April.

Tuckerton Farmers' Market, 120 W. Main St., Tuckerton. Sat from 10 a.m. to 2 p.m., July through September.

Virtua Health Farmers' Market, 1000 Atlantic Ave., Camden. Thurs from 11 a.m. to 3 p.m., late June through late October.

Waretown Farmers' Market, Waretown Lake, Waretown. Tues from 11 a.m. to 5 p.m., early June through mid-October.

Westmont Farmers' Market, Haddon and Stratford Avenues, Westmont section of Haddon Township. Wed from 4 to 7 p.m., May through October.

West Windsor Farmers' Market, Princeton Junction train station, West Windsor. Sat from 9 a.m. to 1 p.m., early May through late October.

Woodbury Farmers' Market, between Cooper and E. Barber Streets, Woodbury. Fri from 2 to 6 p.m., mid-June through late September.

Farms & Farm Stands

DeCou's Farm Market, 860 Main St. (Route 49), Shiloh; (856) 451-7908. You like peaches? DeCou's is the place to visit. They grow 26 varieties of peaches, 6 kinds of nectarines, 10 kinds of apples, plus raspberries, blackberries, corn, cantaloupe, tomatoes, grapes, and other fruit and produce. The folks here also put together custom-made fruit baskets. Open daily, June through Nov.

DiMeo Farms, 366 Middle Rd., Hammonton; (609) 561-5905; www.dimeofarms.com. The DiMeo family operates one of the world's largest blueberry farms, encompassing more than 600 acres. Co-owner Anthony DiMeo III is the fourth generation of DiMeos to work the land; his great-grandfather, Michael DiMeo, started the farm in the early 1900s. Blueberries, raspberries, and strawberries are available at the roadside market, or you can pick your own. Open from 6:30 a.m. to sunset, June through Sept.

Duffield's Farm, 280 Chapel Heights Rd., Sewell; (856) 589-7090; www.duffieldsfarm .com. What better way to start the summer than picking your own strawberries around the first week of June? At Duffield's you can drive directly to the fields and pick the fruit using the containers provided. The original market from the 1950s is now a full-fledged country store, with  produce, bakery, and deli. Homemade potato and macaroni salads, cakes, pies, pastries, soups, and sandwiches are available. You can pick your own pumpkins from late September through October.

Emery's Berry Patch, 346 Long Swamp Rd., New Egypt; (609) 758-8514; www.emerysfarm.com. The best pies in South Jersey can be found right here, in a modest-looking market down a country road. Butch Emery planted his first blueberry bushes 50-plus years ago; today the family farms 25 acres of USDA-certified organic blueberries and an acre of raspberries. You can pick your own. But the pies—about 15 kinds in all—are outstanding. Among the best: the peach berry, fragrant with peaches, cherries, and blueberries; and the blueberry, where the fruit tastes so fresh that you almost expect to find a "Just Picked" tag on the box. Emery's is open daily, 9 a.m. to 6 p.m., from just before Easter through December 23.

Haines Berry Farm, 98 Sheep Pen Hill Rd., Pemberton; (609) 894-8630; www.hainesberryfarm.com. Haines is one of the best-known and most respected sources for blueberries and cranberries in South Jersey. Pick your own blueberries in July, or buy them picked. Blueberries are guaranteed picked the day of purchase. Wagon rides are available to and from the blueberry fields. The owners invite customers to pack a lunch and make use of the picnic tables on the grounds. Open 8 a.m. to 5 p.m. daily July 1 through July 31, and 8 a.m. to 5 p.m. every Sat in Oct.

Hallock's U-Pick Farm, 38 Fischer Rd., New Egypt; (609) 758-8847; www.hallocksupick.com. Doug and Charlie Hallock offer a large variety of fruits and vegetables at their roadside market. Pick your own tomatoes, strawberries, peas, beans, beets, potatoes, cabbage, kohlrabi, okra, collards, onions, broccoli, cucumbers, squash, kale, peppers, pumpkins, rutabagas, and eggplant. From Apr through Nov, open 7 a.m. to 7:30 p.m. Mon through Fri and 7 a.m. to 5:30 p.m. Sat, Sun, and holidays.

Heritage Station, 480 Mullica Hill Rd. (Route 322), Richwood; (856) 589-4474; www.heritagewinenj.com. Bill Heritage—yep, that's his name— still grows peaches, pears, apples, cherries, and plums on a 115-acre farm with his wife, Penni, and their three sons, Richard, Bryan, and Erik., but they're switching over to a

Best Sticky Bun in the State

In an earlier edition of this book, I said Gallo's in Cherry Hill made the state's best sticky bun. Well, I found a better one, and it's at **Aversa's Bakery** (3010 Brigantine Blvd., Brigantine; 609-264-8880; www.aversasbakery.com; $) in Brigantine, just outside Atlantic City. Thick, dense, beautifully cakey, and dripping with caramel goodness, the sticky buns—sold by the half dozen or dozen only—will get you through the day, maybe even the week. I can't tell you how many sticky buns from Aversa's I've had in the last few years, but my waistline can. Aversa's also makes great torpedo and dinner rolls. And the bakery is open year-round, which down the Shore is always a good thing. Other locations at 477 Greentree Rd., Washington Township, (856) 218-8590; 801 S. Black Horse Pike, Turnersville, (856) 227-8005; and 9307 Ventnor Ave., Margate, (609) 487-6600.

vineyard-only operation. They grow Chardonnay, Cabernet Franc, Merlot, and Cabernet Sauvignon grapes. Special activities include harvest and bonfire hayrides in the summer and fall; there is even a "Fish with Rich" program in which kids can try catching largemouth bass and bluegill sunnies on the family pond. Pick your own peaches from early July through early August; apples from early September through October; pears in September; and pumpkins throughout October. And if all that weren't enough, they have a cornfield maze in late summer and early fall.

Johnson's Corner Farm, 133 Church Rd., Medford; (609) 654-8643; www.johnsonsfarm.com. Few are the kids in the Medford area who haven't been to Johnson's Corner Farm sometime in their young lives. The Johnson family has given farm tours to area schoolchildren since the early 1980s. There are plant-your-garden tours, field trips to pick berries and apples, pumpkin- and apple-picking hayrides, even popcorn, peanut, and cotton picking. Plenty of good homemade food here—pies, corn bread, quiche, cake, cobbler, potpies, soups, chili, and cider doughnuts. The market is open daily, 8 a.m. to 8 p.m., from two weeks before Easter through December 24.

Mood's Farm Market, 901 Bridgeton Pike (Route 77), Mullica Hill; (856) 478-2500; www.moodsfarmmarket.com. This is a classic country farm market, marked by a red windmill. The Mood family has been growing apples and peaches in the area since the 1870s. A cider press was added in 1967 for fresh apple cider. There is an extensive pick-your-own program in everything from peaches, blueberries, and blackberries to sweet cherries, Bartlett pears, and Italian plums. Closed Sun.

Red Barn Farm Market, Route 206 and Myrtle Street, Hammonton; (609) 567-3412; www.penzaspies.com. "The most overstuffed, overblown, over-the-top pies I've ever seen" was one customer's evaluation of the pies at Red Barn Market, which started as a small farm market and now includes a cafe, market, bakery, and greenhouse. The pies are justly famous; flavors run from blueberry, peach, double-crusted apple, and apple cherry to strawberry ricotta, frittata, sweet potato, and mincemeat. Other items include a veggie quiche and an Italian taco (veggies, chicken, mozzarella, Romano cheese, sour cream, olive oil, fresh lime juice, garlic, and parsley on a flour tortilla). Open daily, from 8 a.m. to 7 p.m., year-round.

Rottkamp Farms, 780 Shiloh Pike (Route 49), Hopewell Township (Cumberland County); (856) 451-2359. "South Jersey's best sweet corn" is the slogan at this colorful roadside market, painted with signs reading EAT MORE CORN and FIVE VEGGIES DAILY FOR BETTER HEALTH. Corn is the specialty, but you can also get watermelons, honeydew melons, cantaloupes, tomatoes, onions, and other products. Open July through Nov.

Sparacio's Strawberry Farm and Farm Market, 670 Landis Ave., Rosenhayn; (856) 451-4142; www.sparaciofarms.com. Sparacio's offers a wide range of fruit and produce—cherries, pickles, tomatoes, watermelons, corn, squash, asparagus, and peppers, among others—but it is best known for its strawberries. You can pick your own from early May through late June; call ahead for availability.

Springdale Farms, 1638 S. Springdale Rd., Cherry Hill; (856) 424-8674; www.springdalefarms.com. The only working farm left in suburbanized Cherry Hill, 100-acre Springdale Farms produces more than 30 kinds of vegetables. The bakery, though, is where you might want to start. Up to 25 kinds of pies are available, from apple, peach, and blueberry crumb to cherry vanilla, sweet potato crunch, and lemon blueberry. There are also cakes, muffins, breads, cinnamon rolls, brownies, cookies, and rolls, all made on the premises. Springdale offers pick-your-own fruits and vegetables; pick-your-own strawberries are especially popular. The biggest attraction for kids: the Maize Quest, a cornstalk maze generally open from mid-September through early November. Each year, it's a different theme; one re-created the 1804 Lewis and Clark Expedition.

Terhune Orchards, 330 Cold Soil Rd., Lawrence; (609) 924-2310; www.terhuneorchards.com. Cold soil? In name only; this is a bustling, year-round operation run by the Mount family. It's a well-stocked farm market in a century-old barn, with produce, pies, cookies, fruit breads, muffins, and other treats, including fresh-squeezed apple cider. Plenty of farm animals roam about—sheep, chickens, rabbits, dogs, cats, and two white goats named Williams and Waddles. You can even walk the 1-mile nature trail on the property whenever the market's open. Pick your own strawberries, cherries, raspberries, blueberries, blackberries, apples, and pumpkins. Open 9 a.m. to 6 p.m. daily year-round. See Terhune Orchards's recipe for **Apple Rhubarb Slump** on p. 301.

Early April

Dandelion Festival, Vineland; www.vineland.org/history/dande lion/index.htm. The Dandelion Festival was started in 1973 to promote agriculture in Cumberland County, and about 40 years later, it is one of South Jersey's most eagerly anticipated events. The dandelion is one of the most widespread plants on the planet and a rich source of vitamins A and C, calcium, iron, and other nutrients. The name comes from the French *dent de lion,* or "lion's tooth," a reference to the dandelion's serrated leaves. The festival dinner menu includes dandelion-enhanced dishes such as dandelion salad and dandelion soup; ravioli stuffed with dandelion and ricotta; penne with sautéed dandelion and prosciutto; and dandelion-stuffed chicken Florentine. The dinner also includes a variety of meats, vegetables, and desserts. You can also sample varieties of dandelion wine made by local farmers.

Early June

Delaware Bay Days, various locations in Bivalve, Port Norris, and Shellpile (Cumberland County); Bayshore Discovery Project; (856) 785-2060; www.ajmeerwald.org. Billed as "the largest free festival in the tri-state area," the Delaware Bay Days is an exuberant celebration of Delaware Bay life, culture, crafts, and, last but not least, food. The weekend event begins with a parade through the historic oyster town of Port Norris. There are lots of activities for kids,

PIZZA CENTRAL

There may be a greater concentration of pizzerias in New Jersey than anywhere else in the country. Every self-respecting town or community has at least several pizza joints within its borders. Want to start an instant argument in this state? Tell friends or neighbors your pizzeria is better than theirs.

So who makes the best pizza in the state? You asked the right guy. For a six-month-long *Star-Ledger* project, I headed a four-person team with a challenging—and cholesterol-raising—mission: to find the best pizza in Jersey. We visited 350-plus pizzerias, ate 1,000-plus slices, and stirred up a whole lot of comments, and controversy, with the selection of winners and honorable mentions in six categories.

My favorite pizza in the state?: That would be **De Lorenzo's Tomato Pies** (2350 Rt. 33, Robbinsville; 609-341-8480; www .dclorenzostomatopies.com). The saddest food news this year? That the "De Lo's" on Hudson Street in Trenton, with its wooden booths, ancient cash register, tile floors, no credit cards, and no bathroom, was closing. Fortunately, you can get the same pizza at the Robbinsville location, owned by the De Lorenzo family.

Other great pizzerias:

Antonio's Brick Oven Pizza (453 Main St., Metuchen; 732-603-0008; www.slicenj.com). The deep-dish Margherita is amazing.

Bruno's (Clifton Plaza, 1006 Route 46 West, Clifton; 973-473-3339) makes a great Sicilian pizza, with a big, puffy crust and loads of tomatoey goodness.

How many pizza makers are Culinary Institute of America grads? Dave Cambiotti, owner of **Cambiotti's** (102 Shippenport Rd.,

Landing; 970-770-1020; www.cambiottis.com), is. First-rate cheese and a smooth, fresh-tasting sauce make this the best pizza in Morris County, and one of the best anywhere.

DeLucia's Brick Oven Pizza (3 1st Ave., Raritan Borough; 908-725-1322). Allie DeLucia's grandfather, Constantino, opened DeLucia's in 1917 as a bakery; pizza started in the 1930s. Go with the plain pizza.

Denino's Pizza Place (Aberdeen Townsquare, Route 34, Aberdeen; 732-583-2150; www.deninospizzapalace.com). The original Denino's, in Staten Island, is a New York City pizza legend; the Aberdeen Denino's keeps the tradition going. The margherita pizza is terrific.

La Sicilia Pizza & Ristorante (1555 Washington Ave., Belleville; 973-751-5726). Owner Giuseppe Ali makes a range of pizzas, but his Palermo is his best—and most popular. It's a square pizza (thinner than a Sicilian) with fresh mozzarella, marinara sauce, garlic, and grated cheese.

Mr. Bruno's Pizza & Restaurant (439 Valley Brook Rd., Lyndhurst; 201-933-1588; www.mrbrunosrestaurant.com). Mr. Bruno's boasted the best sauce on all the Sicilian pizzas we sampled.

The Sopranos put the brick-walled **Pizzaland** (260 Belleville Tpke., North Arlington; 201-998-9095; www.pizzalandonline.com) on the map; the pizzeria could be seen in the opening credits. The interior is cramped and charmingly low-rent, but the pizza is pretty good. Don't be surprised to see camera-wielding foreign tourists; Pizzaland achieved global recognition because of the HBO mob show.

Star Tavern (400 High St., Orange; 973-675-3336; www.startavern .net). Probably the best-known pizzeria in New Jersey, the Star, with its legendary thin-crust pizza, opened in 1945. It turns out pizza at an astronomical rate—7,000 to 10,000 a month.

everything from games, puppet shows, and face painting to minia-
ture golf, storytelling, and blue crab races. Food? There's plenty of
it—burgers, hot dogs, kettle popcorn, funnel cakes, soul food, and,
of course, good, fresh seafood. Enjoy crab cakes, shrimp, oyster
sandwiches, and more from the likes of the New Jersey Waterman's
Association and Tom's Seafood. River tours, guided wetland walks,
and tours of New Jersey's Official Tall Ship, the historic schooner *A.
J. Meerwald,* are also available. It's all capped off with an evening
concert, a lighted boat parade, and fireworks.

Strawberry Festival, Dutch Neck Village, 97 Trench Rd., Hopewell
Township (Cumberland County); (856) 451-2188; www.dutchneck
village.com. Fresh strawberries, strawberry shortcake, entertainment, and pony rides are featured at the festival. Dutch Neck
Village, located just south of the city of Bridgeton, is a collection
of gift and craft shops, a museum, and a restaurant. Free admission;
fee for parking.

Late June

Whitesbog Annual Blueberry Festival, Whitesbog Village,
120-13 Whitesbog Rd. (Route 530), Browns Mills; (609) 893-4646;
www.whitesbog.org. This is an old-fashioned country festival with
Pine Barrens folk music, blueberry baked goods, blueberry sundaes,
country crafts, children's activities, pick-your-own blueberries,
blueberry pie–eating contests, demonstrations, and Pine Barrens
walking, wagon, and bus tours. Whitesbog Village, in Brendan Byrne
State Forest, is the home of the cultivated blueberry.

Early August

Peach Festival, Dutch Neck Village, 97 Trench Rd., Hopewell Township (Cumberland County); (856) 451-2188; www.dutchneck village.com. This peachy-keen celebration of one of New Jersey's most popular fruits has been held since 1984. Enjoy farm-fresh peaches, homemade peach pies, and other peach-filled desserts. There are burgers, hot dogs, and other foods, too. Free admission; nominal parking  fee. It's held all day on a Saturday. Dutch Neck Village is located just south of the city of Bridgeton.

Mid-August

Garden State Wine Growers Jersey Fresh Wine and Food Festival, Heritage Vineyards, Richwood; www.newjerseywines.com. In just a few years, this has become one of the state's largest food and wine festivals. Held previously in Princeton, at the New Jersey Horse Park, and Mercer County Community College, the festival shifted to Heritage Vineyards. Fifteen of the state's top restaurants, including **Rat's** (p. 199) in Hamilton, Tre Piani in Forrestal Village, Bahr's in Highlands, and John Henry's in Trenton, provide gourmet food for sale. Nearly 20 New Jersey vineyards also participate. Admission charge (children free) includes free wine tasting, souvenir wine glass, and entrance to cooking demonstrations and wine seminars. Other highlights are seafood and produce markets, craft vendors, children's activities, and live entertainment.

Mid-September

Winefest, Valenzano Winery, 1320 Old Indian Mills Rd., Shamong; (609) 268-6731; www.valenzanowine.com. One of the state's biggest wine-related festivals, this weekend event (formerly known as the Jazz and Blues Harvest Festival), features 50-plus craft vendors, four bands, complimentary wine and cheese tastings, gourmet and casual food vendors, free pony rides, free children's face painting, and a tented picnic area. Admission charge.

Late September

Apple Festival, Schoolhouse Museum, 126 S. Main St., Forked River; (609) 971-0467. Apple lovers, rejoice! This 1-day event features delicious baked goods, apple pie–eating contests, candied apples, and apple crafts for sale.

Mid-October

Chatsworth Cranberry Festival, Chatsworth; www.cranfest .org. New Jersey is the third-largest cranberry producer, and the weekend-long Chatsworth Cranberry Festival celebrates both the harvest and the Pine Barrens. More than 150 arts-and-crafts vendors are on hand, and there is live music. Breakfast is served at the Chatsworth Volunteer Fire House each morning. Cranberry recipe contest judging is held on Saturday. Jams, jellies, baked goods, and cranberry ice cream are sold at the White Horse Cafe. Free admission.

Learn to Cook

Atlantic Cape Community Academy of Culinary Arts, Atlantic Cape Community College, 5100 Black Horse Pike, Mays Landing; (800) 645-CHEF; www.atlantic.edu. The academy, billed as New Jersey's largest cooking school, offers 1-day themed workshops on a variety of cooking topics, including pastry baking, confectionary, healthful and vegetarian, American regional, East Asian or Pacific Rim, French, Italian, and other ethnic cuisines. Classes are given by Academy of Culinary Arts faculty. There is also a summer cooking program for kids.

Sur La Table, 500 Rte. 73 South, Marlton; (856) 797-0098; and Freehold Raceway Mall, Route 9, Freehold; (732) 409-9935; www .surlatable.com. "A Cook's Paradise" is the motto of this warehouse-size store, and that is certainly true. Sur La Table stocks high-end kitchenware at reasonable prices, but its big selling point is the amazing variety of cooking classes and seminars held here. For beginners, skilled cooks, and everyone in between, the classes cover a lot of culinary ground. Recent offerings included Salads for Entertaining; Italy on the Grill; Egg Creations; Secrets of Seasoning; When Life Gives You Lemons; Asparagus Festival; and The Greatest Grub, Ever. Classes are generally in the $35 to $55 range. There are even Classes for Young Chefs, for students ages 16 and younger. The store also hosts free demonstrations.

Guilty Pleasure: McMillan's Cream Doughnuts

McMillan's (15 Haddon Ave., Westmont; 856-854-3094), open since 1939, is the quintessential small-town bakery. Located on the main street of Westmont, a section of Haddon Township and east of Camden, it's a small, tidy shop where the women behind the counter ask, "Who's next?" There are brownies, cookies, cakes, pies, doughnuts, and Danish, plus good sticky buns and fat, chewy tea biscuits. But the main attraction here is the cream-filled doughnuts; the three shelves devoted to them attest to their popularity. On the weekend there are often lines out the door. The cream, soft and silky, oozes out of either end of the powdered-sugar-topped doughnut like lava from a volcano, as more than one person has observed. Leave the cholesterol counter at home and indulge your naughty self. One tip: Don't even think of eating them in the car; the cream and powdered sugar will be all over you and your seats in a minute.

Vegetarian Society of South Jersey, PO Box 272, Marlton 08053; (877) WWW-VSSJ; www.vssj.com. This organization regularly hosts natural foods and healthy cooking classes. They typically run 8 weeks and are held at local schools.

Landmark Eateries

Allen's Clam Bar, 5650 Rte. 9, New Gretna; (609) 296-4106; Seafood; $. The folks at this unpretentious little restaurant know their way around a fryer. If you're looking for fancy seafood dishes, go elsewhere. But if you want good fried fish, you won't do better than Allen's. It started as a bait-and-tackle shop; Win Allen opened the restaurant side in the mid-1960s. When he won the state oyster-shucking contest in 1981, business really took off. Can't make up your mind? Go with the combination seafood platter—flounder, shrimp, scallops, clams, and deviled clams, all fried to near perfection. The crab cake sandwich is marvelously mushy. Don't like fish? You'll love the fried chicken here. For a little scenic dining, take your meal down to Allen's Dock (no relation to the restaurant) down the highway, and watch the boats come and go.

The Bait Box, 30 Hancock Harbor Rd., Greenwich; (856) 455-2610; www.hancockharbor.com; Seafood; $$. Least-known or explored county in New Jersey? That would be Cumberland County, nestled between Salem and Cape May Counties. There's a whole lot of peace and quiet down there. One of the best restaurants in South Jersey is the Bait Box. No, it's not a bait-and-tackle shop, but a casual, high-ceilinged restaurant at the edge of the Conhansey River. The sautéed soft-shell crabs, when in season, are outstanding. I love the clams on the half shell, and the irresistible corn and apple fritters, too. In the gift shop next door, you can buy T-shirts that read, "we're all here 'cause . . . we're not all there!"

Barnsboro Inn, 699 Main St., Barnsboro; (856) 468-3557; www.barnsboroinn.com; American; $$. One of the more historic, charming, and romantic dining spots in the state, the Barnsboro Inn has been attracting diners and travelers since 1776, when it opened as a tavern with two guest rooms and stables for guests' horses. Before that, it was a log cabin built by John Budd; Tom Budd, the inn's current owner, thinks he is a descendant of John Budd. The menu is American and continental. Appetizers run from grilled scallop and fried green tomato napoleon to sautéed jumbo shrimp wrapped in prosciutto; the inn's snapper soup is justly famous. Entrees include veal puttanesca, filet mignon a la Diane, hickory-smoked rack of lamb, and pecan-crusted opah. Chef Danielle Crocket has a way with vegetables; desserts are made by Danielle and owner Michael Aliberti.

Blue Claw Crab Eatery, 4494 Rte. 130 North, Burlington Township; (609) 387-3700; www.crabeatery.com; Seafood; $$. It doesn't look like much from the outside—a low-slung, nondescript building with an adult bookstore next door—but the Blue Claw has been packing 'em in since 1961. "With paper on the tables, make as much mess as you want" is the owners' slogan. And you will make a mess, as you tuck into blue claw, snow, Dungeness, Jonah, king, and other kinds of crabs. But Blue Claw is about more than just crabs; they offer a full menu of broiled and fried seafood, plus pasta, burgers, baby back ribs, wings, and wraps. The jumbo lump crab cake is highly recommended. Feeling particularly crabby? You can order the crabs all-you-eat, at prices ranging from about $23 to $36. I repeat, you will make a mess here, and you'll enjoy every minute.

Braddock's Tavern, 39 S. Main St., Medford; (609) 654-1604; www.braddocks.com; American; $$$. Since 1823 food and lodging have been offered on the site where Braddock's now stands. The building operated as an inn and hotel in the 1800s, when it was known as the Medford House Hotel. Charles Braddock bought the property in 1898. Eat in the main dining room or the cozier pub. A few dishes reflect the inn's historic tradition, including Braddock's Colonial Game Pie, made with braised rabbit, duck, and beef, plus fresh mushrooms and russet potatoes, all topped with a pastry crust. Sunday brunch is served from 11 a.m. to 2:30 p.m. Items include eggnog-dipped french toast; Kirby's Apple Cake, the classic Pennsylvania Dutch funnel cake served with warm caramelized apples and country sausage; and seafood strudel, a blend of shrimp, crab, and scallops in a Mornay sauce baked in a flaky pastry.

Caffe Aldo Lamberti, 2011 Rte. 70 West, Cherry Hill; (856) 663-1747; www.lambertis.com; Italian; $$. Aldo Lamberti, who was born in Naples, oversees a small empire of Italian restaurants: 13 Lamberti's Cucina restaurants in New Jersey, Pennsylvania, and Delaware; PastaVino Restaurant and Forno Pizzeria & Grille in Maple Shade; Tutti Toscani in Cherry Hill; and Milano Modo in Mount Holly. Caffe Aldo Lamberti, though, is the flagship restaurant and the place you want to visit for some authentic Italian cooking. Start with an appetizer, such as seafood salad Lamberti (fresh calamari, Florida rock shrimp, and tender young scungilli [conch] tossed in extra-virgin olive oil with fresh lemon juice, sweet celery, and a hint of garlic), and proceed to a main dish, such as fusilli puttanesca, handmade spiral pasta with olives, capers, tomatoes, and anchovies; or the aptly titled *fantasia di mare,* fresh jumbo Ecuadorian white shrimp, langoustine, scallops, littleneck clams, and mussels sautéed in your choice of a fresh pomodoro sauce or while wine sauce. See Chef William Fischer's recipe for **Seafood Risotto** on p. 287.

Crabby's Suds & Seafood, 1413 Rte. 50, Belcoville; (609) 625-2722; Seafood; $$. You can find good crabs up and down the Jersey Shore, but in the Pine Barrens? This fun, friendly, back-roads bar serves them up hot and good. Add a dollar bill to those taped on the ceiling; at the end of the year, they're taken down and donated

Roadside Barbecue

If I had to take one food to my desert island, it would probably be barbecue. Problem is, the desert island would have to be somewhere far from New Jersey because so little top-notch barbecue can be found here. If you want the real deal, head to South Jersey. Route 40, which runs from the Delaware Memorial Bridge to Atlantic City, is not only a great driving road but also home to a dozen or so roadside barbecue stops, many of them of the smoker-and-three-tables-by-the-side-of-the-road variety. Two of my favorites are **Christine's House of Kingfish Barbecue** (926 Rte. 206, Shamong, Burlington County; 609-268-3600) and **Uncle Dewey's BBQ Pavilion** (Mile Marker 40, Route 40, Mizpah, Atlantic County; 609-476-4040; www.uncledeweys .com). Charlie Bryant, aka the Kingfish, was a Route 40 legend; he ran a barbecue stand on the highway for 20-plus years until his death in 2000. Greg Price runs Christine's House of Kingfish, named after Bryant's wife. There are several tables outside as well as seating inside a small cinder-block-walled shack. Excellent ribs here—juicy and tender. Uncle Dewey's is a much bigger operation, a canopy-topped pavilion with picnic tables and coolers of delicious homemade lemonade. Best item here: the brisket, served in a Kaiser roll. I like the coleslaw and potato salad, too. Christine's House of Kingfish is open Thurs through Sun from April 1 to early October, while Uncle Dewey's is open Thurs through Sun from May to Oct.

to charity. Brian Sexton is the chef/manager. Start with his seafood gumbo, or his sherry-flavored he-crab soup. Proceed to the king crab legs or garlic crabs, and finish it all off with strawberry delight, fresh strawberries dipped in granulated brown sugar and sour cream. One stop at Crabby's, and you'll feel anything but.

De Lorenzo's Tomato Pies, 2350 Rte. 33, Robbinsville; (609) 341-8480; www.delorenzostomatopies.com; Pizza; $. The news, in late 2011, was shocking: De Lorenzo's Tomato Pies on Hudson Street in Trenton was closing for good in January 2012. Owners Gary and Eileen Amico were retiring. It was my favorite pizzeria in New Jersey: wooden booths, narrow aisles, and 1950s-style brown glasses; it was like stepping back into the pizza past. No credit cards, no bathrooms, and only pizza on the menu; it was a one-of-a-kind place. Fortunately, you can still get the same great pizza at De Lorenzo's Pizza in Robbinsville, run by Sam Amico, Gary and Eileen's son.

Hudock's Custard Stand, 544 Quinton Rd. (Route 49), Quinton; (856) 935-5224; Ice Cream; $. You can't miss this cute little yellow-roofed, white-shingled landmark, just outside the Salem town limits. Hudock's has been dishing out good custard or soft-serve ice cream since 1949. It's a great place to while away a warm summer afternoon; there's a pleasant picnic area with tables and abundant shade. There are 2 buildings—one for ice cream, the other for hamburgers, foot-long hot dogs, fries, shrimp in the basket, and the renowned Belly Buster, a burger with a half pound of beef, lettuce, tomato, and cheese. Open generally from the end of March through mid-October.

Kibitz Room, 100 Springdale Rd., Cherry Hill; (856) 428-7878; www.kibitzroom.com; Deli; $. Kibitz is Yiddish for "chat," but here you may think it means cholesterol, judging by the waistline-expanding temptations at this classic New York–style deli. "Where size does matter" is the deli's slogan, and the sandwiches, heaped high with meat, may be the biggest anywhere in South Jersey. The corned beef sandwich, hot and steaming, is justly renowned; the hand-carved turkey sandwich also draws raves. The half sandwich is plenty for one person; don't order a whole one unless you haven't eaten in a month or so. There are 40-some kinds of sandwiches, several dozen appetizers and side dishes, salad bowls and platters, steaks, burgers, soups, and main dishes such as roasted chicken, stuffed cabbage, Romanian tenderloin, and tongue with sweet-and-sour sauce. General manager Neil Parish grew up in Baltimore; he worked at the famous Atman's Deli there, serving the likes of Jimmy Carter and Henry Kissinger.

La Campagne, 312 Kresson Rd., Cherry Hill; (856) 429-7647; www.lacampagne.com; French; $$$. La Campagne tops most lists of best French restaurants in South Jersey. The converted home, made to resemble a French country farmhouse, offers rustic yet classy dining—hardwood floors, working fireplaces, tablecloths, candlelight, fresh flowers, classical music. There are several small dining rooms of varying but mute decor. Appetizers include a rosemary and honey-glazed quail and hazelnut-flavored escargots en croute; entrees range from pork olive-crusted red snapper to grilled lamb and pistachio-crusted loin of venison. For those who don't know where to begin, there is a chef's tasting for $49.50 that includes an appetizer, a fish course for 2, a meat course, and dessert. The desserts, including a sampler of Belgian chocolate confections and a tarte tatin, are generally acclaimed to be among the best at any restaurant in the state.

Marsilio's Restaurant, 71 Upper Ferry Rd., Ewing; (609) 882-8300; www.marsilioskitchen.com; Italian; $$. The reason for Marsilio's inclusion here has almost nothing to do with the fact that I ate here nearly every weekend as a kid. The restaurant was formerly located in Chambersburg, Trenton's—and New Jersey's—best-known Italian neighborhood. It is now in Ewing, just outside

Trenton, and is patterned after a Tuscan restaurant, with one of its features a 16-seat family-style farm table. There are also theme nights—clam bakes, old-school Italian, macaroni night, and more. The restaurant's best-known dish is probably its chicken cacciatore; I remember eating it as a kid.

Melange Cafe, 18 Tanner St., Haddonfield; (856) 354-1333; www.melangerestaurants.com.com; Cajun/Italian; $$. Joe Brown, owner of the Melange Cafe, is one of the more entertaining—and ubiquitous—personalities on the South Jersey dining scene. He has appeared on the Food Network and other shows, has been written up in several newspapers, and is the author of *Joe Brown's Melange Cafe Cookbook*. The menu at his Haddonfield restaurant is a creative combination of Cajun and Italian—Big Easy meets Little Italy. His passion for southern cooking was passed down to him by his mother, France. Among the restaurant's most popular dishes are crabmeat cheesecake with pecan crust and wild mushroom sauté; Louisiana sausage and bean soup; chicken, red beans, and rice with France's cheese biscuits; smothered chicken with crawfish mashed potatoes; and crawfish pot pie.

Oyster Creek Inn, 41 Oyster Creek Dock, Leeds Point; (609) 652-8565; www.oystercreekinnnj.com; Seafood; $$. Spend a day in Smithville, then follow Moss Mill Road across Route 9 to this roadhouse overlooking an expanse of marsh, water, and sky. The Oyster Creek Inn is one of those places where you may wonder, "Am I really in New Jersey?" Yes, you are, and, incredibly, just minutes off the jam-packed Parkway. The garlic clams, lemon and pepper scallops, and steamed clams are some of the recommended dishes. You can eat in the spacious indoor dining room or the funky boat-shaped bar, but I like to sit outside on the deck and watch the world go sloooowly by.

Rat's, Grounds for Sculpture, 16 Fairgrounds Rd., Hamilton; (609) 584-7800; www.ratsrestaurant.org; Global; $$$$. With a name

CHEESESTEAK SHOWDOWN

The cheesesteak is, of course, of Philadelphia origin, the city's most familiar, if clichéd, food item. There are hundreds of steak shops in greater Philadelphia and scores more in South Jersey, where shops pride themselves on offering "authentic Philly cheesesteaks." The heated debate over South Jersey's best cheesesteak invariably includes two names: Big John's and Chick's.

Big John's (1800 Rte. 70 East, Cherry Hill; 856-424-1186; www.bigjohns.com; $) is located on busy Route 70 in a sprawling, dinerlike restaurant. Place take-out orders at the front counter. The menu is expansive—steaks, hoagies, salads, wings, hot sandwiches, pizza, burgers, and more. **Chick's Deli** (906 Township Ln., between Virginia and Georgia Streets, Cherry Hill; 856-429-2022; $) is located on a tiny side alley off the same major highway; good luck trying to finesse your car into the tight parking spaces. Chick's sells steaks, subs, hot sandwiches, and that's it. The shelf below the front counter is stocked with Tastykakes and containers of Comet, SOS, and other household cleaners. Big John's cheesesteak is slightly bigger but costs nearly $2 more; on my tasting the meat seemed a bit dried out. Chick's is everything a cheesesteak should be: the meat and cheese melted as one, excellent torpedo roll, juicy but not greasy. Even better is Chick's chicken cheesesteak: shredded, tender chicken covered with your choice of topping, such as mushrooms and onions, barbecue sauce, and hot sauce, among others. Who makes the best Philly cheesesteak in South Jersey? Try both, and judge for yourself.

Other worthy cheesesteak joints: **Gaetano's** (Pennypacker Road, Willingboro, 609-871-6861); **Nardi's Deli** (201 Haddon Ave., West Berlin, 856-767-0908); and **Seagrave's Steaks & Subs** (1 Tilbury Rd., Elsinboro, 856-935-2176). The best cheesesteak website around is **www.bestcheesesteaks.com.**

like that, the food had better be good, and, by all accounts, it's extraordinary. Rat's is owned by Johnson & Johnson heir J. Seward Johnson Jr., a noted sculptor who decided to open a restaurant on his Grounds for Sculpture. Rat's, named after a character in the children's book *The Wind in the Willows*, is a beautiful spot, with aged wood beams and views over a lily pond. Designed to make visitors feel as though they've stepped into a village reminiscent of French Impressionist Claude Monet's beloved town of Giverny, Rat's takes in 3 intimate dining rooms,
a cafe and piano lounge, and the Kabul Kafe, all overlooking the outdoor sculpture and pond. Dishes at the moderately priced Kabul Kafe include tabouli, hummus, marinated olives and almonds, a grilled organic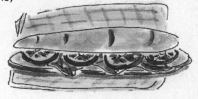
hamburger, and a Cuban sandwich. Appetizers at Rat's include a *foie gras* sandwich with duck bacon, papaya citrus mayonnaise, pickled cipollini onions, and red endive on a toasted brioche. Entrees include rice and tea-smoked duck breast with a crispy Japanese eggplant spring roll, five-rice pilaf, and a black bean hoisin; and wild boar chops with a cranberry apple relish, artichoke hearts, braised red endive, and a game jus. The chef is Eric Martin, formerly of **Stage Left** (pp. 146, 255) in New Brunswick.

Sagami, 37 W. Crescent Blvd., Collingswood; (856) 854-9773; Japanese; $$. Probably the most highly regarded Japanese restaurant in South Jersey, Sagami, on Route 130 just north of the

Collingswood circle, doesn't look promising from the outside, with its squat, boxy, almost ugly exterior. But the rustic, tearoom-like interior is cozy and convivial. Not-so-ordinary appetizers: *gomaae* (boiled watercress with sesame sauce); *sunomono,* a variety of raw fish seasoned in vinegar sauce; and *kushikatsu,* fried pork and onion on a skewer. There are 15 kinds of sushi rolls. The owners are Shigeru Fukuyoshi and his wife, Chizuko. Lunch is available from noon to 2 p.m. Tues through Fri, dinner from 5:30 p.m. Tues through Fri and from 5 p.m. Sat and Sun. Sagami is closed on Mon.

Short Hills Restaurant & Delicatessen, 486 Evesham Rd., Cherry Hill; (856) 429-6900; www.shorthillsrestaurant.com; Deli; $$. Co-owner Jerry Kaplan calls his 200-seat eatery a deli/diner, and it's an apt description. Cozy booths and a monstrous menu that covers breakfast, lunch, and dinner add up to a can't-miss dining experience. The sandwiches are big, the hand-carved pastrami nice and juicy, and the salads first-rate. It's a place to see and be seen, as well as to satisfy serious hunger pangs. If you haven't eaten for a few days, try the Short Hills hoagie, stuffed with pastrami, corned beef, salami, and Swiss. There are good Reubens, coleslaw, and real kosher pickles.

Brewpubs & Microbreweries

Flying Fish Brewing Co., 1940 Olney Ave., Cherry Hill; (856) 489-0061; www.flyingfish.com. The largest of New Jersey's 20-plus craft brewers, Flying Fish produces an impressive range of beers, from IPAs and extra pale ales to Belgian dubbels and imperial espresso porters. A personal favorite: Farmhouse Summer Ale. Many know Flying Fish for its New Jersey Turnpike exit–inspired line of beers, among them Exit 1 (Bayshore Oyster Stout); Exit 6 (Wallonian Rye); Exit 11 (Hoppy American Wheat), and Exit 16 (Wild Rice Double IPA). Open from 1 to 4 p.m. every Sat. Free tour and tasting every Sat; the last tour gets under way by 3:30 p.m.

Iron Hill Brewery & Restaurant, 124 E. Kings Hwy. (Route 41), Maple Shade; (856) 273-0300; www.ironhillbrewery.com. South Jersey's newest brewpub offers a wide-ranging menu (homemade soups, hearth-baked pizzas, beef tenderloin medallions, seafood potpie, and more) and a half dozen house beers, including Vienna Red Lager, Ironbound Ale, and Pig Iron Porter. There are also seasonal releases like Reilly's Chocolate Ale and Apocalypso, an American IPA with hints of pear and apple.

Triumph Brewing Co., 138 Nassau St., Princeton; (609) 924-7855; www.triumphbrew.com. Triumph, according to official company history, was started by a "clan of beer-worshiping Vikings" who came to this country on "a raft of empty beer barrels," eventually landing in Princeton, "with its Old World charm and abundance of natural resources." Whatever. Triumph, right on Princeton's main drag, is a fun place, even if you don't like beer. The menu is ambitious—cassoulet; chicken liver crostini; a harvest salad with Granny Smith apples, Bosc pears, red grapes, blue cheese, toasted walnuts, endive, and an apple cider vinaigrette; honey wheat short ribs; wild mushroom risotto; and other entrees. Seven beers are always available; they include honey wheat, amber ale, Czech pilsner, and coffee and cream stout. See Chef Mark Valenza's recipe for **Honey Wheat Braised Short Ribs** on p. 294.

Wine Trail

Amalthea Cellars, 209 Vineyard Rd., Atco; (856) 768-8585; www.amaltheacellars.com. At the turn of the 20th century, Emilio Caracciolo brought the art of winemaking from the old country to Blue Anchor, a small settlement in southern Camden County. Today his grandson, Louis, who made batches of wine in his dorm room at Pratt Institute in Brooklyn, runs Amalthea Cellars, founded in 1972. Wines include Cabernet Sauvignon, Merlot, Pinot Noir, Chardonnay, Metis (a white Zinfandel–style blush), and Villard, a light, sweet, tropical fruit–style wine. Complimentary tastings are available from 11 a.m. to 5 p.m. Sat and Sun.

Balic Winery, 6623 Rte. 40, Mays Landing; (609) 625-2166; www.balicwinery.com. Another wine immigrant story. Savo Balic, a winemaker from the region along the Adriatic Sea, came to this country and bought 57 acres of land outside Mays Landing. In 1993 his nephew, Bojan Boskovic, arrived from Europe to carry on the family winemaking tradition. Wines range from Chablis, Cabernet Franc, and Chardonnay to country red, cream sherry, blackberry, and raspberry. Free tasting and winery tours available.

Bellview Winery, 150 Atlantic St., Landisville; (856) 697-7172; www.belleviewwinery.com. The climate and soil of South Jersey are nearly perfect for grapevines, according to the owners of this up-and-coming New Jersey winery. Grapevines flourished in this area in the 1800s, hence the name of nearby Vineland (which also produced Welch's grape juice). Varieties produced here include Pinot Grigio, Chardonnay, Syrah, Merlot, blueberry port, and a cranberry sangria. Bellview hosts a number of festivals, including a jazz festival in June and a seafood festival in August.

Hopewell Valley Vineyards, 46 Yard Rd., Hopewell Township (Mercer County); (609) 737-4465; www.hopewellvalleyvineyards .com. Hopewell Valley started in 2002, but owner Sergio Neri's family has been making wine for generations in Italy. The winery, in rural Hopewell Township, west of Princeton, makes for a nice country drive. Learn a little history of the area from historical photos on the wine shop's walls. Wines include a Rosso della Valle, a blend of Cabernet Sauvignon and Chambourcin; and Stony Brook Blush, a blend of Vidal Blanc and Chambourcin. You can even buy extra-virgin olive oil made by Sergio's sister Laura on her Tuscany farm. Winery and wine shop open noon to 5 p.m. Thurs through Sun or by appointment.

Renault Winery, 72 N. Bremen Ave., Egg Harbor City; (609) 965-2111; www.renaultwinery.com. The state's most historic winery, Renault opened in 1870. Before long Renault had become the largest distributor of champagne in the US, earning Egg Harbor City the title Wine City. During Prohibition Renault made sacramental wines and medicinal "tonics." Renault Wine Tonic could be found in drugstores from coast to coast. Today Renault offers a wide variety of wines, many of which have earned praise. Added attractions here are a gourmet restaurant, which also offers a good Sunday brunch, and a golf course. Wines made here range from a vintage Cabernet Sauvignon, a premium dry Merlot, and Chardonnay to a semisweet sangria, white Zinfandel, and blueberry champagne. Special events include an Italian festival in August and a Bavarian-type fall celebration in October.

Silver Decoy Winery, 610 Windsor-Perrineville Rd., Robbinsville; (609) 448-0008; www.silverdecoywinery.com. Growing grapes is not an easy business. Silver Decoy, formed by eight amateur winemakers who decided to raise their craft to the professional level, planted its first vines in the spring of 2001. Their first harvest resulted in 1,000 gallons of wine—not bad, considering they lost much of their crops to a marauding herd of deer. Wines include Black Feather

Chardonnay, Cabernet Franc, Cabernet Sauvignon, and raspberry wine. Open Sat from 10 a.m. to 4 p.m., and Sun from noon to 5 p.m.

Tomasello Winery, 225 White Horse Pike (Route 30), Hammonton; (800) MMM-WINE; www.tomasellowinery.com. One of the state's biggest and best wineries, Tomasello has been growing grapes in Atlantic County since 1933. Wine critics have taken notice. Robert M. Parker Jr., of the authoritative *Parker's Wine Buyer's Guide,* said he's had "several delightful Chardonnays" from Tomasello, and *Philadelphia Inquirer* wine columnist Deborah Scoblionkov said Tomasello's Chambourcin "appears to be emerging as the Philadelphia area's most consistently superior red wine." Wines range from Atlantic County Chardonnay, Tomasello Cape May White, and Traminette (a Gewürtztraminer-style white wine) to Tomasello Burgundy, Atlantic County Cabernet Sauvignon, and the popular Rkatsiteli, a slightly sweet wine with melon and pear flavors. Open 9 a.m. to 8 p.m. Mon through Sat; 11 a.m. to 6 p.m. Sun.

Valenzano Winery, 1090 Rte. 206, Shamong; (609) 268-6731; www.valenzanowine.com. Tony Valenzano and his sons, Anthony and Mark, started making wines as a hobby in 1990. Their passion soon turned into a business, as the vineyards expanded from 3 to 30 acres. Located in the heart of New Jersey's Pine Barrens, Valenzano now makes 18 wines, from white Cabernet, Chardonnay, Shamong Red, and Pinelands Blush to cranberry, apple cider, strawberry, and blueberry wines. Tasting room open from 11 a.m. to 5 p.m. Thurs and Fri and 11 a.m. to 4 p.m. Sat and Sun. The vineyard hosts an annual jazz and blues festival (p. 188).

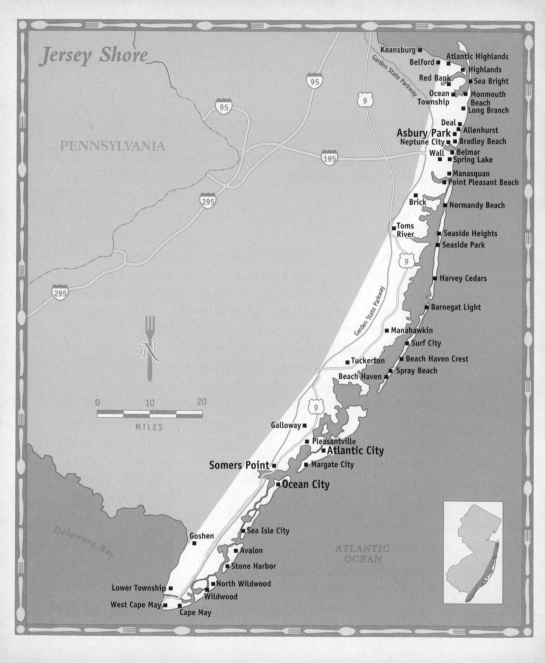

Jersey Shore

The Jersey Shore is 127 miles of sun-kissed beaches and predominantly small towns, from Sea Bright in the north to Cape May in the south. Boardwalk and short-order food rules "down the shore," at least in the summer. There are plenty of places to satisfy any hunger. The boardwalk sausage-and-peppers sandwich is a fixture, as are slices of gloriously greasy pizza, gooey sticky buns, sugary funnel cakes, curly fries, and other bad-for-you-but-oh-so-good fare.

When the sun goes down, visitors and locals head to their favorite Shore restaurants (prepare for waits on the weekend in most places), whether white-tablecloth Italian or neighborhood pizzerias, upscale fish restaurants or dilapidated seafood shacks, resort hotel bars or peanuts-on-the-floor sports joints. There are scores of cafes and juice bars for healthy eating and places where you can throw caution and cholesterol-counting to the wind. Roadside markets abound; who can resist taking some fresh Jersey tomatoes home after a day on the beach? There are one-of-a-kind, not-to-be-missed stops, like the state's most classic drive-in and the best Irish pub-restaurant, as well as Cape May's exclusive restaurants.

The Jersey Shore is fancy and stuffy, casual and easygoing; you can find many of the state's most elegant restaurants here, along with its scruffiest seafood shacks and most bare-bones barbecue joints. And they're all good, if you know where to look.

In this breezy, sunny chapter, we'll pay a visit to Mud City and Boulevard Clams, learn about fudge and saltwater taffy, and find out where to buy red, white, and blue cheesecake. The Shore's best pizza, the state's best wings—they're here, too. Have you always wanted to literally scream for your ice cream? We'll tell you where to go.

Made Here

Blair's Hot Sauces, PO Box 363, Highlands 07732; (800) 98-BLAIR; www.extremefood.com. Blair—he goes by one name only—is a former restaurant owner who was so aggravated by late-night drunks that he offered to serve them another drink only if they tried some of his hot-sauce-coated wings. That grew into a challenge—eat four wings and you'd get them for free, although only one in 100 people managed to do that—and later into a business. His original sauce, in 1989, was Death Sauce, which won a Golden Chili Award for best overall hot sauce. His best-known product is Sudden Death Sauce; the most popular is Blair Q Heat Habañero Mango, with fresh orange habañeros. His priciest is 3 a.m. Reserve—100 times hotter than a jalapeño. And don't forget Death

Best Doughnuts Down the Shore

Picking up a dozen doughnuts on a Sunday morning is a Jersey Shore tradition, especially for those who rent houses and apartments near the beach. Picking the best doughnut shops is a mighty challenge, but I'll do it anyway!

Shore Good Donuts (1211 Long Beach Blvd., Ship Bottom; 609-492-0100). One of the newer Shore doughnut shops is owned by two plumbers (but of course). Everything's made to order; fill out one of the forms and take it to the counter. Lots of creative choices; the maple doughnut tastes like breakfast in the Vermont woods. Doughnuts don't get any fresher, or finer, than this.

Brown's (110 Boardwalk, Ocean City; 609-391-0677; www .brownsocnj.com). Doughnuts are made right in front of you at this boardwalk stand, tumbling down a conveyor into a hot oil-filled bin. There are just six kinds available, including cinnamon-sugar, chocolate glazed, and powdered sugar. Be prepared to wait in a long line on weekends, but it moves pretty quick.

Ob-Co's Donuts (547 Fischer Blvd., Toms River; 732-270-3882; www.obcosdonuts.com). This doughnut shack just off busy Route 37 opens at 6:30 a.m., but be warned: When they run out of doughnuts, they close, and it can be before noon. The "croissant doughnut" bears no resemblance to a croissant; it's a cinnamony-twist treat. Many doughnuts are supersize; try both the chocolate and cream doughnuts if you can't make up your mind. The apple fritters are enormous; there are nearly 50 doughnuts and pastries in all. Park in the gravel lot, walk up to the counter, and worry about your diet tomorrow.

Rain Nitro, "the hottest dry spice ever," according to Blair. He rates his sauces from "mild" ("enjoyable to most palates") to "hot" ("will cause a bead of perspiration on forehead") to "crazy hot" ("1 or 2 drops at a time will have lingering heat for up to 30 minutes") to "!!!!!" ("use with the most extreme caution; remember to wash hands well after"). Why are the sauces called Death? "Because they take you to the brink of heat intoxication and drop you off just short of eternity," Blair explains. The sauces are available online and at select gourmet and specialty shops.

Bread and Cheese Cupboard, 246 96th St., Stone Harbor; (609) 368-1135; www.breadandcheesecupboard.com. Every bakery from Long Beach Island south, or so it seems, offers sticky buns. The reason? Sticky buns are a longtime Philly favorite, and many of those who populate Wildwood, Sea Isle City, Ocean City, and other southern-shore resorts come from Philly, or their parents or grandparents did. Despite their ubiquitousness, a good sticky bun is not always easy to find down the Shore; often, you'd be better off buying them at your local supermarket. The Bread and Cheese Cupboard serves up one of the Shore's best sticky buns: thick, sweet, gooey with caramel. Buy a half dozen—plain or with raisins or pecans—and try to resist the urge to down them all right on the spot. The Bread and Cheese Cupboard also advertises "56 different gourmet breads."

Charlie's Cafe/Farm Market, 491 Rte. 35, Normandy Beach; (732) 793-3305. How Jersey is this: What may be the Shore's best cheesecakes can be found at a market in the middle of a traffic island. Charlie's is a cafe and farm market, but you might as well call it Cheesecake Charlie's. Owner Teri Lightner and staff make 5,000 cheesecakes every summer, and just on Monday and Tuesday, although you can buy them any day. "The main ingredient in [many] cheesecakes is ricotta cheese," Teri explains. "We don't use it; we just wanted a nice light cheesecake." She uses Philly Cream Cheese or Axelrod's. Teri literally buys it by the ton. One other difference with her cheesecakes: They are not baked but are made fresh and then put directly in the freezer. It keeps the heavy cream and heavy cream cheese from congealing in the pan, she says. Her regular cheesecake is so light that it practically floats above the plate. Around the Fourth of July, you can get a red (cherries), white (bananas), and blue (blueberries) cheesecake. You're not sure whether to eat it or fly it.

Country Kettle Chowda/Country Kettle Fudge, 9th and Bay Avenue, Beach Haven; (609) 492-2800; www.bay villagelbi.com/country-kettle-chowda. The annual Chowder Cook-Off at Chowderfest in Beach Haven in early October (p. 243) attracts thousands of chowder and seafood lovers to

Long Beach Island. Country Kettle Chowda has won the chowder title several times, and for good reason. It's the real thing, thick and hearty. Country Kettle Fudge, part of the same operation, is equally renowned. Fudge comes in 26 flavors, including triple chocolate, Oreo crunch, and chocolate peanut butter. There is another Country Kettle Chowda/Country Kettle Fudge at 20th and the Boulevard in Surf City, also on Long Beach Island. The stores are open daily from mid-May through Chowderfest in October, then weekends until New Year's, then from Presidents' Day through mid-May.

Cravings Gourmet Desserts, 310 Main St., Allenhurst; (732) 531-7122. "The Shore's Premiere Dessert Shop" lives up to its name. A modest storefront in sleepy Allenhurst, Cravings makes delectable desserts for area restaurants—and you. Boston cream pie. Carrot cake Bundt. A chocolate malt mousse. Mosaic fruit torte. Their Ring Ding would never be confused with the commercially produced snack of the same name; it's chocolate cake with a sweet, fluffy buttercream filling and a chocolate ganache icing. Chocolate Decadence means different things to different bakers; here it means a chocolate Kahlúa mousse followed by a darker Jamaican rum mousse with a chocolate crust. A personal favorite: the Very Berry Pie, a 10-inch deep-dish pie filled with strawberries, blackberries, raspberries, and apples. And for a quick, bite-size treat, it's tough to beat their rugalach, which come in cinnamon-raisin, chocolate, and apricot flavors.

Flaky Tart, 143 1st Ave., Atlantic Highlands; (732) 291-2555; $. Marie Jackson's bakery is not located in the center of Atlantic Highlands, but just off busy Route 36, and she loves it; her three kids attend school right across the street. Jackson cooked for her husband's beach club before opening the Flaky Tart in 2007. Don't go expecting a staggering array of baked goods; Jackson emphasizes quality over quantity, with a selection of pastries, Danish pastries, scones, and yes, tarts. It's impossible to single out a few, but I'll do it anyway—the old-fashioned chocolate cake, the macaroon kisses, the cheese brioche, lemon meringue tarts, and many others. A sign inside Flaky Tart reads MAKING THE WORLD A SWEET PLACE. Indeed it does. *Inside Jersey* magazine named the Flaky Tart the state's best bakery in 2010.

Hinck's Turkey Farm, 1414 Atlantic Ave., Wall; (732) 223-5622; www.hincksfarm.com. Hinck's, a Shore roadside institution, is not just about turkeys, although the farm, in Wall, raises 30,000 birds a year for sale in four retail stores as fresh, oven-ready, or cooked, or as the base product in salads, soups, potpies, burgers, and other items. The farm, just off the Manasquan (Route 35) circle, features a year-round zoo, plus hayrides in the fall. Hinck's turkeys are justly popular, but you can also buy sandwiches (turkey club, turkey Reuben, roast beef, lobster melt, and others) and individual dinners. Richard Hinck started in the turkey business in 1938, selling fresh turkeys to his retail egg customers.

Best Hoagies at the Jersey Shore

The hoagie, or sub, is New Jersey's favorite sandwich. Piled high with meats, laden with lettuce and tomatoes, it is a fast, filling lunch or dinner. Every beach town has a sub shop. I've tried subs up and down the Shore, but no shop can match **Primo Hoagies** (500 Brick Blvd., Brick; 732-920-2334; $). It all starts with good bread, from Liscio's Bakery in Glassboro, plus good meat—they use Thumann's—and loads of it. One twist: They won't put vinegar in your sub unless you ask for it. "We don't believe in vinegar," says slicer Dan Dennis. "You put lemon in milk, it spoils the milk. You throw vinegar on these, it'll curdle the meat." They may be onto something there. Nearly 50 subs and sandwiches are available. Besides the Brick shop, there are 8 other Primo Hoagies down the Shore—in Avalon (3252 Dune Dr.; 609-368-8600); Cape May (605 Lafayette St.; 609-884-1177); Egg Harbor Township (3143 Fire Rd.; 609-407-6063); Margate (3 S. Frontenac St., 609-822-8281); North Wildwood (1209 New Jersey Ave.; 609-522-1300); Ocean City (656 Asbury Ave.; 609-399-7746); Sea Isle City (29 John F. Kennedy Blvd.; 609-263-1005); and Wildwood Crest (6105 New Jersey Ave.; 609-523-6590).

Hoffman's Ice Cream, 804 Richmond Ave. (Route 35), Point Pleasant Beach; (732) 892-0270; www.hoffmansicecream.net. Hoffman's is one of the best-known and most beloved ice-cream stores along the Jersey Shore. It started as a Carvel in 1955; Bob Hoffman bought it in 1956. The store closed in early 2004; it reopened in May 2004 under new ownership. Lines snaking out the door into the parking lot attest to Hoffman's popularity. On a Saturday night Hoffman's goes through about 50 three-gallon tubs of ice cream. On all weekend nights you have to take a number. The wait will be worth it; the chocolate ice cream may be the best you'll taste down the Shore. Vanilla is the most popular ice-cream flavor at just about every ice-cream stand on the planet. Not here; the most popular flavor at Hoffman's among kids is chocolate chip; adults' top picks include coconut joy, almond turtle, and butter pecan. There are also stores in Little Silver (79 Oceanport Ave.; 732-530-3773) and Spring Lake (569 Church St.; 732-974-2253).

Holiday Snack Bar, 401 Centre St., Beach Haven; (609) 492-4544; www.holidaysnackbar.com; $. The Holiday Snack Bar, with its curvy counter, chalkboard menu, and chairs that look like they came from your grandma's attic, has been open 60-plus years, and will probably continue at least another 60 more. You can get burgers, onion rings, and BLTs here, but you go for the cakes and pies. You can go the slice or whole pie route; besides apple, cherry, blue-berry, pecan, and lemon meringue, choices include the Lady Lord Baltimore cake (yellow and chocolate cake with chocolate and white icing) and the delicious angel food cake.

Johnson's Popcorn, 660 Boardwalk, 828 Boardwalk, and 1360 Boardwalk, Ocean City; (800) 842-2676; www.johnsonspopcorn .com. Johnson's Popcorn has been in business on the Ocean City boardwalk since 1940, and the salty-sweet caramel corn they sell by the bag and bucket has earned legendary status. As a testament to the popularity of this treat, there are now 3 Johnson's Popcorn shops—still sporting their hallmark red-and-white facades—on the boardwalk, and at the height of the season you may have to wait in line even then. The caramel corn, made on the spot, is produced in prodigious amounts. And while the mixing of the popcorn in the 19 copper kettle furnaces always draws a crowd, it's the sweet buttery fragrance wafting down the boardwalk that really brings the people in. Johnson's caramel popcorn is available in cups, bags, tins, and tubs. You can also purchase plain popcorn and peanut brittle.

Laura's Fudge, Wildwood and Ocean Avenues, Wildwood; (609) 729-1555 or (800) 4-LAURAS; www.laurasfudgeonline.com. The splendid neon sign alone should be enough to draw you to Laura's. The center of the sign reads FUDGE, framed by two fudge makers stirring their pots; chocolate-covered strawberries blaze in red neon above it. Laura's bills itself as "the greatest name in fudge," and it's hard to argue with that. The store opened in 1926. They say the difference between Laura's fudge and others is the quality of ingredients: real dairy cream, 100 percent natural chocolate liquor, pure vanilla, and high-quality nuts, coconut, and peanut butter. You can buy almond buttercrunch, chocolate-covered marshmallows, peppermints, coconut clusters, and cordial cherries, but if you miss the star attraction here, you'd really be fudging things.

Mallon's Homemade Sticky Buns, 1340 Bay Ave., Ocean City; (609) 399-5531 or (800) 880-BUNS; www.mallonsstickybuns .com. When a shop does one thing, you expect it to do it well, and Mallon's does not disappoint. Sticky buns—is any food more accurately named?—are a dime a dozen along the Jersey Shore, but Mallon's stands out. The business started in 1988. The recipe is of course a closely guarded secret, but owners Ger and Jody Mallon admit to using "lots of butter, sugar, and cinnamon."

You can order online, and the Mallons say the buns can be frozen for later use. The original store, at 14th and Bay in Ocean City, closes in the fall and reopens Easter weekend. The other stores are open from May through Sept. They are at 55th and Central Avenue, Ocean City; 14th and Boardwalk, Ocean City; 2105 Ocean Dr., Avalon; and 5008 Landis Ave., Sea Isle City.

Scone Pony, 305 Washington Ave., Spring Lake; (732) 280-8887; www.thesconepony. I have a weakness for scones; the only problem is that so few bakeries around the state make good ones. The Scone Pony, as befits its name, delivers; the scones are buttery-soft, silky, just crumbly enough. But there's much more here: croissants, tarts, cupcakes, turnovers, muffins, and cakes. The coconut cake, creamy and dense, is flat-out great.

Pizza Paradise at the Shore

Ask 100 Jerseyans to name their favorite pizzeria, and you'll get 100 different answers. If I had to single out one at the Jersey Shore, let it be **Maruca's** (Boardwalk and Porter Avenue, Seaside Park; 732-793-0707; www.marucaspizza.com). The business started in 1950 just 1 block north, in Seaside Heights. The owners were four Maruca brothers: Anthony, Dominick, Pasquale, and Joe, nicknamed, respectively, "Jake," "Spike," "Patsy," and "Slippery." The current owner is Domenic Maruca, Anthony's son. Maruca's has plenty of crusty competition; there are 30 pizzerias alone on the Seaside Heights and Seaside Park boardwalk. But his plain cheese pie is just plain terrific. And if you like sausage, you'll like Maruca's sausage pie; the sausage comes from Esposito's in Brooklyn. Maruca's stays open through the winter, but on weekends only.

Farther south, try **Manco and Manco** (formerly Mack and Manco's). Mack and Manco's traces its roots to 1956, when Duke Mack and Kay and Frank Manco opened a pizza joint at 8th and Boardwalk in Ocean City. Pizza makers put on a show here, adroitly spinning dough over their heads in full view of customers. The thin-crust version is good and fresh, with none of the warmed-over taste you get at many places. One of the newer additions to the menu is the Venetian pizza, with whole sliced Jersey tomatoes. There are 3 locations, all in Ocean City: 758 Boardwalk, 920 Boardwalk, and 12th and Boardwalk. The 920 Boardwalk location (609-399-2548; www.mackandmancos.com) is open year-round.

Maybe the best sausage pizza in the state can be found at **Tony's Baltimore Grill** (2800 Atlantic Ave., Atlantic City; 609-345-5766; www.baltimoregrill.com). The Baltimore Grill is a local haunt, 2 blocks from the boardwalk and casinos. Much of the food is undistinguished; yet the pizza is so good you almost think you're eating in two different places. The sausage comes from Delaware Market in nearby Ventnor.

Wildwood boasts two pizza legends—**Mack's Pizza** and **Sam's Pizza Palace**. Anthony and Lena Macaroni opened Mack's (3218 Boardwalk, Wildwood; 609-522-6166; $) on the Wildwood boardwalk in 1953; they sold exactly eight pizzas. Today, Mack's is doing much better, thank you. The pizza is thin-crust and the sauce is strong and assertive. Sam's Pizza Palace (2600 Boardwalk; 609-522-6017; www.samspizzawildwood.com; $) is anything but—call it a spacious boardwalk cafeteria. They opened in 1957, four years after Mack's. Good plain pizza, with excellent crust.

Thin crust? Probably the best-known of that variety down the Shore is **Pete and Elda's** (Route 35 South, Neptune City; 732-774-6010; www.peteandeldas.com). It's a crunchy, crackly crust, more seasoned than most others. Call it a pie with attitude. Love the sign: No CELL PHONE USE WHILE IN DINING ROOM. Eat a large pie by yourself, and you'll get a free T-shirt. It's not my favorite Shore pizza; then again, the parking lot is always jammed in the summer.

Gelato in Jersey

There's nothing like an ice cream cone on a hot summer day—unless it's a serving of gelato. Creamy, cool, with lower butterfat content—and thus it's lower in fat than ice cream. In recent years, several dozen gelateria have popped up around the state. Here are some notable ones:

Angelato Heavenly Ice Cream (187 Columbia Tpke., Florham Park; 973-295-6430; www.angelatoheavenlyicecream.com; $). You put "heavenly" in your name, you'd better be good, and Angelato is. This casually stylish shop—it would look at home in Venice or Milan—offers 30-plus flavors of gelato, from strawberry, death by chocolate (a personal favorite), and sea salt and caramel to cannoli cream.

Casa Di Dolci (539 Cookman Ave., Asbury Park; 732-807-3777; $). This shop in suddenly resurgent Asbury Park seems to boast more "grown up" flavors than most gelaterias I've visited, and it's not just because of the Grand Marnier in the zuppa inglese gelato. The gelati all seem creamier, richer, more complex than most. Recommended: the kiwi, coconut, and pistachio.

Gigio's (11 High St., Nutley; 973-368-8240; $). Giampiero Giannico and his wife Katharina could easily pass as models: they're that striking-looking. Giannico's tiny shop offers traditional flavors, plus several unconventional ones—*nociola* (hazelnut), *straciatella, amarena* (wild cherry), and *bacio* (chocolate truffle).

Lickt Gelato (at farmers' markets in Maplewood, South Orange, Green Brook and Mendham Township; www.licktgelato.com; check

Facebook page for days, times, and locations). Margaret Asselin Woods walked away from a cushy corporate job at M&M Mars to open Lickt Gelato. She once served her gelati and sorbet in a shop; now she shuttles between area farmers' markets. She uses fresh seasonal ingredients—rhubarb custard in the spring, for example. Her flavors push the gelato envelope—blueberry lemonade, Saigon cinnamon, watermelon mint, and more. My favorite flavor is one of her sorbets—the cran-pome-lime.

Mara's Cafe & Bakery (25 Main St., Denville; 973-625-0901; www.marascafe.com; $). Mara's makes excellent cheesecake in its Morristown bakery (p. 24); what many people don't know is there is a Mara's cafe in Denville, and that the store, besides offering baked goods, breakfast, and lunch, also makes and sells its own gelati. When it comes to ice cream, I'm all about the chocolate (you mean there are other flavors?), and Mara's chocolate gelato is sooo good. Close behind are the white chocolate strawberry and chocolate-covered strawberries gelati.

Sotto Zero (89 Ridge Rd., North Arlington; 551-580-7829; www.sottozero.com; $). Sotto Zetto does not look like a classic gelateria, with its cinder-block walls and exposed duct work, but this spacious shop offers some unconventional flavors, including mascarpone with cognac, Tony Mangia's Cambellone con Nutella (takes longer to say it than eat it), and the outrageous chocolate chili—creamy, smooth, and fiery all at once.

Serene Custard, 2336 Northwest Blvd., Vineland; (856) 692-1104. Vineland is the largest municipality by size in New Jersey; the 70-square-mile Cumberland County town seems to stretch forever. Finding Serene is no easy task; you might want to use, or buy, a GPS. And the location isn't exactly appealing; the neon-lit ice-cream stand is situated at a lonely country crossroads, on the other side of railroad tracks. But the custard is superb—velvety-smooth, wonderfully creamy, and reasonably priced besides. The mint chocolate chip is refreshing and bracing, and there are unique flavors like B-berry, with the unlikely combination of beets, blueberry, orange, and marshmallow fluff. They have ice cream, but you go to Serene for the custard.

Springer's Homemade Ice Cream, 9420 3rd Ave., Stone Harbor; (609) 368-4631; www.springersicecream.com. The lines in the summer outside this Shore ice-cream parlor attest to its enduring popularity; Springer's has been open since Prohibition. Nearly 50 kinds of ice cream are available, along with sorbets, gelati, and ices. Recommended: the black raspberry and Springer chip ice cream. Less mainstream choices include butterscotch brickle, teaberry, and the Almond Joy–like Emotionally Nuts.

The Sweet Life Bakery, 601 E. Landis Ave., Vineland; (856) 692-5353; www.thesweetlife bakery.com. This attractive, spacious storefront is run by a young couple, Jill McClennen and

Stephen Wilson. She's from South Jersey, he's from Florida, and the two culinary school grads spent a month in Paris learning about pastry and food and wine before opening Sweet Life. They make pastries, croissants, cookies, cakes, and brownies, and you can order sandwiches made with their own bread. Two of my favorites here: the chocolate brownies and the coconut macaroon.

Specialty Stores & Markets

Beach Haven Fishery, 2115 Long Beach Blvd., Spray Beach; (609) 492-4388; www.beachhavenfishery.com. There are dozens of seafood restaurants and "shacks" on Long Beach Island, known to locals and visitors alike as LBI. Where do you begin? Try Beach Haven Fishery, just north of Beach Haven in Spray Beach. "Nobody on this island is fresher than me," boasts owner John Perrotti. "There ain't no fish on the whole island fresher than this." If you make a statement like that, you'd better be able to back it up, and John and his young staff do. The restaurant and adjoining market offer flounder, tuna, swordfish, and mako shark (from Jersey waters); king crab (from Russia); shrimp (Brazil); mussels (Prince Edward Island); and fish from other countries. "We are not your grandmother's fish market," John explains. "We don't have scrod or whiting, any of that." Spread your containers on one of the picnic tables in the glow of the Japanese lanterns for the ultimate Jersey seafood shack experience.

Belford Seafood Co-op, 901 Port Monmouth Rd., Belford; (732) 787-6508. There are two seafood co-ops on the Jersey Shore, in Point Pleasant Beach and Belford, both owned by local commercial fishermen. While much of their catch is sold to wholesale markets in the Mid-Atlantic states, New York, and southern New England, both establishments supply fresh seafood directly to local consumers through their dockside retail seafood markets.

Boulevard Clams, 2006 Long Beach Blvd., Surf City; (609) 494-9494; www.boulevardclams.com. The key to opening a clam, according to the Boulevard Clams website, is to chill it thoroughly—relaxing the muscle—by submerging it in ice or putting it in a freezer for at least 45 minutes. Not only will you learn how to prepare shellfish and seafood here, but you'll also learn how to eat well. Clammer Michael Sulish opened Boulevard Clams in 1979; today the market

sells 30,000 clams a week in season. The restaurant features a long list of fresh, creative seafood—clams and oysters on the half shell and steamed littlenecks, of course, but also barbecued mako bits, fresh steamed tuna salad, Brazilian shrimp salad, jumbo wine and garlic crabs, and other items. Don't leave without trying some of the good lobster bisque. You can even throw your own clambake; bring a pot, and the crew will fill it with mussels, clams, lobster, shrimp, and sweet corn to be steamed.

Dean's Natural Food Market, 1119 Rte. 35, Ocean Township; (732) 517-1515; and 490 Broad St., Shrewsbury; (732) 842-8686; www.deansnaturalfoodmarket.com. The Ocean Township flagship location—more than 5,000 square feet of space—offers Monmouth County's largest selection of fresh organic produce and discount vitamins. Choose from natural and specialty foods, kosher vitamins and foods, "cruelty-free" cosmetics, plus herbs, vitamins, and sports supplements. Dean's also has a takeout organic salad bar and juice bar.

Jean Louise Candies, 1205 3rd Ave., Spring Lake; (732) 449-2627; www.jeanlouisecandies.com. You can literally eat a house al Jean Louise Candies, one of the Shore's distinctive specialty shops. In addition to their creative made-of-chocolate buildings, owners Meg and Robert Bannick offer wonderful chocolate-covered fresh fruit confections and delicious chocolate creams. Other temptations abound. The best-selling item, though, is the buttercrunch candy. As part of a global Internet project called My Town Is Important, local kids were asked to name the most important thing about

DAFFY OVER TAFFY

There's no salt and very little water in saltwater taffy, and the origins of this chewy soft-candy treat are shrouded in sweet mystery. What is known is that taffy was being sold on the Atlantic City boardwalk in the 1880s, if not sooner. It was known by different names, including ocean wave taffy and sea foam taffy, but saltwater taffy was the name that stuck. The two big names in the taffy trade are **Fralinger's** (800-93-TAFFY; www.jamescandy .com), based in Atlantic City, and **Shriver's** (877-66-TAFFY; www .shrivers.com), in Ocean City.

Joseph Fralinger took over a taffy stand on the Atlantic City boardwalk in 1885. He wasn't the only taffy maker; the 1899 Atlantic City Directory listed 42 confectioners, many of whom made taffy, fast becoming a household name. By 1909 there were four Fralinger's stores in Atlantic City. In June 1932 the family opened a Depression Store, where candy "seconds" were sold— at cheap prices. Today Fralinger's—the oldest retail business on the world's most famous boardwalk—makes between 5,000 and 10,000 tons of taffy every day in the summer. About 20 flavors are available—from chocolate, vanilla, and banana to molasses mint, spearmint, and teaberry.

Shriver's has been on the Ocean City boardwalk since 1898. "Saltwater taffy actually started in Atlantic City," according to the Shriver's website. "We in Ocean City just made it better." You can watch candy of all kinds being made in Shriver's; the company makes 50,000 pounds of fudge and 100,000 pounds of taffy every summer. One floor is devoted to the making of macaroons. The retail store features an old-time store soda fountain and a minimuseum of candy. Taffy has become such a Shore souvenir that you almost feel guilty spending a weekend and not bringing a box home.

bucolic Spring Lake. "The Jean Louise candy shop," a first grader at the H. W. Mountz School replied. "I like their candy. The gummi worms are the best. The town has great parks. This is a good town for having fun. Even school is fun sometimes. But the most important thing about Spring Lake is the Jean Louise candy shop."

Joe Leone's, 400 Rte. 35 South, Point Pleasant Beach; (732) 701-0001; www.joe leones.com. How tough is it to make good bread down the Shore? The salt air kills yeast, essential to bread making. Before he opened his Italian bakery and specialty store, Joe Leone made bread in various Shore locations in an attempt to discover the right amount of salt. "I was mixing dough on the boardwalk, then I was out on Route 70," he recalls, laughing. "My parents thought I was nuts." His shelves are stocked with imported treats—Fondo di Toscana arborio rice, Sclafani gnocchi, Delverde lasagna, and other items. His cookies and cannoli are first-rate. Leone sells his homemade sauce, plus pasta from **Vitamia & Sons** in Lodi (see separate entry in North Jersey chapter, p. 44). Gourmet salads, focaccia sandwiches, and hot entrees also are available. There is another store at 527 Washington Blvd., Sea Girt; (732) 681-1036.

Klein's Fish Market, 708 River Rd., Belmar; (732) 681-1177; www.kleinsfish.com. Ollie Klein opened his fish market in 1929;

today Klein's includes indoor and outdoor restaurants, a sushi bar, and a take-out section in addition to the fish market. The outdoor seating, on the Shark River, is particularly pleasant, with front-row viewing of commercial and party boats. Some of the freshest fish you'll find anywhere can be found in the market—tuna, swordfish, lobster, clams, scallops, shrimp, oysters, and many other selections. As far as the restaurant goes, the salads, the sushi appetizer, and the seafood diablo are all good here, and make sure to leave room for the homemade Key lime pie.

Lusty Lobster, 88 Bay Ave., Highlands; (732) 291-4100 or (800) 347-4409; www.bestlobster.com. Lusty Lobster owners Dick and Douglas Doughty sell a wide range of fish and shellfish at their retail market in Highlands, the town just before the entrance to Sandy Hook. The operation opened in 1981, and the Doughtys pride themselves on obtaining the best fish from suppliers in port from Nova Scotia to Florida, including, of course, New Jersey. Besides a wide selection of fresh fish, they carry crab cakes, fish cakes, and deviled crabs fully prepared and cooked, plus tuna, seafood, and lobster salads.

Mario's Italian Market, 1905 Long Beach Blvd., Surf City; (609) 361-2500; www.mariositalianmarket.com. Mario's is squeezed into a strip mall on Long Beach Island's main drag, and you may have trouble squeezing out of the place with all the bags of goodies you'll likely be lugging. Mario Aversa is the charming owner; his wife, Phyllis, is behind the counter; and their sons, Mario Jr. and Peter, who have taken over the day-to-day operation, can usually be found in the kitchen. Mario does not suffer from lack of confidence. "There isn't a store from here to Brooklyn that does this cooking," he boasts. The spacious, spotless shop is crammed with cold cuts, cheeses, olives, pastas, breads, soups, and a staggering range of prepared foods, from homemade lasagna, Capellini cake, and chicken cacciatore to pies, pastries, and cheesecake. One irresistible item: Mario's fried ravioli, one of the most wicked, wonderful pleasures you'll run across down the Shore, or anywhere. Bet you can't eat just one.

Piancone's Deli and Bakery, 800 Main St., Bradley Beach; (732) 775-4870. Italians are the largest ethnic or ancestral group in New Jersey, which has the second-largest Italian-American population (1.5 million) in the US. So the listing of several Italian delis or specialty shops should not come as a surprise. Piancone's, run by the same family since the mid-1960s, is one of the better ones anywhere. Antipasto, salads, meats, cheeses, fresh mozzarella and ricotta, bread, pastries, homemade sauces, more than 50 prepared entrees—it's all here. Love the nearly 2-foot-long pizza loaves, jammed with mushrooms, peppers, sun-dried tomatoes, and other toppings.

Sarah's Tent, 100 Norwood Ave., Deal; (732) 531-5560. Deal, one of the most exclusive communities on the Jersey Shore, is dotted

Best Jersey Shore Diner

Singling out one Jersey Shore diner as the best from several hundred is a nearly impossible task, but I'll cast my vote for **Mustache Bill's** (8th and Broadway, Barnegat Light; 609-494–3553; $). It's a classic 1950s diner at the north end of Long Beach Island, an easy stroll from Barnegat Light. Owner Bill Smith worked at the diner as a dishwasher while in college; seven years later he bought the place. The diner's name came from a newspaper's mistaken description of Bill as having a mustache. It's open weekends only, even in the summer. The omelets—eggy, fluffy, and fresh—alone are worth the long ride, but everything from the grits to the greasy burgers is good. The best thing is that he's the cook and is always there; if you have a special request or complaint, you can take it right to the boss. This classic Shore diner won a James Beard Foundation award in the America's Classics category in 2009.

with multimillion-dollar homes in every architectural style imaginable. Many of Deal's residents are of Middle Eastern background, so Sarah's Tent, with a large American flag in the window, is a natural. The owners, Rochelle and Jack Shemueli, are Jewish, but you'll find a wide selection of Middle Eastern snacks, cakes, candies, cheeses, and other items here: baba ghanoush, tahini, hummus, kibbe; Syrian cheese; juices from Israel; dried nuts, fruits, figs, and dates; roasted peppers with parsley; avocados in oil and garlic; spices; and olive oils from various countries. It's one-stop Jersey Shore shopping for Middle Eastern treats. Not all items are priced, so ask first. There's a surprisingly good selection of pasta and sauces and a smattering of American-made barbecue and hot sauces, too. There's a self-serve olive bar; try the hot olives, on the far left.

Spike's Fish Market Restaurant, 415 Broadway, Point Pleasant Beach; (732) 295-9400. Spike's is an unpretentious little place that is always busy in the summer. Spike Layton opened the fish store in 1926. The store sells all the usual fish and shellfish as well as calamari, seafood, and seaweed salads. NONE OF OUR FOOD IS DEEP FRIED, reads a sign. There is an L-shaped bar, and a mounted sailfish is displayed on the wall. At every table are giant shakers of La Baleine White Sea Salt, for that little extra seasoning. Recommended dishes include the stuffed shrimp, red snapper New Orleans style and flounder française. Excellent desserts too, especially the Swedish apple pie and Key lime pie.

Farmers' Markets

The best source of up-to-date information about dates and times for roadside markets, pick-your-own farms, and community markets along the Jersey Shore is the state Department of Agriculture's Jersey Fresh website, **www.jersey fresh.nj.gov.** Community market hours often change from year to year.

Asbury Park Farmers' Market, Main Street and Sunset Avenue, Asbury Park. Sat from 8 a.m. to 1 p.m., mid-June through late October.

Atlantic City Farmers' Market, Center City Park, Atlantic and South Carolina Avenues, Atlantic City. Thurs and Sat from 10 a.m. to 4 p.m., early July through early October.

Atlantic Highlands Farmers' Market, Veterans Park, 111 1st Ave., Atlantic Highlands. Fri from noon to 6 p.m., early May through early October.

Avalon Produce Market, 2931 Ocean Dr., Avalon. Daily from 8 a.m. to 8 p.m., late May to early September.

Belmar Farmers' Market, Main Street and 9th Street, Belmar. Sat from 9 a.m. to 1 p.m., late May through late August.

Carousel Farmers' Market, First and Ocean, Asbury Park. Thurs from 4 to 7 p.m., late June through early October.

Highlands Farmers' Market, Bay Avenue and Waterwitch Avenue, Highlands. Sat from 9 a.m. to 2 p.m., early June through late October.

Lower Township Farmers' Market, 2600 Bayshore Rd., Villas. Call (609) 886-7880 for schedule.

Manahawkin Farmers' Market, 657 E. Bay Ave., Manahawkin. Fri, Sat, and Sun from 9 a.m. to 3 p.m., July to Sept.

Manasquan Farmers' Market, Miller Preston Way, Manasquan. Thurs, from 9 a.m. to 3 p.m., late June through early September.

Margate Community Farmers' Market, Amhearst and Monroe Avenues, Margate. Thurs from 9 a.m. to 12:30 p.m., late June through early September.

Ocean City Farmers' Market, 5th Street and Asbury Avenue, Ocean City. Wed from 8 a.m. to 1 p.m., late June through early September.

Point Pleasant Beach Farmers' Market, Route 35 North and Arnold Avenue, Point Pleasant Beach. Sun from 10 a.m. to 2 p.m., late June through mid-September.

Sea Isle City Farmers' Market, JFK Boulevard, Sea Isle City. Tues from 8 a.m. to 1 p.m., late June through late August.

Seaside Park Farmers' Market, J Street and Central Avenue, Seaside Park. Mon from 11 a.m. to 5 p.m., mid-June through mid-October.

St. Paul's Farmer Market, Routes 9 and 166, Beachwood. Tues from 1 p.m. to 7 p.m. mid-June through late October.

Stone Harbor Farmers' Market, 95th Street and 2nd Avenue, Stone Harbor. Sun from 8 a.m. to 12:30 p.m., late June through early September.

Toms River Farmers' Market, Water Street, Toms River. Wed from 11 a.m. to 5 p.m., early June through late October.

West Cape May Farmers' Market, Borough parking lot, Broadway, West Cape May. Tues from 3 to 7:30 p.m., late June through late August.

West End Farmers' Market, 139 Brighton Ave., Long Branch. Thurs from 11 a.m. to 6 p.m., mid-June through mid-November.

Farms & Farm Stands

Atlantic Farms, 1506 Atlantic Ave. (Route 524), Wall; (732) 528-8680. This is a popular stop for Manasquan, Spring Lake, and Sea Girt day-trippers heading home after a day on the beach. It offers a good selection of fruits and vegetables; your kids will love the petting zoo. Next door is **Hinck's Turkey Farm** (see separate entry under Made Here, p. 215). Open daily, 9 a.m. to 7 p.m., year-round.

Foster's Farm Market, 400 N. Bay Ave., Beach Haven; (609) 492-1360. The folks here pride themselves on finding and selling the freshest produce—lettuce, citrus fruits, and onions from local farms and the Philly produce market; blueberries from Hammonton; giant mushrooms from Kennett Square, PA; #1 grade unblemished Jersey beefsteak tomatoes, Jersey zucchini, peppers, strawberries, cucumbers, and more. Sandwiches and salads are available in the deli. Open daily from 8 a.m. to 8 p.m., from the third week of Mar through early Oct.

Manahawkin Pick Your Own Berry Farm, 178 Beachview Ave., Manahawkin; (609) 597-3437. As the name suggests, here you can pick your own strawberries, raspberries, blackberries, blueberries, tomatoes, and figs. Open daily from 8:30 a.m. to 7 p.m., June 1 to October 31.

Myers Farms, 425 Rte. 47 North, Goshen; (609) 465-8777. Spending a week or weekend in Cape May, Wildwood, or Avalon?

This is a good source for fresh fruits and vegetables, especially tomatoes, cantaloupes, watermelon, sweet corn, peaches, plums, peppers, beans, and sweet potatoes. Open daily from 8 a.m. to 8 p.m., June through Nov. Route 47, which runs west and north from Wildwood and connects with Route 55, makes for a nice country road trip.

No Frills Farm, 1028 Seashore Rd., Cape May; (609) 884-8209. Specialties here are corn, cantaloupes, tomatoes, peaches, pumpkins, and herbs. Bedding plants, flowers, mums, and Indian corn are also available. Open daily, Apr through Oct; hours vary.

Rea's Farm Market, 400 Stevens St., West Cape May; (609) 884-4522. This market offers fresh produce in season. You can also buy plants, flowers, homemade jams and jellies, spaghetti sauce, honey, and cider. Hayrides to the pumpkin patch are offered in the fall. Open daily from 9 a.m. to 6 p.m., May through Nov.

Silverton Farms, 1520 Silverton Rd., Toms River; (732) 244-2621. Silverton Farms, at 6 acres one of the state's smaller farms, is a bit off the beaten path, but it's well worth finding. Owner Tom Nivison grows and sells certified organic produce, including strawberries, raspberries, green beans, and cherry tomatoes, all of which you can pick on your own. Park your car in the circular gravel driveway. He also sells his own honey and eggs. Open Tues through Sun from 10 a.m. to 5 p.m. from mid-May through November 5.

Smith's Farm Market, 2810 Allaire Rd., Wall; (732) 449-1928. Joe and Jane, the owners of this open-air farm market across the road from the Wall Township municipal building, sell peaches, corn, tomatoes, and other vegetables. There are homemade doughnuts and cookies, and salads and sandwiches. But the main reason to stop here is for the pies—apple, blueberry, peach, and others, all with a slightly sweet and altogether irresistible crust. Open daily from 8 a.m. to 7 p.m., April 1 through December 23.

Food Events

Mid-May

New Jersey State Chili and Salsa Cook-Off, Washington Street between Main Street and Hooper Avenue, Toms River; (732) 341-8738; www.downtowntomsriver.com/chili/chefs.htm. Held since 1989, this is the International Chili Society's only New Jersey–sanctioned event. More than 50 chili and salsa makers vie for honors, and you can sample their creations. Past winners have included Top Secret Chili, Doctor's Choice Chili, and No Antidote. The event also includes live music, craft vendors, and children's entertainment. Contest fee, no admission charge.

Early June

Let Them Eat Fish Fest, Barnegat Light Firehouse, 10th Street and Central Avenue, Barnegat Light; (609) 494-9196. This is one

GUILTIEST PLEASURE

The Jersey Shore is rife with temptation and vice of the food variety. Pizza, hot dogs, sausage sandwiches, funnel cake, cotton candy, ice cream—anyone who loses weight after spending a week or two down here in the summer deserves a medal. If I had a last-meal request, it might well be the cheesesteak-stuffed pizza at **Slice of Heaven** (610 N. Bay Ave., Beach Haven; 609-491-1900; $). You heard right. Think the best cheesesteak you've ever tasted, minus the roll and grease, inside a first-rate Sicilian pizza. The result: pizza nirvana. Bring plenty of friends when you order one of these. It is a monster molten pie, weighing in at an astounding 6 pounds.

of the smaller, but better, seafood festivals down the Shore. It's an all-you-can-eat affair; admission is $15. Commercial fishermen donate their fresh catch; tuna, sea bass, flounder, bluefish, scallops, swordfish, and other fish are baked, broiled, steamed, and grilled. Homemade desserts also available.

New Jersey Seafood Festival, Belmar; www.belmar.com. Held in Silver Lake Park, right across from the ocean, the festival features food from 30 or so vendors, plus a wine tent, artists and craftspeople, and entertainment. Admission is free; pay for food as you go along. Everything from shrimp, clams, and lobster to gator bites and seafood sausage are available, from such well-known local restaurants as Matisse and Jack Baker's Seafood Shanty.

Mid-July

New Jersey State Barbecue Championship, Anglesea Volunteer Fire Company, New Jersey Avenue, North Wildwood; (856) 881-8062; www.njbbq.com. One of the more fun—and filling—festivals in New Jersey, the New Jersey State Barbecue Championship draws 40,000 people over 3 days. Barbecue teams from around the country compete for about $10,000 in prize money, cooking straight through Saturday night for Sunday's judging. Vendors such as Papa Woody's BBQ Sandwiches and Butch's Smack Your Lips BBQ sell mouthwatering ribs, pulled pork, chicken, and sauce. It's a weekend of good barbecue, beer, and blues; the Anglesea Blues Festival runs concurrently.

Late July

New Jersey State Ice Cream Festival, Washington Street between Main Street and Hooper Avenue, Toms River; (732) 341-8738; www.icecreamfest.com. Held for the first time in 2003, this proved to be a popular and fun event, with contestants vying for the title of Best Ice Cream in New Jersey. You can cast your vote, too; there's a special People's Choice award. Live music, food, and craft vendors.

Early August

Clam Fest, Huddy Park, Bay and Waterwich Avenues, Highlands; (732) 291-4713; www.highlandsnj.com. One of the more popular Jersey Shore food happenings, Clam Fest has been held since 1994.

The Thursday-through-Sunday event attracts thousands of seafood lovers for just-off-the-boat fresh fish and shellfish. Sample seafood prepared by local restaurants such as Bahrs and Doris and Ed's. One highlight is the annual competition known as Battle of the Clam Shuckers. There are also a baby costume contest, rides, and entertainment.

Late August

West Cape May Tomato Festival, behind the West Cape May Borough Hall, 732 Broadway, West Cape May. For information, contact Greater Cape May Chamber of Commerce, (609) 884-5508. Little West Cape May has had so much fun with the Lima Bean Festival (see subsequent entry for early October) that it decided, in 2003, to launch an annual tomato festival. Jersey tomatoes have never been rightfully celebrated in the Garden State, according to the event's organizers, and the festival aims to do something about that. You can buy tomatoes and tomato sauce, and you'll also find a pig roast, antiques, art and craft items for sale, music, and a dunk tank.

Mid-September

Seafood in Seaside, Grant Avenue, Seaside Heights; www.seaside heightstourism.com. This popular 1-day festival features food and craft vendors and live entertainment. Sample fish dishes, sandwiches, and platters from local restaurants such as the Crab's Claw Inn, Berkeley Seafood, and Seaside Clam Bar.

Late September

Cape May Food & Wine Festival, various locations, Cape May; sponsored by the Mid-Atlantic Center for the Arts; (609) 884-5404 or (800) 275-4278; www.capemaymac.org. For the foodie this is festival heaven. There are seminars and cooking classes; wine tastings hosted by restaurant professionals; a chowder contest; gourmet luncheons; a 3-hour restaurant tour; and a lobster bake at the Marquis De Lafayette Hotel. Then there's the restaurant relay race, where teams from local restaurants compete in various events—who can set the fastest table, fold the fanciest napkin, or deliver a cocktail without spilling a drop? Admission to the restaurant relay race is free, but there is a charge for other events. A $150 full package plan gives you entry to all events, plus a limited-edition cookbook. Most events are held within walking distance of each other. Want to live, and eat, like a king? Enroll in the Chefs' Dine-Arounds—5 courses at 5 different restaurants each night for 5 nights.

Early October

Chowderfest, 9th Street and Taylor Avenue, Beach Haven; (609) 494-7211; www.chowderfest.com. Chowderfest, an annual event since 1989, is serious stuff. Chowder makers from near and far compete to see who makes the best New England and Manhattan clam chowder. The event includes food, vendors, entertainment, and shuttle parking; the event draws 15,000 or more people. Grand prize winner in New England chowder five times between 1997 and 2004: **Country Kettle Chowda** (see earlier entry in the Made Here section, p. 213). Stefano's California Grill won the top award for Manhattan clam chowder in 2001, 2002, and 2003.

Lima Bean Festival, Wilbraham Park, West Cape May. For information, contact Greater Cape May Chamber of Commerce; (609) 884-5508. West Cape May, nestled between Cape May and Cape May Point, is known as the Lima Bean Capital of the World for the many acres of lima beans once grown on local farms. Now only a few farms remain in lower Cape May County. The town pays tribute to its agricultural tradition with the Lima Bean Festival, a colorful weekend event. Highlights include food (lima bean soup, lima bean chili, barbecued limas, etc.), craft items, a lima-bean-tossing contest, and the crowning of the Lima Bean King and Queen. You can buy lima-bean-covered birdhouses and other items and an official Lima Bean Festival cap.

Learn to Cook

The Gables Restaurant and Inn, 212 Centre St., Beach Haven; (609) 492-3553; www.gableslbi.com. Restoration of this historic Long Beach Island B&B began in November 2005 under the supervision of new owners Sondra and Stephen Beninati. The Victorian-pretty The Gables, one of the Jersey Shore's more celebrated restaurants, offers a 2-day workshop in professional cooking led by Executive Chef Richard Diemer and his team. Classes, held from January through May, and from September to December, range from pastry baking and healthy or vegetarian food to Italian, French, American regional, and other cuisines. Call for schedule.

Learn about Wine

Cape May Wine School, Washington Inn, 801 Washington St., Cape May; (800) 275-4278. Sponsored by the Mid-Atlantic Center for the Arts, the Cape May Wine School is limited to 65 students. You can enroll in individual classes for $30 or take the entire 10-week course for $200. Topics include the Elements of Tasting, German and Austrian Wines, Country Wines of France, Australian Reds, and the Different Faces of Chardonnay. All classes held at the Washington Inn from 1 to 3 p.m. Sun. Attendees must be age 21 or older.

Landmark Eateries

Allenwood General Store, Allenwood-Lakewood Road, Wall; (732) 223-4747; www.allenwoodgeneralstore.com; Deli; $. Old-time general stores are a disappearing breed in New Jersey; this

75-year-old store is not only a treasure trove of antiques, signs, magazines, and other knickknacks but also a great place for breakfast. Pork roll egg and cheese is practically the state sandwich; Allenwood's version, served in a top-notch roll, is exemplary. The pancakes, nice and fluffy, are surprisingly good. There's a small deli section; don't forget to order a container of "rustic coleslaw," with tomatoes, radishes, carrots, and cucumbers.

At the Table, 311 Bond St., Asbury Park; (732) 455-5093; Southern/Soul Food; $$. Janice Murphy's southern/soul food restaurant really is a family affair; her husband, daughter, son, sister, aunt, and niece all work here. Murphy, a former cook at the acclaimed Delta's in New Brunswick, offers all the southern standards—perfectly seasoned fried chicken; superbly tender beef short ribs; fried-just-right whiting. The sides are super—nutmeg-flecked yams; black-eyed peas, and potato salad. Murphy doesn't allow patrons to bring wine or beer into her restaurant; she doesn't want younger family members around alcohol.

Chef Vola's, 111 S. Albion Place, Atlantic City; (609) 345-2022; Italian; $$. Trying to get a table at this small, homey hideout is not easy. Neither is finding it. Look for the white house with the Blessed Virgin Mary statue out front, and then head downstairs. Don't bother looking for a big sign; there is none. Reservations are

THE SECOND ODDEST EATERY IN THE STATE

It's difficult to edge out **Charlie's Pool Room** in Alpha (p. 28) as the state's most eccentric eatery, but **El Jose** (Gulf Gas Station, 980 E. Bay Ave., Manahawkin; 609-597-5099; Mexican; $) comes close. How many Mexican restaurants you know of are located inside gas stations?

At El Jose, you really can eat here and get gas. Walk past the cans of motor oil and the shelves stocked with Bimbo sweet bread and Kranky chocolate corn flakes, and give your order to Jorge Salazar. He works the counter, while his wife, Elsa, does the cooking. They make an entertaining duo. "We have been married 27 years," Jorge says. "Now my other three wives..."

"Authentic Mexican food" may be the three most overused words in the culinary lexicon, but food made by two Mexico City natives is authentic enough for me. No fancy touches or sauces here, and it's takeout only. Good tamales and first-rate chorizo tacos. You can even get *menudo*—not the boy band, the Mexican tripe and hominy soup. Maybe there should be more restaurants in gas stations.

absolutely required, and when you call, "act like you know someone's brother's second cousin's hairdresser," as one patron put it. It's not that difficult, but you may need to call a week ahead. The wait should be worth it. Chef Vola's serves up heaping portions of homemade Italian food in a small, crowded, dimly lit dining room. Regulars rave about the desserts, especially the banana cream pie and the hot apple ricotta. Chef Vola's is a great way to begin—or end—an Atlantic City excursion. Bring plenty of cash; Chef Vola's does not accept credit cards. In 2011, the restaurant won the coveted James Beard Foundation America's Classics award, given to "special dining establishments" that "bring their communities together around the table."

Circus Drive-In, 1861 Rte. 35, Wall; (732) 449-2650; www.circus drivein.com; American; $. The nation's first drive-in restaurant was the Dallas Pig Stand, opened by one J. G. Kirby on the premise that "people with cars are so lazy that they don't want to get out of them to eat." New Jersey's best remaining drive-in is the Circus Drive-In, on busy Route 35 in Wall. Open from the beginning of Apr generally to the end of Sept, the Circus is marked by a splendid smiling-clown neon sign. Richard Friedel has been the Circus's sole owner since 1954. "I can't match the fast-food places," he says. "The only way I can beat them is by giving people good food and a lot of variety." The soft-shell crabs are especially popular here; the restaurant goes through 800 a day. The menu is circus-themed (Bareback Betsy, the Wild Animal Special, the Daredevil, and so on). Good fried chicken, better than you might expect, and excellent pink lemonade. A must-stop in any Jersey Shore summer.

BEST WINGS

Practically all the bars in New Jersey—and more than a few restaurants—offer some variation on wings: plain, buffalo, southern fried, whatever. Most are instantly forgettable; you can make them better at home. **The Broadway Bar & Grill** (106 Randall Ave., Point Pleasant Beach; 732-899-3272; $$), with its houseboatlike interior, opened in 1992; the building housed Nelly's Long Bar for 50-plus years. This wing lover has eaten wings at scores of restaurants around the state; no one has yet matched the Broadway's. Fat, crispy, slightly blackened on top, they are coated with a smooth, tangy, tomato-tinged sauce. The secret? The wings are deep-fried, then finished off on the grill. Best wings in the state? Right here.

The Crab Shack, 74 Mantoloking Rd., Brick; (732) 477-1115; Seafood; $. The Crab Shack is an unassuming little Jersey Shore market/restaurant—call it a glorified shack—where you know you'll find the freshest crabs, clams, and scallops. Crabs of different sizes claw for space in baskets at the front counter. There are just a half dozen tables, all supplied with paper towels, which you'll definitely need. The soft-shell crabs are meaty and marvelous, and don't miss the red crab soup.

Drew's Bayshore Bistro, 28 E. Front St., Keyport; (732) 739-9219; www.bayshorebistro.com; Gulf/Low Country; $$$. Andrew

Araneo always wanted to open a restaurant in his hometown. "The whole goal," he says, "is to be self-employed." His menu features Gulf and Low Country cuisine—shrimp and grits, jambalaya, muffuletta salad, and more, plus American standards such as strip steak and pan-roasted garlic and herb chicken. Araneo loves the pig; his "pork du jour" dish features some variation of pork. "We change the pork nightly," he explains. I've had the barbecue pork struedel (BBQ pork and crispy phyllo) and the chili-rubbed pork tenderloin, both memorable.

Ebbitt Room, Virginia Hotel, 25 Jackson St., Cape May; (609) 884-5700 or (800) 732-4236; www.virginiahotel.com; American; $$$. Even in Victorian-happy Cape May, the small, elegant Virginia Hotel stands out. The inn, built in 1879 by Alfred and Ellen Ebbitt, operated as a small hotel through several owners until it was sold in the 1960s. In the early 1980s the structure was condemned but survived the wrecking ball. The hotel was completely renovated, and it reopened in 1989; the restored dining room was named the Ebbitt Room. It's one of Cape May's, and the Shore's, classiest restaurants, consistently ranking at or near the top of the state's best hotel restaurants and most-romantic dining stops. The Ebbitt Room also won *Wine Spectator*'s award for excellence in 2001, 2002, and 2003. The private dining room, the Richmond Room, is available for birthdays, reunions, and other events.

410 Bank Street, 410 Bank St., Cape May; (609) 884-2127; www.410bankstreet.com; Creole/Caribbean; $$$. Set in a beautiful house filled with lush greenery, 410 Bank Street is one of the Jersey Shore's top dining destinations. The menu is Creole-Caribbean; entrees include blackened sea scallops with a Louisiana remoulade sauce; Gulf Stream crab terrine with fresh tomatoes and avocado; and, for those not feeling particularly fishy, home-smoked Cowboy Steak, a 28-day-aged Black Angus New York strip served with a red pepper coulis and green chile relish. Reservations recommended.

Good Karma Cafe, 17 E. Front St., Red Bank; (732) 450-8344; www.goodkarmacafenj.com; Vegetarian; $$. It was a sad day when Down to Earth, one of the state's most-beloved vegetarian restaurants, closed in Red Bank. Fortunately, Good Karma filled the vegetarian void, and it may even be better. It's a charming, almost trippy space, with hardwood floors, psychedelic artwork on the walls, and friendly, helpful waitstaff. Of the belief that vegetarian means boring? Go to Good Karma. The "live"—as in not cooked— pastas are uniformly excellent. The live spaghetti combines angel hair zucchini noodles, sundried tomato sauce, nut-and-veggie meatballs, and Parmesan-style cashew cheese.

Harvey Cedars Shellfish Co., 7904 Long Beach Blvd., Harvey Cedars; (609) 494-7112; www.harveycedarsshellfish.com; Seafood; $$.

Hot Dogs with a Difference

Hot dog stands and carts line the Jersey Shore, but two manage to stand out in this crowded wiener world.

The first of our doggie duo is **Max's** (25 Matilda Ter., Long Branch; 732-571-0248; $). Here you can find the Hot Dog Queen of the Jersey Shore, by official proclamation of the state legislature. She's Celia Maybaum. Her late husband, Milford Maybaum, took over a legendary hot dog stand on the Long Branch boardwalk named after its original owner, Max Altman. Today everyone calls Celia "Mrs. Max." Max's is no ordinary hot dog stand; the wall is filled with colorful food signs and photos of luminaries—everyone from Danny DeVito to Bruce Springsteen—who have paid Max's a visit. There are good chili dogs, and Mrs. Max makes a mean cheesecake. Seating for 100-plus patrons, and beer on tap.

Picnic benches comprise the only seating at **Maui's Dog House** (806 New Jersey Ave., North Wildwood; 609-846-0444; www.mauisdoghouse .com; $). Co-owner Mike D'Antuono was a chef at restaurants from Hawaii to the Jersey Shore. He got tired of other people making money and told his wife he wanted to open his own place. "Put your money where your mouth is," Liz D'Antuono replied. They opened Maui's in 1999. "We wanted to do something different," Liz says. "This town is basically cheesesteaks, gyros, and pizza." There were lean years at first, but business steadily improved. A lot of people still haven't heard of Maui's. The draw here is the creative range of toppings, as well as the choice of traditional hot dog or a "Whitey," made with veal. Maui's offers nearly 30 kinds of hot dogs, all served in dog bowls. Order a Dressed Horse (hot dog, spicy ground beef sauce, raw onions, and Maui's fiery "horsey" mustard), an order of cheese-topped "cardiac fries," and some "salty balls" (fresh small potatoes cooked in a brine of salt and spices and served with drawn butter). You'll be in doggie heaven.

This seafood market/restaurant has come a long way since its opening in 1976 in a renovated beach house. There were just two items on the menu then (a lobster platter and shrimp platter, each $3.95). The menu now includes such singular seafood dishes as Louisiana crawdads (spicy, messy, and good); sautéed clams and mussels over garlic bread (a staggeringly large plate that only Gulliver, with an army of Lilliputians, could finish); and sautéed Maryland soft-shell crabs. The piped-in music is a baby boomer's dream: "Hurdy Gurdy Man," "Down in the Boondocks," and other hits from the '60s and '70s. Harvey Cedars is at the north end of Long Beach Island. For more good seafood, also visit **Beach Haven Fishery** (see Specialty Stores & Markets section, p. 225).

Hot Dog Tommy's, Jackson Street, just off the beach, Cape May; (609) 884-8388; www.hotdogtommys.com; Hot Dogs; $. You'll meet a lot of characters down the Shore, but none more colorful than Tommy Snyder, owner with his wife Mary, of this hot dog hole-in-the-wall. You can't miss Tommy; just look for the guy wearing the bright yellow hot dog hat. He's a former college dean of admissions and Black Hills buffalo tour guide; in the winter he and Mary head south in their RV. Tommy is a jokester, but his dogs are the real deal; they're plump and juicy, and you can get all kinds of toppings, including baked beans, banana peppers, and salsa. Don't forget to try Mary's homemade cranberry coleslaw.

Inlet Cafe, 3 Cornwall St., Highlands; (732) 872-9764; www.inlet cafe.com; Seafood; $$$. For a waterfront setting, it's hard to beat this restaurant, with its views of Sandy Hook and, in the distance, the New York skyline. The "cafe" moniker is misleading; this  is a full-scale bar/restaurant, with indoor and outdoor seating. On the weekend you may have to wait a bit, but it'll be worth it. The sesame-crusted ahi tuna is near perfect; it comes with a side of delicious seaweed salad. The Inlet Scallops are melt-in-your-mouth good.

Irish Pub and Inn, 164 Saint James Place, Atlantic City; (609) 344-9063; www.theirishpub.com; American; $$. If you're looking for a great, local, reasonably priced bar and restaurant in Atlantic City, head over to the Irish Pub and Inn. Established in 1972, this Victorian-looking inn may seem out of place next to the minarets and towers of the Trump Taj Mahal, but it's a colorful change of pace from the brightly lit, sanitized casino scene. There are daily "Poor Man's Specials," and the menu features hearty pub fare—burgers, jumbo sandwiches, meatball subs, pasta, steak, and such Irish standards as fish-and-chips and Guinness. The atmosphere is casual and friendly, but the best thing about the Irish Pub and Inn is that it never closes. You can often find co-owner Richard Burke in a corner booth, right by the Joe DiMaggio memorabilia; the Yankee Clipper was a regular.

BEST BURGER IN NEW JERSEY

In 2010, *Inside Jersey* magazine did something no one had done before: stage a "Food Fight" among North, Central, and South Jersey to see which part of the state would come out on top. There were five categories—pizza, burgers, ice cream, baked goods, and subs/hoagies. Teams of tasters—one for each category—fanned out around the state, sampling and evaluating food.

Stage Left in New Brunswick (p. 146) was judged the state's best burger. Premium beef, smoked bacon, quality tomato, red onion, fresh spring greens and chipotle mayo and a brioche bun added up to burger perfection. Other worthy contenders: **The Iron Horse** (20 Washington Ave., Westwood; 201-666-9682; www.theironhorse.com); **White Manna** (358 River St., Hackensack; 201-342-0914), and **Frankie's Bar & Grill** (414 Rt. 35 south, Point Pleasant Beach; 732-892-6000; frankiesbarandgrille.com).

Kaya's Kitchen, 817 Belmar Plaza, Belmar; (732) 280-1141; www.kayaskitchenbelmar.com; Vegetarian; $$. Mark Rasmussen opened Veggie Works, for a decade the Jersey Shore's best-known vegetarian restaurant, in 1994. In 2005 Kaya's Kitchen, owned by his brother-in-law, Omer Basatemur, took its place, continuing the fine vegetarian tradition. Judging by the reviews, Kaya's Kitchen hasn't missed a beat. There are tried-and-true standards such as vegan burgers, spinach quesadillas, and vegan meat loaf, plus new dishes such as hot jambalaya, Rocky Mountain stew, and curried coconut delight. A visit to Kaya's Kitchen may not make you want to change the world, but it may make you change your diet.

Kelsey & Kim's Soul Food and Bar-B-Que, 53 Main St., Pleasantville; (609) 484-8448; www.kelseyandkim.com; Southern/Soul Food; $. Finding barbecue, much less good barbecue, in New Jersey is a difficult if not thankless mission. There just isn't a lot of it out there. Chain barbecue restaurants have sprung up in recent years, but for the real thing you must wander farther afield. Thousands of people drive through Pleasantville every day on their way to Atlantic City, but few ever stop there. Now there is a reason. Kelsey Jackson's Main Street take-out joint is barebones; his barbecue is anything but. Nothing

sits around under a heat lamp here; food is prepared to order. Standout items: the ribs, the pulled-pork sandwich, and Jackson's sauce. They also own the **Southern Cafe,** 201 Melrose Ave., Atlantic City; (609) 350-6800.

Knife & Fork Inn, Albany and Atlantic Avenues, Atlantic City; (609) 344-1133; www.knifeandforkinn.com; Steak/Seafood; $$$. The distinctive Flemish turrets of the Knife & Fork Inn are the first major landmark as you enter Atlantic City on Route 40. Established in 1912 as a private gentleman's club, the Knife & Fork has been in

Best Soft-Serve Ice Cream

Soft ice cream has long taken a backseat to "hard" ice cream, but along the Jersey Shore soft ice cream—also known as soft-serve and custard—reigns supreme. The best-known soft-serve stands are **Kohr's** and **Kohr Bros.**, with 20 stands in Seaside Heights, Point Pleasant Beach, Wildwood, Ocean City, and elsewhere. The businesses are owned by descendants of the five Kohr brothers who opened an ice-cream stand on Coney Island in 1919. On their first weekend they sold 18,460 cones at a nickel apiece. The demand has scarcely lessened; on a hot summer day, there is nothing like a smooth, cold, creamy Kohr's—or Kohr Bros.—cone for instant relief. (Visit www.kohrstheoriginal.com [Kohr's] and http://kohrbros.com [Kohr Bros.]) Other recommended soft-serve stops around the state: the **Margate Dairy Bar** (9510 Ventnor Ave., Margate; 609-822-9559), with its green-awninged, pink-lettered, fluorescent-lit facade; the **Polar Cub** (388 Rte. 22 West, Whitehouse; 908-534-4401), and **Jersey Freeze** (120 Manalapan Rd., Freehold; 732-462-3008).

the Latz family since 1927. The food had seemed to slip in quality in recent years, but a new cook and other changes have restored the Knife & Fork to its prior standing as one of the Jersey Shore's top restaurants. It is, in any case, an atmospheric change of pace from the casino scene. The restaurant is particularly known for its lobster and other seafood dishes.

Mad Batter, at the Carroll Villa Hotel, 19 Jackson St., Cape May; (609) 884-5970; www.madbatter.com; Seafood; $$$. I've tasted many a crab cake up and down the coast; I judge an annual crab cake contest at Monmouth Park every summer. I've yet to taste a crab cake better than the one served at Mad Batter, the popular breakfast/brunch spot at the Carroll Villa Hotel. The Maryland crab cake sandwich, with a marvelous remoulade on a Kaiser roll, is the stuff of lasting summer food memories. The blackened grouper sandwich and the Chesapeake Bay Benedict are not far behind. Right across the street is **Hot Dog Tommy's** (p. 253).

Matisse, 1300 Ocean Ave., Belmar; (732) 681-7680; www.matisse-catering.com; American; $$$. Belmar, Party Central of the Jersey Shore, would seem an unlikely spot for an upscale restaurant, but owner Anthony Wall has found a home amid the crowded bars and boardwalk scene. And in a converted McDonald's, of all places. "I am very particular about what I buy and how I prepare the food," says Tony, a globe-trotting cook who has worked in South America, Asia, Europe, and North America. "Today the nou-veau way to serve food is to stack it, but have you ever watched anyone try to eat something served like that?" Appetizers include corn-meal-crusted bluepoint oysters and New England clam and bacon chowder. Entrees show off Tony's worldly vision; they include pan-seared salmon fillet with apple-braised red cabbage and English mustard sauce; skillet-braised duck breast with goat cheese polenta, sun-dried cherry jus, and herb salad; and roasted free-range chicken with spiced Italian sausage, escarole, and cannellini in garlic broth.

Mud City Crab House, 1185 E. Bay Ave., Manahawkin; (609) 978-3660; www.mudcitycrabhouse.com; Seafood; $$. For the story on good, fresh seafood, go see a Magazine. That's Melanie Magazine, co-owner of Mud City Crab House, which may serve up the best seafood in the Long Beach Island area. The restaurant is located just off Route 72, minutes from the bridge to LBI. Be prepared to wait; the roadside patio is a good place to have a beer or a glass of wine as you wait for a table at this BYOB spot. It serves great Maryland crab chowder, with fat chunks of tomatoes. Recommended entrees: blackened grilled salmon, blackened tuna, marinated tuna, grilled mako. After a visit or two to Mud City, you'll come up with your own favorites. There is a newer location at 17 Lacey Rd., Forked River; (609) 978-3660.

My Kitchen Witch, 29 Beach Rd., Monmouth Beach; (732) 229-3033; www.mykitchenwitch.com; American; $. The Kitchen Witch is the Shore equivalent of the **Blue Rooster** (p. 105) in Cranbury: a cozy retreat from the outside world and inclement weather, or both. Owner Karyn Jarmer is, shall we say, obsessed with witches; her cell phone plays the *Wizard of Oz* instrumental score. She ran a catering business for 15 years with many high-profile clients, including Rosie O'Donnell and Regis and Kathie Lee. The focus here is on healthy choices and quality ingredients. The Broomstick Hilda salad, with shredded chicken, apples, red seedless grapes, Craisins, and onions, is bewitching, and the grilled cheese sandwich, with white cheese, spinach, and tomato on Texas toast, is comfort food supreme.

Off the Hook, 20th and Bayview, Barnegat Light; (609) 361-8900; www.vikingoffthehook.com; Seafood; $$. The seafood at this takeout-only restaurant/market at the tip of Long Beach Island is literally right off the boat. The owner is Kris Panacek, whose father, John Larson, owns Viking Village, home to both a collection of fishing-shacks-turned-gift shops and a commercial fishing fleet. Five million pounds of seafood are packed here annually, including two million pounds of scallops a year. One of the scallop boats, the *Lindsay L,* was used in the movie *The Perfect Storm*. The seafood dishes you'll find at Off the Hook are near perfect; I love their scallops—fried, broiled, or grilled. The soft-shell crab and tuna teriyaki are also excellent, as are the pasta dishes topped with shrimp, scallops, or crabmeat. Even the fruit salsa—pear, lime juice, cilantro, honey, vinegar, salt, and onion—is given star treatment. There are benches nearby for seating. You have to drive to the very end of Long Beach Island, but it's worth it. This place really is off the hook.

Park Seafood, 1808 Boardwalk, Seaside Park; (732) 793-5001; www.seasideparkseafood.com; Seafood; $$. Bobby Dionisio left Martell's Shrimp Bar in Point Pleasant Beach to open Park Seafood on Jersey's wildest boardwalk. Those expecting the usual selection of

steamers and oysters on the half shell will be surprised by the quality and range of food at this outdoor stand. Recommended dishes include the grilled shrimp with pineapple and rice, the chipotle oysters, grilled grouper, and the no-mayo lobster roll. You can't miss Park Seafood; it's just across the way from the Sawmill, the legendary boardwalk bar.

The Pier House, Beach Drive and Pittsburgh Avenue, Cape May; (609) 884-1717; www.thepierhousecapemay.com; Mediterranean; $$$. The Pier House, formerly known as Water's Edge, remains Cape May's premier dining spot. The seaside setting, classy but casual dining room, and black marble bar add up to a memorable experience. The menu is billed as a "gastronomic symphony of Mediterranean rim–inspired flavors," with such Greek favorites as *keftedes*, octopus, lamb chops, and saganaki, plus American standards such as lobster tail and New York strip steak. Breakfast includes eggs, pancakes, omelets, brioche-style french toast, and a hot-iron Belgian waffle. In the summer, try to snag a table at the outdoor terrace overlooking the ocean.

Pinky Shrimp's Seafood Company, Long Beach Boulevard and 83rd Street, Beach Haven Crest; (609) 492-4545; www.lobzilla.com; Seafood; $. Pinky's is a classic Jersey seafood shack, a low-slung building with multicolored banners and a wooden sign atop the roof that reads CLAMS SHRIMP LOBSTER TAKEOUT. This is a fun place, a market and take-out restaurant that offers "the best dang seafood in Jersey." The froth on top of the 1,000-gallon tank just inside the front door makes it look like the world's biggest bubble bath, but it's actually a holding tank for lobsters. A helpful sign on the wall lists lobster prices; the highest are for "Lobzilla," anything four pounds or more. The New England and Manhattan clam chowders are both recommended. The creative menu includes jambalaya, catfish New Orleans, Caribbean coconut shrimp, fish kebabs (tuna, swordfish, mako shark), seafood Creole, fried oyster sandwich, even ribs and the Big Ol' Burger, a charbroiled 8-ounce "all beef patty nude or with cheddar cheese." See Pinky Shrimp's recipe for **Thai Chicken and Shrimp** on p. 285.

Ragin' Cajun, 1102 River Rd., Belmar; (732) 280-6828; www.ragin cajunnj.com; Cajun; $$. A breezy, fun atmosphere surrounds this pleasant outdoor eatery across the highway from the Belmar Marina; owner Tracie Orsi can be found chatting up customers—or busing tables when its gets especially busy. The rambling old house where the restaurant is housed may or may not be haunted, and the tables look right out of a yard sale, but the food is memorable. Try the alligator bites (tastes like gator, not chicken), Nola BBQ shrimp, the terrific chicken Creole, and the spiced-just-right jambalaya. If you find yourself talking to Orsi, be prepared for a "Dude, gotta cook!" as she dashes off to the kitchen.

Roadside Diner, Routes 33–34, Collingwood Circle, Wall; (732) 919-1199; www.theroadsidediner.com; American; $. Why single out the Roadside Diner among the scores of diners in this part of Jersey? First, it's beautiful, or beautiful in the way only diners can be, with a striking red railroad-car-style roof, yellow awnings, and a stainless-steel sheen. The diner had fallen into diner limbo until Dimitri and Toula Gerakaris bought it and spent 3 months cleaning and renovating it. Nothing fancy here; you'll go for the atmosphere (check out the sliding glass door and tiny bathrooms), friendly banter, and good food. The diner was the center of action in John Sayles's 1983 movie *Baby It's You.* It's a great place to hang out and watch the world—and the traffic on Route 34—go by.

Schooner *American*/Lobster House, Fisherman's Wharf, just outside Cape May in Lower Township; (609) 884-8296; http://the lobsterhouse.com/restaurant/; Seafood; $$. Plenty of restaurants up and down the Shore offer scenic waterfront dining; the Schooner *American* takes it one atmospheric step better. The boat, a great spot for drinks or appetizers (full menu not available) at sunset, is docked behind the Lobster House. This is a seafood Disneyland, with indoor restaurant, outdoor cafe, various raw bars, and gift shop. The dory fishing schooners, of which the *American* was an example, may have been the fastest working boats ever built. The complex itself dates to the 1920s, when Jess Laudeman opened a wholesale fish business. Today his grandson, Keith, runs the operation. The family owns several of the 20 to 30 fishing boats that supply fish to the Lobster House and its adjoining market. Don't forget to pay your respects to the monstrous 37-pound lobster mounted on a wall inside the restaurant. And in the market, say hello to employee Sandy Brown, who does a wicked Woody Woodpecker imitation.

Show Place, Centre Street and Beach Avenue, Beach Haven; (609) 492-0018; www.theshowplace.org; Ice Cream; $. Want to scream for ice cream? At this ice-cream emporium, you can. Waiters and waitresses frequently break into song and dance. Conga lines are not unheard of. At least one person at every table is asked to sing, dance, or do something crazy for their dessert, and later everyone is treated to a cabaret show featuring the "waitri," who are all professional performers. Some of them come from the Surflight Theatre, a summer-stock company, next door. The Show Place's parlor is open from 6 p.m. to midnight from Memorial Day through Labor Day (weekends only in early June); the take-out window is open from noon to midnight July 1 through Labor Day. The most extravagant item on the menu: the Anything Goes, with 12 flavors of ice cream, 2 sorbets, 7 toppings, banana wheels, wet walnuts, whipped cream, and cherries.

Smitty's Clam Bar, 910 Bay Ave., Somers Point; (609) 927-8783; Seafood; $. Pull up a stool outside Smitty's Clam Bar and enjoy the view: boats bobbing, gulls squawking, and an endless line of traffic inching over the bridge to Ocean City. It's a fun, casual spot, with indoor and outdoor seating. The colorful menu covers are drawn by local kids—fish swimming, fish grinning, fish leaping from the sea. I love the grouper burger here—strips of lightly fried grouper on a soft roll. The fried shrimp is excellent, crispy, and crunchy, and the New England clam chowder is terrific. There's a breakfast shop out back called, well, the Breakfast Shop. You can buy T-shirts with the slogan—"you can't lick our clams."

Sonny's Southern Cuisine, 574 Cookman Ave., Asbury Park; (732) 774-6262; Southern/Soul Food; $$. When he was a teen in Florida, William Wiley dreamed about being a famous R&B singer. He moved to East Orange to pursue the dream, but it didn't quite happen. Patrons of his southern and soul food restaurant in Asbury Park can thank heaven for small favors. William, who spent more than 20 years working for the railroad (Amtrak), opened Sonny's (named after his late brother) in 2001 to near instant acclaim. Catfish, fried chicken, barbecued ribs and chicken, chopped barbecue, crab cakes—all the southern and soul food standards are here and well

THE BEST BAGELS

On no other food in the state—with the possible exception of pizza—is opinion as divided as it is on bagels. Go to 10 bagel places, and you'll get 10 different bagels and 10 sets of loyal customers who will swear their favorite bagels are far superior to the guy's down the street. The problem is that we all like our bagels different ways—soft and chewy or hard and crusty, New York–style (boiled, then baked) or not (just baked), plain or cinnamon raisin, poppy or sesame, and so on. I love bagels and have a particular weakness for a good old-fashioned egg bagel with nothing on it. Or a cinnamon raisin with extra cream cheese.

A half dozen or dozen bagels is a Jersey Shore breakfast tradition, and the best can be found at **JT's Bagel Hut** (918 Lacey Rd., Forked River; 609-971-5151). Their French toast bagels are legendary, but I love their egg bagels: fat and pillowy. Turnover is high with all the bagels, so chances are you can get a nice warm one. They have excellent coffee, too. **Bagels N Beyond** (336 Rte. 18, East Brunswick; 732-390-4477) and **Bagel Bazaar** (590 Milltown Rd.,

executed. And don't leave without trying some of the homemade sweet potato pie and peach cobbler.

Sunset Landing, 1215 Sunset Ave., Asbury Park; (732) 776-9732; Breakfast; $. This is one of the coolest and still relatively unknown breakfast hangouts on the Jersey Shore. The dozens of surfboards perched on the rafters in this log cabin–like luncheonette are not

North Brunswick; 732- 247-2880) may be the best bagels in Central Jersey. I also like the cinnamon raisin crumb bagel and the power bagel at **Warren Bagels & Deli** (125 Washington Valley Rd., Warren; 732-868-0565), The heaviest and heartiest bagel I've come across can be found at the **Bagel Box** (642 Eagle Rock Ave., West Orange; 973-731-4985). The shop's Healthy Bagel, a sinewy combination of black pumpernickel, oatmeal, raisins, and walnuts, weighs in at nearly half a pound. Now that's a bagel! **Sonny's** (123 S. Orange Ave., South Orange; 973-763-9634) is a Jersey bagel icon. Another highly recommended spot: **Kosher Bagels Supreme** (252 Mountain Ave., Springfield; 973-376-9381).

But if I had to take just one bagel to my desert island, it would have to be the Cinn-a-Bagel from **Jersey Boy Bagels.** It's a fat bagel with a flaky, cinnamony crust, a sweet, chewy cross between a bagel and a doughnut. It's baked, not fried. There are four locations: 16 South St., Morristown, (973) 455-7222; 1731 Rte. 10, Morris Plains, (973) 984-0744; 62 Rte. 10, East Hanover, (973) 887-4445; and 1594 Rte. 10, Randolph, (973) 252-3003.

just for decoration; owners Donna Logdon and Rob Pruszynski have been known to catch a wave before putting on their aprons and preparing breakfast. Sit inside, or on the deck with scenic views of Deal Lake, and watch Donna's 30 or so "adopted" ducks waddle around outside. Good french toast and pancakes—buttermilk, blueberry, even cranberry/pecan and Nestle Crunch/banana. They've got grits—smooth and piping hot—but you have to ask for them;

they're not on the menu. This is a great place to while away a rainy day at the Jersey Shore.

Whispers, Hewitt Wellington Hotel, 200 Monmouth Ave., Spring Lake; (732) 974-9755; www.whispersrestaurant.com; Seafood; $$$. Nestled in a beautiful 19th-century Victorian mansion, Whispers rates among the top romantic Jersey Shore food experiences. It's a splurge, but worth it for the food and view—rambling porches, manicured grounds, and the lake. Tapestry-covered armchairs, plush carpets, and a formal white and rose dining room will instantly make you forget about the nearby boardwalk scene, or the sand still between your toes. The menu is predominantly seafood— Norwegian salmon fillet; Japanese bread crumb–crusted halibut; and nori-crusted swordfish stuffed with jumbo lump crabmeat, the chef's signature dish. This is a restaurant worthy of Spring Lake's understated elegance.

White House Subs, Arctic and Mississippi Avenues, Atlantic City; (609) 345-1564; Sandwiches; $. All you have to know about the White House is this: The Beatles, Tiny Tim, Frank Sinatra, and countless Miss Americas have eaten at this legendary sub shop.

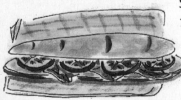

Serving simple and simply great subs since 1946, the White House is cramped, busy, chaotic—and absolutely not to be missed. Take a number and wait your turn. The guys behind the counter at times can be brusque and cranky, but once you become a regular, you're treated like family. On the walls are photos of celebrity visitors and various souvenirs, including the towel Sinatra used in his last Atlantic City performance. Sandwiches are wrapped in orange butcher paper and a double layer of nuclear-war-proof waxed paper; you don't have to worry about them leaking on your car seats. There is now a White House Subs shop in the Trump Taj Mahal in Atlantic City.

Brewpubs & Microbreweries

Cape May Brewing, 1288 Hornet Rd., Lower Township; (609) 849-9933; www.capemaybrewery.com. The state's southernmost brewery is located in an industrial park next to Cape May Airport. The owners are Bob Krill; his son, Ryan; and Ryan's friend Chris Henke. Brews include Sweet Stout, Honey Porter, and Cape May Wheat. Tours generally held on weekends; check the Facebook page for updates.

Carton Brewing, 6 E. Washington St., Atlantic Highlands; (732) 654-BEER; www.cartonbrewing.com. Cousins Chris and Augie Carton, and their favorite home brewer, Jesse Ferguson, opened Carton in a turn-of-the-century brick warehouse. Brews include Launch Golden Ale, Boat Beer, and the curiously-titled Brunch.Dinner.Grub, a brown country ale.

East Coast Brewing Co., 528 Arnold Ave., Point Pleasant Beach; (732) 202-7782; www.beachhausbeer.com. Owners Brian Ciriaco and John Merklin are high school and college buddies who spent 2 years making beer and drafting business plans before opening East Coast in November 2009. Their first release was Beach Haus Classic American Pilsner; Winter Rental Black Lager was introduced in fall 2010.

Tun Tavern, 2 Miss America Way, Atlantic City; (609) 347-7800; www.tuntavern.com. The Tun, Atlantic City's only brewery-restaurant, is a spin-off of the legendary Tun Tavern in Philadelphia, which opened on the waterfront in 1685. On November 10, 1775, the Continental Marines—now the US Marine Corps—were formed there. In the 1740s it was known as Peggy Mullan's Red Hot Beef Steak Club at Tun Tavern; patrons included George Washington and Thomas Jefferson—which probably accounts for the Thomas Jefferson Tiramisu on the Atlantic City restaurant's menu. There's a full range of appetizers, sandwiches, steak, and fish, but the homebrews are the draw. Selections include Devil Dog Pale, a classic-style English pale ale; Bullies Brown Ale, with a roasty, toasty flavor; Tunfest Lager, a German Oktoberfest amber lager; and Freedom Ale, a barleywine-style ale with hints of bourbon and vanilla. The Tun, part of the Sheraton Hotel, is located across the street from the Atlantic City Convention Center.

Wine Trail

Cape May Winery, 711 Townbank Rd., Cape May; (609) 884-1169; www.capemaywinery.com. This winery, New Jersey's southernmost, acquired a new owner in 2003, when Toby Craig, owner of the Washington Inn, took over. Toby's mission: to take the winery to new levels and to make Cape May a wine destination. His future plans include areas for weddings and celebrations, as well as wine festivals and special events. Open year-round. Tours are given at 3 p.m. daily from June to Sept, and 3 p.m. on Sat from Oct through Dec. The wine shop is open from noon to 5 p.m., daily; a wine tasting—choose any 6 wines—costs $6 and includes a souvenir glass.

Recipes

Jersey is no longer New York's—or Philadelphia's—disrespected cousin. In recent years, the state's food scene has expanded, with new restaurants, stores, and markets opening, and many thriving, despite challenging economic times. The state itself is difficult to stereotype, and so is its bounty. The Jersey tomato is justly famous, but the state is a major grower of blueberries, cranberries, and other fruits and vegetables. Its wholesale seafood industry generated nearly $150 million last year. The recipes here reflect that diversity, everything from fruit pies, baked apples, and seafood salad to chili and steak made from home-raised bison and ostrich.

Thanks to all of the folks, restaurants, and shops for allowing me to use their recipes, many of which reflect the abundance and diversity of New Jersey–grown produce.

Appetizers

Soups

Main Dishes

South Jersey–Style Clams Casino

This recipe is from Debbi Halter of Millville through the state Department of Agriculture's Jersey Fresh program.

Serves 4–6

- **48 littleneck clams**
- **½ cup (1 stick) butter, melted**
- **1 large Jersey Fresh bell pepper, diced**
- **1 pound bacon, sliced and diced**
- **1 (8-ounce) package shredded cheddar cheese**

Preheat oven to 350°F.

Scrub clams under cold running water until clean. Steam the clams in a large pot until they open and remove one shell from each clam.

Place the clams on the half shell on a baking sheet; dab each clam with half a teaspoon of melted butter.

In a large skillet, fry together the diced bell pepper and the bacon until well done. Drain on paper towels to remove grease. Crumble the bacon and place some bacon and pepper on each clam. Cover with the shredded cheese.

Bake in the oven for 3–5 minutes, or until the cheese is melted.

Courtesy of Debbi Halter

Fresh Raspberry Crostini

Nancy Wyant, owner of the Gingercreek Cooking School, draws on 25 years of tested recipes for her school and personal use. She loves to use ingredients "that can be found at their best in New Jersey." She says her recipe for raspberry crostini, developed to serve during raspberry season, is "light and beautiful with a pure sort of complexity in flavor." It's also perfect for the Christmas holiday season when imported raspberries are available.

Makes 24

- 1 French baguette, sliced ¼-inch thick on diagonal
- 6 ounces feta cheese, crumbled
- 2–4 teaspoons extra-virgin olive oil
- ½ pint fresh red raspberries
- ¼ cup warmed wildflower honey
- 4 teaspoons freshly snipped parsley

Preheat the oven to 350°F. Place the baguette slices side by side on a parchment-lined baking sheet.

In a small bowl, cream together the feta cheese and enough olive oil for a spreading consistency (you may refrigerate the feta mixture up to 1 week).

Slather the bread slices with a thin layer of the feta mixture and bake about 5 minutes just to warm the bread and cheese. Remove baking sheet from oven; place 2 large or 3 small raspberries lengthwise on each slice of bread.

Warm the honey in the microwave 45–60 seconds; drizzle very lightly (about ½ teaspoon per slice) over each raspberry-topped slice.

Transfer crostini to serving plate and sprinkle lightly all over with snipped parsley. Serve at room temperature within 60 minutes.

Courtesy of Nancy Wyant, Gingercreek Cooking School (p. 69)

Garden State Vegetable Soup

Tim Schafer, owner of Tim Schafer's Cuisine in Morristown (82 Speedwell Ave., Morristown; 973-538-3330; www.timschafersrestaurant.com), is renowned for the use of beer in his restaurant; even the watermelon and goat cheese salad served in his restaurant is "beer enhanced." He writes a regular column for Ale Street News, *the beer periodical. Tim loves New Jersey, especially for its abundance of fresh vegetables. This Schafer recipe shows off the bounty of the Garden State.*

Makes 6 large servings

- 1 white onion
- 1 carrot
- 1 turnip
- 1 parsnip
- ¼ rutabaga
- 2 stalks celery
- 1 tablespoon olive oil
- 3 cloves garlic, minced
- ½ teaspoon dried thyme
- ½ teaspoon dried oregano
- ½ teaspoon dried basil
- 2 quarts chicken stock, heated
- 1 teaspoon chopped fresh herbs (optional)
- 1 beefsteak tomato
- 2 leeks
- 1 small zucchini
- 1 small yellow squash
- 1 cup corn kernels
- 1 cup sliced mushrooms
- 8 ounces fresh spinach
- 1 teaspoon salt
- Fresh cracked black pepper to taste
- Dash of Worcestershire sauce
- Dash of Tabasco

Peel and/or wash all vegetables, then dice into ½ x ½-inch pieces, keeping the vegetables separate.

In a 4-quart soup pot, heat the olive oil, add the onion, and sauté until tender.

Add the carrot, turnip, parsnip, rutabaga, and celery. Stir, then add the garlic and dried herbs. Stir again, then cover and cook the vegetables for 3–4 minutes, stirring occasionally.

Add the hot chicken stock and remaining herbs and vegetables, excluding the spinach and seasonings. Stir well. Add spinach and seasonings last, after the squash is tender. Season to taste with salt, pepper, Worcestershire, and Tabasco.

Courtesy of Tim Schafer, Tim Schafer's Cuisine

Roasted Butternut Squash Soup

You may not be able to duplicate The Manor's furnishings—Limoges porcelain, candlesticks once used by President Woodrow Wilson, and a silver serving cart from the Queen Mary—but you can create this popular dish from the acclaimed restaurant.

Serves 6

- **2 whole, medium-size butternut squash, peeled, seeded, and cut into 1-inch cubes**
- **Olive oil**
- **Salt, pepper, and nutmeg to taste**
- **4 cups chicken broth**

- **2 cups heavy cream (optional)**
- **2 slices white bread, diced into tiny cubes and toasted to make croutons**
- **4 slices thinly cut prosciutto, diced**

Preheat the oven to 300°F.

In a large bowl toss the squash with olive oil to coat lightly. Sprinkle with salt and pepper and dust with nutmeg.

Place the squash cubes on a baking sheet and roast in the oven for about 40 minutes, or until golden brown.

Heat the chicken broth in a large stockpot. Add the browned squash and simmer for 10–12 minutes.

Remove from heat and puree with a handheld blender until smooth. If desired, add the cream and bring to a boil. Reduce the heat and simmer for 5–7 minutes. (The use of heavy cream is optional since pureeing the squash in itself will thicken the soup. The cream, however, adds a silky texture to the soup as well as added flavor.)

Season with salt, pepper, and nutmeg to taste. Garnish each serving with crou-tons and diced prosciutto. (Nutmeg is a very strong spice and should be used sparingly. If too much is used, it could, and possibly will, ruin your dish.)

Courtesy of Wade Knowles, The Manor, Highlawn Pavilion, Ram's Head Inn (p. 83)

New Jersey Clam Chowder

The Ram's Head Inn (9 W. White Horse Pike [Route 30], Absecon; 609-652-1700; www.ramsheadinn.com), just outside Atlantic City, is a Shore institution. The Knowles family, which also owns the acclaimed Highlawn Pavilion and The Manor in West Orange, took over the Ram's Head in 1979. Its wood-burning fireplaces and soft candlelight enhance the dining rooms, and the glass-enclosed veranda, with its view of the beautiful gardens, provides a great setting for parties and special functions. This recipe, from the inn's Executive Chef, Luigi Baretto, is a showcase for top-flight Jersey ingredients—tomatoes, asparagus, corn, and, of course, clams.

Serves 8

2 dozen fresh clams

10 ounces fresh New Jersey asparagus

2 pints milk

2 cups clam juice

olive oil

½ medium onion, chopped

½ teaspoon chopped garlic

2 tablespoons flour

3 New Jersey tomatoes, seeded and chopped

1 cup fresh New Jersey corn from the cob

1 cup diced white potatoes

½ teaspoon thyme

A few bay leaves

Salt and pepper to taste

1 cup heavy cream

Steam and chop clams. Set aside.

Clean and cook asparagus. Puree in food processor. Set aside.

Combine milk with clam juice; bring to a boil.

In a soup pot, sauté onion and garlic in olive oil until golden. Add flour, stirring; when smooth, add hot mixture of milk and clam juice.

Whip until smooth; add the puree of asparagus and then the tomatoes, corn, potatoes, thyme, bay leaves, salt, and pepper, mixing well.

Bring to a boil and simmer for 15 minutes, stirring often.

Finish with 1 cup of heavy cream, clams, and asparagus.

Courtesy of Luigi Baretto, Ram's Head Inn

D'Artagnan Duck Bacon Carbonara

If there's anyone who can make a delectable dish out of wild game and birds, it's D'Artagnan. Wild boar bacon, duck prosciutto, and gizzards confit are only a few of the products available from this company. Here is one of its recipes.

Serves 4

- 1 pound black truffle tagliatelle pasta
- 8 ounces duck bacon, julienned
- 8 ounces ventreche (bacon substitute), cubed
- ¾ cup sliced shallots
- 2 tablespoons chopped garlic
- 1 cup white wine
- 1 cup heavy cream
- 1 cup grated gruyère cheese
- Salt and pepper to taste
- Black truffle oil
- 1 tablespoon chopped parsley

Bring water to a roiling boil, add pasta, and cook according to package instructions.

Meanwhile, sauté duck bacon and ventreche over low heat until crisped and combined.

Add the shallots and sauté until caramelized. Combine with the garlic and cook for a few seconds, then pour wine into pan and deglaze.

Add the cream and gruyère cheese, and mix together. Season with salt and pepper to taste. Toss in cooked pasta, and drizzle with a few drops of truffle oil. Garnish with parsley.

Courtesy of Isabelle Abrard, D'Artagnan (p. 17)

Thai Chicken and Shrimp

The name is unusual, and so are many of the dishes at this Long Beach Island seafood shack. Owner Christian von Gorski was good enough to contribute this long-popular dish at Pinky Shrimp's to this book. "No one down here offers something like that; it separates us from the fried-fish houses," he says. Serve it over steamed short-grain rice. A side of mango slices with fresh mint leaves is always a nice touch.

Serves 4

- **4 cups coconut milk, cream and milk mixed***
- **2 teaspoons red curry paste***
- **½ cup julienned red bell pepper**
- **½ cup julienned carrots**
- **4 ounces snow peas, snipped**
- **1 (8-ounce) can bamboo shoots, sliced**
- **10–12 ounces boneless chicken breast, sliced in ½-inch strips**
- **16 shrimp, size 26–30 count, peeled and cleaned**
- **½ cup canned straw mushrooms**
- **½ cup unsalted peanuts**
- **1 teaspoon fresh lime juice**
- **3 teaspoons fish sauce***
- **1 teaspoon turbinado sugar (or substitute light brown sugar)**
- **1 dried red chile, seeded**
- **½ cup roughly chopped fresh basil leaves**
- **¼ cup roughly chopped fresh cilantro**
- **Kosher salt to taste**

*available in most Asian food markets

In a wok or large frying pan, bring 1½ cups of the blended coconut milk to a boil. Reduce heat and gently simmer for 5 minutes.

Whisk in red curry paste, breaking up clumps.
Simmer for another 3 minutes.

Add remaining coconut milk, red bell pepper,
carrots, snow peas, and bamboo shoots. Simmer
for 5 minutes.

Add chicken, shrimp, straw mushrooms, peanuts,
lime juice, fish sauce, sugar, and dried chile
pepper. Cook, gently stirring, until chicken is just
slightly pink in the center. By the time it hits the table, the chicken will be
cooked perfectly. If mixture gets too dry, add a tiny bit of water.

Gently stir in basil and cilantro. Add kosher salt to taste.

Courtesy of Christian von Gorski, Pinky Shrimp's Seafood Company (p. 261)

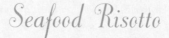

Seafood Risotto

Here's one of the favorite recipes of Chef William Fischer of Caffe Aldo Lamberti. He knows something about seafood; before entering the culinary world, he worked as a commercial fisherman. Caffe Aldo Lamberti, the flagship restaurant in Aldo Lamberti's family of restaurants, specializes in fresh fish and shellfish dishes.

Serves 8 as entree or 12 as appetizer

6 cups clam stock

6 cups water

¾ cup chopped onion

1 tablespoon whole butter

¼ cup olive oil

2 garlic cloves, sliced

2 pounds Italian rice (Arborio), uncooked

1½ cups Chablis

½ pound each calamari, scallops, rock shrimp, clams, firm-fleshed fish

1 pound mussels

⅛ cup chopped parsley

½ pound plum tomato, chopped

½ pound yellow tomato, chopped

⅛ teaspoon crushed red pepper flakes

Place stock and water in 3-quart stockpot and bring to boil.

Separately in another 3-quart stockpot, sauté onion in butter and oil till wilted, then add garlic and sauté without browning till wilted and aromatic.

Add uncooked rice to the onion and garlic mixture and stir to coat with oil. Add wine and half the stock-water mixture. Cook over high heat and stir frequently.

Meanwhile, cook all the seafood in order of sequence, one at a time in stock until just done. Remove each with a slotted spoon before adding the next, and reserve for addition to the rice when it has thoroughly cooked.

Note: As the rice cooks you will need to add additional stock to prevent burning. The rice absorbs the liquid and will surely stick, so stir it frequently. By the time you have cooked all of the seafood, the rice will need the remainder of the stock. Add it all and test for doneness while the last stage of cooking continues.

Rice is always best served al dente, so be careful not to over-cook it. As soon as the rice is ready, add all the seafood and blend it with the chopped parsley, plum tomatoes, yellow tomatoes, and red pepper flakes. Serve immediately.

Courtesy of William Fischer, Caffe Aldo Lamberti (p. 194)

Garden State Seafood Salad

New Jersey is renowned not just for its fruits and vegetables but also for its seafood. In 2010 the state harvested nearly 200 million pounds of seafood; the industry employs about 5,000 fishermen, processors, dockworkers, and truckers. "New Jersey seafood is pristine and high quality," says Jim Weaver, head chef at Tre Piani Restaurant (120 Rockingham Row, Plainsboro; 609-452-1515; www.trepiani.com) in Plainsboro's Forrestal Village in Central Jersey. Jim represented the state in the Great American Seafood Cook-Off in New Orleans in July 2004. He developed this recipe for the competition.

Serves 2

- ½ cup large diced Jersey tomato
- ½ cucumber, julienned
- ½ fennel bulb, julienned (reserve a few fronds for garnish)
- 2 garlic cloves, sliced
- 1 scallion cut on the bias into thin slices (reserve green top for garnish)
- 4 basil leaves, chiffonade, plus several whole leaves for garnish
- ½-inch bread cubes (from one large baguette)
- 3 ounces monkfish
- 8 littleneck clams
- 4 large sea scallops
- 3 ounces calamari
- ½ cup extra-virgin olive oil
- ½ teaspoon sea salt, plus extra as needed
- Black pepper to taste
- 1 cup water
- 3 teaspoons lemon juice

Set aside the diced tomato, julienned cucumber and fennel, sliced garlic and scallions, and basil chiffonade. Keep chilled until ready to use.

Lightly toast the bread cubes in a 350°F oven and set aside.

Prepare the seafood. Skin the monkfish and cut into bite-size pieces. Rinse the clams of any sand. Peel the abductor muscle from the sides of the sea scallops. Keep chilled until ready to cook.

Peel and clean the squid; pull the tentacles and all that are attached from the tube. Cut the tentacles off just above from where they start and discard the beak and eyes. Also remove the tough clear membrane from within the tube and discard. Slice the squid into ¼-inch rings. Keep well chilled until ready to prepare.

Heat a large sauté pan and add the olive oil.

Season the scallops and monkfish with salt and pepper and sear them until browned on the outside; remove from the oil and reserve on a plate.

Add the garlic to the pan and let brown slightly; add the calamari and give a quick toss.

Next add the clams and the water, and season lightly with salt and pepper. Cover until the clams begin to open and then return the scallops and monkfish to the pan.

Cook, covered, until all the clams open or about 1 minute. You may have to add more water if the clams do not open. You want to make sure that you have about ½ cup liquid left when the dish is finished.

Put the cut vegetables into a large bowl and season with salt and pepper. Add the bread cubes and toss with the vegetables.

Toss in the hot seafood and half of the cooking liquid.

Portion onto plates, garnish with the scallion tops and fennel fronds, and pour the remaining seafood broth around each plate. Serve immediately.

Courtesy of Jim Weaver, Tre Piani

Wild Striped Bass
with Red Beet Agrodulce Jus

Fascino (331 Bloomfield Ave., Montclair; 973-233-0350; www.fascino restaurant.com) is a family affair. Owner-Chef Ryan DePersio started cooking when he was 13 under the tutelage of his mom, Cynthia. Today Cynthia is pastry chef at Fascino; she also designed the restaurant's gold and burgundy dining room. Ryan's brother, Anthony, is general manager. The restaurant is particularly known for its seafood dishes. Here is one featuring striped bass, a popular New Jersey fish among commercial and sports anglers.

Serves 4

3 large fresh beets with greens attached

Agrodulce Jus

1 cup dry white wine
1 cup red wine vinegar

½ cup sugar

Fish

4 (6-ounce) fillets striped bass or any sea bass with skin attached
1 teaspoon salt
1 teaspoon finely crushed fennel seeds

½ teaspoon freshly ground black pepper
2 tablespoons canola oil

Salad

1 tablespoon extra-virgin olive oil

1 teaspoon fresh lemon juice
Pinch of salt

Preheat oven to 450°F.

Cut greens off beets about 2 inches above the stem and reserve. Wrap each beet in foil and place on baking sheet. Bake about 1½ hours, until a knife can pierce the beet easily to the center.

Unwrap beets and pull skin away from beets with paper towel and discard. Slice beets thinly with a very sharp knife. Stack slices and cut in half. Keep warm.

Meanwhile, rinse beet greens and dry well, then tear into bite-size pieces. Chill in plastic food bag.

Bring wine, vinegar, and sugar to a boil in a heavy-bottomed, nonreactive, medium saucepan.

Sprinkle fillets evenly with salt, fennel seeds, and pepper. Heat the oil in a 12-inch nonstick ovenproof skillet over medium heat. Add fillets skin side down and cook 5 minutes without moving. Transfer to oven and bake 2 minutes.

Toss greens with oil and lemon juice.

Divide warm sliced beets among four large, shallow pasta bowls. Divide agrodulce jus among bowls.

Top with hot fish, skin side up. Arrange beet green salad on top in center and serve immediately.

Courtesy of Ryan DePersio, Fascino

Bison Chili

"You're not going to notice any difference in the chili whether it's bison or beef," says Erick Doyle, co-owner of the Readington River Buffalo Co. *"It tastes so much like beef, you'll be surprised it wasn't. And bison is so much lower in fat."* And let's hear it for New Jersey grass; Readington River's buffalo graze on mostly orchard grass and timothy, an alternative to the sage and tumbleweed often found on buffalo farms in the prairie states. *"Our grass is green,"* Erick says. *"Their grass is bluish and tan."*

Serves 10

2 pounds buffalo burger

5 cloves garlic, minced

4 red onions, chopped

1 green pepper, chopped

1 cup finely chopped celery

12 ounces beer (alcoholic or nonalcoholic)

1 teaspoon dried basil

1 teaspoon cumin powder

2 tablespoons chili powder

1 (53-ounce) can red kidney beans or black beans, undrained

Freshly ground pepper to taste

1 teaspoon dried oregano

1 (28-ounce) can tomatoes packed in thick tomato puree

2 dashes Tabasco sauce

1 tablespoon cider vinegar

2 beef bouillon cubes

1 tablespoon brown sugar

1 teaspoon salt (optional)

¼ cup ketchup

Sauté buffalo burger, garlic, onions, green pepper, and celery.

Combine with the remaining ingredients in large stockpot. Bring to boil and simmer for 2–3 hours.

Courtesy of Erick Doyle, Readington River Buffalo Co. (p. 111)

Honey Wheat Braised Short Ribs

Some of the state's best, most original food can be found in its brewpubs. Triumph Brewing in Princeton is no exception. The menu includes such surprising fare as Japanese paella, brie-stuffed strawberries, and shrimp po'boys. Chef Mark Valenza's honey wheat braised short ribs is a year-round crowd pleaser.

Serves 2

Salt

4 beef short ribs (butcher can saw each rib into 3 pieces)

2 cups all-purpose flour

½ cup vegetable oil

2 large Spanish onions, rough chopped

2 carrots, rough chopped

4 celery ribs, rough chopped

2 (48-ounce) cans Italian peeled tomatoes

2 bay leaves

2 quarts honey wheat beer

1 teaspoon whole black peppercorns

Salt and pepper to taste

Salt short ribs and coat in flour.

Heat vegetable oil in a roasting pan and brown ribs.

Add everything else to roasting pan (onions, carrots, celery, canned tomatoes, bay leaves, honey wheat beer, and peppercorns).

Cover with foil, put into a 425°F oven, and braise for 2 hours or until meat is tender. Serve with mashed potatoes, polenta, rice, or your favorite vegetable.

Courtesy of Mark Valenza, Triumph Brewing Co. (p. 203)

Siren of the Sea

Mark Rasmussen, former owner of one of the state's best-known vegetarian restaurants, offers this recipe. He is the author of the Veggie Works Vegan Cookbook, *a collection of 375 of his favorite recipes, available on amazon.com.*

Serves 1–2

½ block (½ pound) firm tofu
1 tablespoon olive oil
1 teaspoon crushed garlic
½ cup vegetable stock*
6–8 broccoli florets
¼ cup soaked and chopped wakame sea vegetable (available at Asian markets and most good health food stores)
6 spears asparagus

4 cups loosely packed raw spinach, rinsed
¼ cup orange juice
Juice of ½ lemon
½ teaspoon Old Bay Seasoning
2 pinches salt
1 pinch black pepper
1 teaspoon cornstarch
2 tablespoons water

*If you don't have homemade vegetable stock, canned vegetable stock can be used or, alternatively, mix 1 vegetable bouillon cube with 2 cups boiling water.

Slice the tofu into 5 or 6 thin fillets and set aside.

In a heated skillet, add olive oil. Lightly brown garlic in skillet and then add half the vegetable stock to the garlic and oil mixture.

Combine broccoli, wakame, asparagus, and spinach and toss or stir into skillet.

Add remaining vegetable stock, orange juice, lemon juice, Old Bay Seasoning, salt, and pepper.

Next add tofu fillets and cover skillet. Turn heat down to medium and simmer for 5 minutes.

Mix cornstarch with 2 tablespoons water and add this to sauté pan. Toss or stir and serve immediately over precooked brown rice or pasta.

Courtesy of Mark Rasmussen

Summer Pasta Salad with Fresh Rigatoni

Casa di Trevi in Roselle Park not only makes the state's best ravioli, they offer great pasta of all shapes and sizes. Pick up their homemade rigatoni for this fresh, summery pasta dish.

Serves 10–12

2 pounds fresh Casa di Trevi rigatoni, cooked al dente

1 tablespoon olive oil

1 red bell pepper

1 yellow bell pepper

1 pint cherry tomatoes

1 small red onion

1 small head broccoli

1 8 oz. wedge provolone cheese

1–2 packets Good Seasonings Italian Dressing, per your taste

white vinegar

olive oil

water

Pinch of garlic powder

Salt and black pepper to taste

Cook the pasta until al dente. Drain the pasta and rinse under cold water. Toss with 1 tablespoon olive oil to prevent sticking.

Cut the peppers, tomatoes, onion, broccoli, and provolone cheese into small pieces.

Mix the Good Seasonings Italian Dressing packets, white vinegar, olive oil, and water according to package directions.

Toss the pasta with all ingredients and dressing.

Add a pinch of garlic powder and salt and black pepper to taste.

Courtesy of Casa di Trevi (p. 17)

Dandelion Pesto

Vineland's Dandelion Festival (p. 183) is one of the most popular and longest-running food-related festivals in New Jersey. Launched in 1973 to promote farming in Cumberland County, it includes a dinner where all the dishes are dandelion-enhanced. Merighi's Savoy Inn (4940 E. Landis Ave., Vineland; 856-691-8051; www.savoyinn.com) is one of the best-known restaurants in Vineland.

Makes about 1½ cups

- 4 cups thoroughly cleaned dandelion greens
- 2 tablespoons olive oil
- 1 tablespoon grated Pecorino Romano cheese
- 1 tablespoon toasted pine nuts
- ½ cup chicken stock
- 1 teaspoon minced garlic
- Salt and pepper to taste
- Pinch of onion powder
- ⅓ cup heavy cream (optional)
- 1 teaspoon softened butter (optional)

Place all ingredients, except cream and butter, in a blender and blend until well combined.

Place blended mixture in a saucepan over low heat and stir while heating. If using cream and butter, stir in until thoroughly incorporated.

Add pesto to hot cooked pasta, or serve with grilled chicken.

Courtesy of Tom Merighi, Merighi's Savoy Inn

Bobby's Famous Spicy Barbecue Sauce

The crab cakes at Robert Sliwowski's Bobby Chez restaurants (www.bobbychez crabcakes.com) are legendary; you may not find better between Boston and Maryland. But the owner, who started in the food business by selling fruit-flavored snowballs from his small wagon when he was 8 years old, is particularly proud of his barbecue sauce.

"One day I was playing around, and came up with the recipe," he recalls. The key: the chipotle chiles. "They give a nice smoky flavor rather than burning hot. And the sweetness of the brown sugar you add comes through." The restaurant is located in Collingswood, Washington Township, Cherry Hill, Margate, Mount Laurel, and Egg Harbor Township.

Makes 3–4 quarts

- **2 cups ketchup (Heinz preferred)**
- **1 cup sautéed tomatoes and onions**
- **½ cup dark brown sugar**
- **½ cup water**
- **1 teaspoon liquid smoke**
- **2 tablespoons Worcestershire sauce (Lea & Perrin's preferred)**
- **3 chipotle chiles (from jar or can)**

Blend all ingredients in food processor and store in a tightly sealed container.

Courtesy of Bobby Sliwowski, Bobby Chez Seafood Specialties

Corn Slaw

Peter Melick, co-owner of Melick's Town Farm, calls his recipe for corn slaw "an excellent side dish for any summer meal." Its centerpiece is fresh-picked Jersey corn. "My personal favorite is to serve it under crab cakes," he says.

Serves 4–6

- **5 ears fresh-picked Jersey corn**
- **1 cup chopped red cabbage**
- **½ bell pepper, chopped**
- **2 finely chopped green onions (scallions)**

- **¼ cup red wine vinegar**
- **⅓ cup mayonnaise (Hellmann's recommended)**
- **¼ teaspoon cayenne (optional)**
- **Salt and pepper to taste**

Husk and de-silk the corn. Wrap in a damp paper towel and microwave on high for 4½ minutes.

Cut corn from the cob and combine with all other ingredients. Serve immediately; it's best if served warm.

Courtesy of Peter Melick, Melick's Town Farm (p. 127)

Apple Rhubarb Slump

Slump is the New England name for a fruit dessert topped with a sweet dumpling mixture. On Cape Cod, slumps are called grunts; in other parts of the country, cobblers. "Apples are great in combination with other fruits," says Pam Mount, co-owner of Terhune Orchards. "Rhubarb gives a tartness to the dish, which reminds everyone of dinner at Grandmom's. It's an early spring treat."

Serves 8

Filling

4 medium-size apples

2 cups rhubarb, cut into 1-inch pieces

¾ cup sugar

½ teaspoon ground cinnamon

½ teaspoon ground ginger

¼ teaspoon ground cloves

Topping

1 cup all-purpose flour

1½ teaspoons baking powder

2 tablespoons sugar

3 tablespoons butter

½ cup milk

1 tablespoon vanilla extract

Heavy cream for serving

Preheat oven to 400°F. Grease a 2-quart baking dish.

Peel, core, and slice apples into ½-inch pieces. Place pieces in a saucepan and add the rhubarb, ¾ cup sugar, cinnamon, ginger, and cloves. Cover pan and cook over low heat for 10 minutes, stirring once or twice until apple slices are soft but not falling apart. (Or, put in microwave in a 2-quart glass dish and cook until apples are tender.)

In medium-size bowl, sift together flour and baking powder. Stir in remaining 2 tablespoons sugar and cut in butter until mixture resembles crumbs.

Stir milk and vanilla extract into the crumb mixture until just blended. Do not overmix.

Pour hot apple-rhubarb mixture into greased baking dish.

Spoon dough mixture in dollops over the top.

Bake for 20–30 minutes until topping is golden brown. Serve warm with heavy cream.

Courtesy of Pam Mount, Terhune Orchards (p. 182)

Blueberry Bavarian Pie

The blueberry, thanks largely to a group of fourth graders in Brick, was named New Jersey's state fruit in 2003. The organizers of the New Jersey State Fair thought it only fitting to add a blueberry category to the annual fair's food competition, and in 2004 Sue DeCamp of Blairstown won first prize for this recipe, which was adapted from a 1992 Crisco recipe.

Makes 1 10-inch pie

- 1½–2 ounces white chocolate baking bar
- 1 (10-inch) pie crust, baked and cooled
- 5 cups fresh blueberries, divided
- 1¼ cups sugar
- ¼ cup cornstarch
- 2 teaspoons lemon juice
- 1 envelope unflavored gelatin
- ¼ cup cold water
- 1 cup fresh blueberries
- ¼ cup plus 1½ teaspoons sugar
- 1½ cups whipping cream
- Sweetened whipped cream
- Fresh blueberries for the garnish

Melt the baking bar in the top of a double boiler over hot water. Brush on the inside of the baked crust.

For the filling, place 2½ cups blueberries in a large saucepan. Crush the berries. Stir in 1¼ cups sugar and the cornstarch. Cook and stir on medium heat until the mixture comes to a boil and thickens. Cool.

Stir in the remaining 2½ cups blueberries and lemon juice. Refrigerate.

For the Bavarian layer, place the gelatin in cold water to soften. Puree 1 cup of blueberries. Heat the puree in a small saucepan on low heat. Add gelatin to puree and stir until dissolved. Stir in ¼ cup plus 1½ teaspoons sugar. Remove from heat. Cool until almost set.

Beat whipping cream in a small bowl of an electric mixer set at high speed, until stiff peaks form. Fold one-third of the cream into the puree. Fold puree into the remaining whipped cream and refrigerate.

To assemble, spoon two-thirds of the filling into the coated crust. Cover with the Bavarian layer. Spoon the remaining filling into the center of the Bavarian. Top the pie with whipped cream and garnish with fresh berries. Refrigerate until firm.

Courtesy of Sue DeCamp

Jersey Summer Fruit Crisp

This classic fruit crisp is enlivened with Laird's Apple Jack, made in Colts Neck. The recipe is from Patricia Mack of Hackensack through the state's Jersey Fresh program.

Serves 12

10 cups Jersey Fresh peaches (peeled), strawberries, plums, and/or blueberries(any combination), cut up

½ cup granulated sugar, or to taste

¼ cup Laird's Apple Jack

1 tablespoon fresh lemon juice

3 tablespoons plus ¼ cup flour

1 cup chopped walnuts, divided

1 cup rolled oats

1 tablespoon brown sugar

1 teaspoon cinnamon

⅓ cup butter, softened

Whipped cream (optional)

Preheat oven to 375°F. Spray a 9 x 13-inch pan with nonstick cooking spray.

Gently toss fruit with sugar, Apple Jack, and lemon juice. Sprinkle with 3 tablespoons flour. (If fruit is very juicy, drain some or add a bit more flour.) Toss gently. Spread fruit in prepared pan; set aside.

To make the topping, process ½ cup walnuts until fine in a food processor or blender; transfer to a bowl. Add oats, brown sugar, cinnamon, and remaining flour. Using a pastry blender, cut butter into oat mixture until crumbly. Add remaining chopped walnuts. Sprinkle mixture evenly over fruit.

Bake 20–25 minutes, until fruit is tender and topping is golden brown.

Serve warm, with whipped cream, if desired.

Courtesy of Patricia Mack

Cinnamon Apple Butter Cheesecake

"Cheesecake is the number one dessert in the country," insists Ed Simpson, owner of Muirhead of Ringoes. "This is one of about 10 million recipes." He likes this one because it brings a "little sweetness" to the traditional cheesecake recipe.

Serves 12–16

Crust

1¼ cups graham cracker crumbs

½ cup chopped pecans

¼ cup firmly packed brown sugar

¼ cup melted butter

Filling

3 (8-ounce) packages cream cheese

1 cup sugar

2 tablespoons all-purpose flour

3 eggs

1 jar Muirhead Cinnamon Apple Butter

Preheat oven to 350°F.

Mix all crust ingredients. Press in bottom of ungreased 10-inch springform pan.

In large bowl beat cream cheese and sugar at medium speed until smooth and creamy. Add flour to bowl and blend well. At low speed add eggs one at a time, beating just until blended. Add Muirhead Cinnamon Apple Butter to bowl and beat until well blended. Pour into pan.

Bake at 350°F for 30 minutes. Turn off oven and allow cake to remain in oven for 1 hour or overnight. Do not open the oven.

Courtesy of Ed Simpson, Muirhead of Ringoes (p. 109)

Mrs. Barclay's Baked Apples

Using this recipe in a book about New Jersey foods is only fitting, according to Donna Annunziata, bakery manager at Delicious Orchards. Janet Barclay, for whom the recipe is named, started the company's fabled pie-making business in the 1950s, baking apple pies in her home. The pies became so popular that her living and dining rooms were turned into a bakery operation, as peach, blueberry, cherry, and other kinds were added to the lineup. Now Delicious Orchards makes about 500 pies a day.

Serves 6

6 baking apples, cored
1½ cups cider
¼ cup sugar

¼ teaspoon cinnamon
⅛ teaspoon nutmeg

Preheat oven to 350°F.

Place apples in baking dish. Pour cider over apples. Sprinkle sugar, cinnamon, and nutmeg on top of the apples and cider.

Bake for 30–45 minutes. Baste apples several times during baking.

Courtesy of Donna Annunziata, Delicious Orchards (p. 115)

Mrs. Sickles's French Silk Chocolate Pie

Bob Sickles, owner of Sickles Market, remembers this pie well. "It's one of my favorites," he says fondly. "My mother used to make it all the time when I was growing up. It's very decadent."

Serves 8

¾ **cup sugar**
½ **cup butter, softened**
2 **ounces unsweetened chocolate, melted**
1 **teaspoon vanilla**

2 **eggs**
1 **(8-inch) baked pastry shell (or a graham cracker crust)**
Whipped cream and walnuts or shaved chocolate (optional)

In a small mixing bowl, combine sugar, butter, chocolate, and vanilla. Blend well.

Add eggs, one at a time, beating at medium speed for 3–5 minutes after each (make sure the sugar is dissolved).

Pour into baked pastry shell. Chill at least 2 hours.

Top edges with whipped cream, walnuts, and/or shaved chocolate if desired.

Courtesy of Bob Sickles, Sickles Market (p. 118)

Strawberries with Crème Anglaise

In a town filled with beautiful inns and bed-and-breakfasts, Alexander's (653 Washington St., Cape May; 609-884-2555; www.alexandersinn.com) manages to stand out. The antiques-appointed Victorian inn caters to honeymooners and couples on romantic getaways. This light, delightful dish comes courtesy of innkeepers Diane and Larry Muentz. "Crème anglaise is a classic, and classics are things that are so good they survive trends," Diane says. "This recipe is good because there are no shortcuts, no compromises on calories or price, and it takes some skill to execute. Take your time and do it right; the reward is there."

Serves 8

1 quart strawberries	1 cup heavy cream
6 egg yolks	1 cup milk
¾ cup sugar	1 teaspoon vanilla extract

Wash, hull, drain, and slice strawberries into a serving bowl.

Place egg yolks, sugar, and heavy cream in the top of a double boiler over low heat.

Heat, constantly stirring the mixture until it is totally blended and coats a spoon, about 15 minutes.

Remove from heat and stir in milk and vanilla. Pour mixture through a fine mesh strainer and into a bowl.

Pour mixture, warm or at room temperature, over strawberries and serve immediately. (If making it the day before, store it in the refrigerator and bring it to room temperature before serving.)

Courtesy of Diane K. Muentz, Alexander's Inn

Appendices

Appendix A: Index of New Jersey Eateries

Appendix B: Specialty Foods, Markets & Purveyors

Appendix C: Index of Food Events

July

All-American Barbecue
(Sergeantsville), 132

New Jersey State Barbecue
Championship (North
Wildwood), 241

New Jersey State Ice Cream
Festival (Toms River), 241

St. Ann's Feast, Church of St. Ann
(Hoboken), 66

August

Annual Bluegrass Music Festival
(Cream Ridge), 133

Clam Fest (Highlands), 241

Garden State Wine Growers Jersey
Fresh Wine and Food Festival
(Richwood), 187

Middlesex County Fair (East
Brunswick), 133

New Jersey State Fair/Sussex
County Farm and Horse Show
(Augusta), 66

Peach Festival, Hopewell Township
(Cumberland County), 187

West Cape May Tomato Festival
(West Cape May), 242

September

Apple Festival (Forked River), 188

Cape May Food & Wine Festival
(Cape May), 243

Fruit Crush and Pig Roast Festival
(Cream Ridge), 134

Gourmet Food & Gift Show, Garden
State Convention & Exhibit
Center (Somerset), 134

Seafood in Seaside (Seaside
Heights), 242

Winefest, Valenzano Winery
(Shamong), 188

October

Chatsworth Cranberry Festival
(Chatsworth), 188

Chowderfest (Beach Haven), 243

Country Jamboree and Chili
Cook-Off (Keyport), 134

Garden State Wine Growers Harvest
Festival (Finesville), 135

Lima Bean Festival (West Cape
May), 244

Index

Harvest Square Farmers' Market, 47
Harvey Cedars Shellfish Co., 251
Hasbrouck Heights Farmers'
    Market, 48
Haworth Farmers' Market, 48
Healthier Heart Farmers' Market at
    Trinity Cathedral, 173
Heritage Station, 178
Highland Park Farmers' Market, 122
Highlands Farmers' Market, 235
High Point Wheat Beer Co., 95
Hightstown Farmers Market, 174
Hinck's Turkey Farm, 215
Hiram's, 82
Historic Downtown Special
    Improvement District Farmers'
    Market, 48
Hobby's, 79
Hoboken Farmers' Market, 48
Hoboken Uptown Farmers'
    Market, 48
Hoffman's Ice Cream, 216
Holiday Snack Bar, 217
Holley's Gourmet to Go, 90
Honey Wheat Braised Short
    Ribs, 294
Hopewell Community Farmers'
    Market, 174

Hopewell Valley Vineyards, 205
hot dog hangouts, 82
hot dogs, 252
Hot Dog Tommy's, 253
Hot Grill, 82
Hudock's Custard Stand, 196
Hunterdon Land Trust Farmers'
    Market, 123

I

Iberia Peninsula, 96
Iberia Tavern & Restaurant, 96
ice cream, soft-serve, 257
Inlet Cafe, 254
Inn at Millrace Pond, 79
Irish Pub and Inn, 254
Ironbound neighborhood
    (Newark), The, 96
Iron Hill Brewery & Restaurant, 203
Iron Horse, The, 255

J

Jean Louise Candies, 227
J. Emanuel Chocolatier, 22
Jeremiah's, 80
Jersey Boy Bagels, 267
Jersey City Farmers' Market I, 48
Jersey City Farmers' Market II, 48

London Food Company, 31
Long Valley Pub and Brewery, 95
Lower Township Farmers'
    Market, 235
Luca's Ristorante, 140
Lucey's Berry Farm, 62
Lucy's Ravioli Kitchen & Market, 162
Lusty Lobster, 230

M

Mack's Pizza, 221
Madame Claude Cafe, 82
Mad Batter, 258
Madison Farmers' Market, 49
Main Street South Orange Farmers'
    Market, 49
Mallon's Homemade Sticky Buns, 219
Manahawkin Farmers' Market, 235
Manahawkin Pick Your Own Berry
    Farm, 237
Manasquan Farmers' Market, 235
Manco and Manco, 220
Manischewitz, 23
Manor, The, 83, 152, 281
Maplewood Farmers' Market, 50
Mara's Cafe & Bakery, 24, 223
Margate Community Farmers'
    Market, 235

Margate Dairy Bar, 257
Mario's Italian Market, 230
Market Roost, 109
Market Square Farmers' Market, 50
Marsilio's Restaurant, 198
Martell's Tiki Bar, 153
Maruca's, 220
Matisse, 258
Maui's Dog House, 252
Max's, 252
Maxwell's Farm, 62
Mazur's, 25
McMillan's, 190
Medford Lakes Farmers' Market, 174
Melange Cafe, 198
Melick's Town Farm, 127, 300
Merchantville Farmers' Market, 174
Metuchen Farmers' Market, 123
Middlesex Borough Farmers'
    Market, 123
Middlesex County Fair, 133
Miel Patisserie, 167
Mi Gente Cafe, 83
Millburn Deli, 51
Millburn Farmers' Market, 50
Mitsuwa Marketplace, 31
Moghul, 148
Moghul Express, 148